"*Tom Lawry reminds us that the health care industry (* when it needs to. Given the right tools, we can evolve from health systems to systems of health, baked with Responsible Intelligence to do good while embedded with respect, inclusion, and transparency. Health citizens deserve Tom's vision to emerge.*"

Jane Sarasohn-Kahn
Health Economist
Author of *Health Citizenship: How a Virus Opened Up Hearts and Minds*

"*One of the most comprehensive compilations of groundbreaking AI topics that are fundamentally shaping healthcare today. Tom Lawry shines the light on these complex solutions in a simple and consumable manner. A must read for anyone wanting to learn more about how AI is transforming the world of healthcare in this post-pandemic world.*"

Ankur Teredesai, PhD
Professor, University of Washington
Founding Director, Center for Data Science
Healthcare AI Entrepreneur

"*In a substantive and brilliant follow-up to his prior impactful book AI in Health, Tom takes us on a futuristic journey of just how AI and its escalating panoply of tools can be in synergy with humans and concomitantly the necessary solution to our healthcare conundrum. In* Hacking Healthcare, *Tom astutely educates us on the myriad of nuances of AI in healthcare with his unique perspective as National Director of AI for Health and Life Sciences at Microsoft.*

"*I applaud Tom for this outstanding work as a clarion call for all of us to take part in this 'intelligent health revolution.' As we face the inevitable possibility of a shorter lifespan for our population, we owe Tom a debt of gratitude for his timely and insightful book that offers what we all very much need for our next generation: hope.*"

Anthony Chang, MD, MBA, MPH, MS
Founder of Artificial Intelligence in Medicine (AIMed)
Author of *Intelligence-Based Medicine*
Chief Intelligence and Innovation Officer,
Children's Health of Orange County (CHOC)

"*This is an exquisitely written one-of-a-kind book. The author masterfully helps bridge the understanding between healthcare administrators and physicians in the complex landscape of healthcare AI*"

Eric Eskioglu, MD, FAANS
Neurosurgeon
Executive Vice President – Chief Medical & Scientific Officer
Novant Health

Hacking Healthcare

In this original work, Tom Lawry takes readers on a journey of understanding what we learned from fighting a global pandemic and how to apply these learnings to solve healthcare's other big challenges. This book is about empowering clinicians and consumers alike to take control of what is important to them by harnessing the power of AI and the Intelligent Health Revolution to create a sustainable system that focuses on keeping all citizens healthy while caring for them when they are not.

Hacking Healthcare
How AI and the Intelligence Revolution
Will Reboot an Ailing System

Tom Lawry

A PRODUCTIVITY PRESS BOOK

First published 2023
by Routledge
605 Third Avenue, New York, NY 10158
and by Routledge

2 Park Square, Milton Park, Abingdon, Oxon, OX14 4RN

Routledge is an imprint of the Taylor & Francis Group, an informa business

ISBN: 978-1-032-26016-7 (hbk)
ISBN: 978-1-032-26015-0 (pbk)
ISBN: 978-1-003-28610-3 (ebk)

DOI: 10.4324/9781003286103

Typeset in Garamond
by KnowledgeWorks Global Ltd.

To those who believe health and medicine are
noble causes and strive to make them so.

[Handwritten annotation:] This is what we do!

[Handwritten inscription:] All the best in your AI journey!! Tom

Contents

Foreword

The COVID-19 pandemic exposed the profound vulnerabilities of American healthcare, with disproportionately poor outcomes in underrepresented minorities and the indigent. The United States had the highest per capita mortality rate of any industrialized nation, with more than 1 million deaths. Although only comprising 4% of the world's population, US fatalities accounted for more than 16% of the pandemic deaths through 2021. Poor clinical outcomes for the US pandemic were not at all new for this country. Even with over $4 trillion spent on healthcare in 2021, outstripping all countries in the world, the lifespan of its residents, along with maternal and infant mortality metrics, are the worst of all 38 Organisation for Economic Co-operation and Development (OECD) member countries. If there is a better example of when you don't get what you pay for, I don't know of it.

In *Hacking Healthcare*, Tom Lawry, the National Director for AI, Health and Life Sciences at Microsoft, explores the intersection of the pandemic and the Intelligent Health Revolution. There are few examples for AI having a substantive impact on the pandemic. One medication, baricitinib, an anti-inflammatory JAK-kinase inhibitor used for treating rheumatoid arthritis, was identified by data mining and ultimately proved, by randomized clinical trials, to achieve mortality reduction for severe COVID. Many other AI data mining efforts to repurpose existing drugs have not been successful, despite subsequent testing in clinical trials. Another way AI made a difference in the pandemic was in Greece, whereby an algorithm was launched to determine which travelers should be tested for COVID. It turned out to be two to four times more efficient than random testing.

Literally, thousands of studies claimed that AI could accurately diagnose COVID via a chest X-ray or CT scans. But an in-depth review of the best 62 papers (of 2,212 preprints or publications) categorized them as "Frankenstein datasets" and concluded: "None of the models identified are of potential clinical use due to methodologic flaws and/or underlying biases." That exemplifies the hype of AI, that its overall impact for the pandemic was modest at best, and that it is still early in the real-world clinical validation and acceptance of AI tools.

This book, however, gets into the remarkable promise that AI has for the future. Let's take the potential for AI to reduce health inequities. In Africa, India, and many remote parts of the world, smartphone ultrasound is now being used to make a diagnosis. Noteworthy is that the person obtaining the ultrasound is not necessarily a doctor or clinician; the AI is starting to direct an uninitiated individual to obtain the desired image and do an auto-capture of a picture or video loop of interest. Algorithms are also being developed to provide immediate and accurate interpretations of the images obtained. Once fully validated, this creates a "closed-loop" without the need for trained personnel to rapidly and inexpensively obtain preliminary diagnoses anywhere in the world. We're not there yet, but the early experience suggests it may be eminently achievable. Even now there is leveling of the earth with the smartphone attached probe that acquires an image that can be shared in the cloud and interpreted by an expert remotely.

It's important to underscore, however, that AI tools could easily make inequities worse, if they are only available to affluent people. We have already seen too many examples of how bias can creep into algorithms and how AI tools can be used in practice that may unwittingly promote discrimination and unfairness. Attention to these concerns is vital if AI is ever going to reduce health inequities.

It took decades for clinical researchers to finally determine that the social determinants of health were just as important, if not more so, than traditional risk factors such as diabetes or hypertension. While helpful, a person's zip code is far too rudimentary to get a handle on this risk factor. Early studies that are noted in the book show how such data are starting to get imputed with natural language processing of electronic medical records including education, economics, neighborhood, access to health, health literacy, and social context.

During the pandemic, the Hospital at Home (HaH) concept was tested by several health systems in the United States by default, since the faculties were overloaded with patients and the idea was to use remote monitoring of those who were not as sick with COVID at presentation to the Emergency Department. Some health systems used a multi-sensor device from Current Health placed on the upper arm that continuously monitors all vital signs except blood pressure: temperature, oxygen saturation, heart rate and rhythm, and respiratory rate. There haven't been any randomized clinical trials or publications that prove remote monitoring with this device or other similar biosensors is as safe as admitting patients to the hospital for monitoring but the HaH concept and the tools to test it – the hardware and AI analytics – are now becoming available. Interestingly, Best Buy acquired Current Health, so that surprise should be an indicator of some unpredictable combinations and directions AI will take us in the years ahead. Hopefully less need for hospitalizations will be one of them.

The cost of American healthcare is such an outlier in the world. Lawry reviews many ways AI can help this dire situation such as with streamlining operations, billing, detection and prevention of fraud, optimizing staffing, avoiding hospital readmissions, and clinic no-shows. Reducing hospitalizations would certainly put a dent in it. They alone account for over $1 trillion in the annual US healthcare expenditures, but they also represent important revenue streams for hospitals. The American Hospital Association is one of the largest lobbyist organizations in the country. Unlike countries with universal healthcare, there is no incentive in the United States to actively promote HaH, owing to perverse incentives. AI cannot fix our lack of universal healthcare, a deep lesion that is holding us back in so many ways. The lack of access to healthcare for the under-represented and indigent is a by-product of our fee-for-service model. The points that the promise of AI has limitations, that the field is still early, and there are critical obstacles to overcome cannot be emphasized enough.

That brings me to the human capital narrative in American healthcare. We keep adding jobs to this sector at a torrent pace, which is already the largest labor force and well over the traditional major sectors of retail and manufacturing. Yet there's still a marked shortage of personnel. The pandemic has magnified the issue greatly with not only intensification of clinician burnout, which had already manifest as a global crisis, but now there are resignations or early retirements at scale. We are losing an enormous number of nurses, doctors, and other clinicians from the American healthcare workforce. This is an area we urgently need AI to come to the rescue, to augment the productivity efficiency and accuracy of each clinician remaining, along with the new ones to join. On top of my list, and what we came to when I did the review of the National Health Service of the United Kingdom is keyboard liberation. That is using natural language processing and machine learning to eliminate or greatly reduce any need for clinicians to function as data clerks, with synthetic notes generated by the conversation between the patient and doctor – AI, not human, scribes. Just a first base for what AI can conceivably do to make the practice of medicine the way it was before clunky electronic medical records for billing purposes took over.

However, if AI is misused such that doctors and nurses are getting "squeezed" to do even more, that will only exacerbate the conditions that the pandemic ushered in. Therein lies the rub of managers and administrators, the overlords of the American health system, who focus on revenue and not morale, who are interested in implementing AI tools but may not be aware of what must be regarded as the cardinal objective. The people who went into medicine did so because they, for the most part, want to take care of patients. Reciprocally, patients want to know their doctors have a presence and have their back, that they really care for them. If clinicians feel they cannot provide care effectively, which has clearly been the case during the pandemic, their interest for staying in medicine will be lost. Using AI to make doctors see more patients faster, or read more scans, or slides, is not the fix that we need. The overarching goal of AI in healthcare, as I wrote extensively in *Deep Medicine*, needs to be to restore the human connection, the precious patient-doctor relationship, the essentiality of medicine, and its humanity. Let's hope as healthcare is rebooted and hacked, we will get there someday

Eric J. Topol, MD
La Jolla, California

Preface and Acknowledgments

All things are ready, if our mind be so.

William Shakespeare

For as long as humans have walked the earth, we have been trying to predict things. The Druids built rock alignments like Stonehenge to predict the change of seasons. The Babylonians predicted weather from cloud patterns while the Greeks divined the future by studying the flight patterns of birds.

Predictive *science* was born in 1687 when Sir Isaac Newton penned *Mathematical Principles of Natural Philosophy*. This treatise established concepts of modeling and put forward the notion that mathematical equations could be used to predict how systems evolve. Shortly thereafter, enterprising companies like Lloyds began using this new science to risk rate sea voyages in exchange for risk-adjusted insurance premiums.

Our quest to predict things hasn't changed. What has changed is the growing array of tools and the massive amounts of data that make us better at trying to predict and shape what lies ahead. Your smartphone today has a million times more processing power than the NASA computers that sent humans to the moon. When it comes to data, the internet is now a trillion times larger than it was in 1996.

And so it goes. We're now moving from merely predicting things to imbuing machines with capabilities once only within the purview of humans. Our techno-creations have already reached human parity in speech, vision, knowledge extraction, and other capabilities previously unique to the human brain.

This body of work and its capabilities is known as artificial intelligence, or simply AI.

By chance, I find myself writing this on the second anniversary of the first death in America due to COVID-19. All of us have shared this experience. The pandemic has given us stories of so many losses: loved ones, jobs, our sense of security and safety. But it has also given us stories about resilience, tenacity, heroism, perseverance, and hope. Each story is different, but the themes running through them will forever bind us together.

Much has changed in just over two years. Since that first COVID-casualty, we've learned a great deal about the importance of health and well-being for ourselves, our families, and the world in general. We've seen how our current health system works. We've also witnessed its fragility and where it is failing us.

My last book, *AI in Health: A Leader's Guide to Winning in the New Age of Intelligent Health Systems* was a technology treatise. I wrote it as a primer on the emerging use of artificial intelligence in healthcare.

This book is different. It is ostensibly about AI in health, but it's more about how the Intelligent Health Revolution will help us take what we've learned from our COVID-19 experiences and apply our newfound knowledge to solving healthcare's other big challenges.

You see, even before the pandemic, something has been niggling at many of us for too long. Whether you are a practicing physician or nurse, medical researcher, health executive, elected official, volunteer caregiver, or health consumer, somewhere deep in our brains has been this simple truth: the current health system isn't working, and it will only get worse if we don't do something about it.

It took a planetary health crisis to bring greater focus to the importance and impact of getting healthcare right. It's time for a deeper discussion about the crises of today and the problems that are coming. It's a dialogue about what we want from our healthcare system. Beyond talking, it's about taking action. We can and must do better.

You'll learn more about the role of the Intelligent Health Revolution throughout this book, but it can be summarized with this simple equation:

Humans + Artificial Intelligence = Superpowers for Change.

Another key theme of this book is that AI is not the answer to fixing healthcare. Humans are. We were smart enough to create artificial intelligence, now we must harness it for the good it can do in health and medicine.

The pandemic accelerated the use of AI in health and medicine, but we are still early in its use and application. As such, I sometimes come across pundits and critics debating the *"risks"* of AI in health as if it could be stopped. When I hear this, I find myself wondering about conversations our early ancestors must have had about fire.

Kai-Fu Lee is one of my favorite authors and leaders. He's the former president of Google China and senior executive at Microsoft, SGI, and Apple. He's also the bestselling author of *AI Superpowers*. In his latest book *AI 2041*, Lee gives us a glimpse of what an AI-driven world will look like two decades from now. Here's what he has to say about the Intelligent Health Revolution:

> ***When we look back in (the year) 2041, we will likely see healthcare as the industry most transformed by AI.***

And so, ready or not, the Intelligent Health Revolution is upon us. This book is about harnessing the power of this movement to create a health system that better serves all of us in the next century.

On the subject of "Hacking" Healthcare – When presenting my proposal for this book to my publisher Taylor and Francis, one of the reviewers admonished me to drop the word *"hacking"* from the title as it implied someone sitting in a dark room doing nefarious things.

And while there may be someone downloading my credit card information and personal profile as I write this, the term "hacking" has a very different meaning in the circles in which I travel.

Hacking is not anything negative. It's a term that describes a free-form way of seeing a problem and then experimenting with ways of solving something that seems unsolvable. Drew Endy, a biohacker and bioengineering professor at Stanford, said it best: *"I come from a tradition where hacking is a positive term, and it means learning about stuff by building and trying to make things and seeing what happens."*[1]

A national focus with global impact – My last book was published in seven languages and distributed worldwide. To me, this is a proxy measure for how it was relevant across geographies.

While much of this book focuses on the United States, the challenges defined and concepts presented are relevant to all geographies. The Intelligent Health Revolution is universal and not something that will be contained by historical boundaries.

The data explosion in health and medicine is not confined to select geographies, whether we are talking about better managing the needs of aging populations in the United States, Japan, or South Korea. Instead, our ability to break down data barriers within and across borders through data and secure, intelligent cloud services holds great promise for everything from improving maternal and child health to preventing the next pandemic.

Roll the credits – While my name is on the cover, this book is based on the collective wisdom and experience of so many people.

From public health challenges to space medicine, I have been blessed to serve in roles where I get to help health and medical practitioners solve problems. Along the way I've learned much from those on the frontlines. In this regard, I'm reminded of an adage of an early mentor of mine: *"None of us is as smart as all of us."* And so, many of the views reflected in this book come from working alongside countless people who have the collective desire to make healthcare better.

I am also fortunate and grateful to brush up against some amazing luminaries in the field that have assisted in shaping the content of this book:

Eric Topol, MD, is one of the strongest voices for change and transformation in healthcare today. He's the author of several best-selling books including *Deep Medicine, The Creative Destruction of Medicine, and The Patient will See You Now*. Dr. Topol is the founder and director of the Scripps Research Translational Institute, and a professor of Molecular Medicine at The Scripps Research Institute.

Ken Dychtwald, PhD, is a psychologist, gerontologist, and best-selling author of 19 books on aging-related issues, including *Bodymind, Age Wave: The Challenges and Opportunities of an Aging Society, Age Power and How the 21st Century Will Be Ruled by the New Old, Healthy Aging*. In preparing to write this book, I spent a day with Dr. Dychtwald at the Esalen Institute in Big Sur getting his take on the challenges of aging in today's world and the value and use of technology to help close the gap between healthspan and lifespan (more on this in Chapter 9 – Intelligent Aging is Healthcare's Moonshot).

Ann Mond Johnson is the CEO of the American Telemedicine Association (ATA). Long before the pandemic put telehealth in the public eye, Ann and her team were steadfast in championing the value and benefits of innovating health delivery by expanding the reach of clinicians using telehealth and virtual care services.

Greg Caressi is Sr Vice President and Global Client Leader responsible for Frost & Sullivan's Healthcare and Life Sciences practice. In this role, he engages with industry leaders across the globe regarding tech trends while leveraging insights from the firm's research to identify growth opportunities and needed solution capabilities for healthcare stakeholders. He was especially helpful in providing guidance on the changing nature of Retail Health.

Harry Pappas is the founder and CEO of the Intelligent Health Association. He is a convener of health and medical leaders across the globe who are on the leading edge of new ways of improving health through AI and digital breakthroughs.

Eric Eskioglu, MD, is SVP and Chief Medical Officer at Novant Health. He's a tireless advocate and a frontline AI practitioner who is improving the quality of health services across the care continuum.

Ankur Teredesai, PhD, is a professor of Data Science at the University of Washington and a serial entrepreneur who is applying AI to improve digital therapies. He is also one of the leading minds in the use of AI and advanced Nudge Theory to improve the health of citizens at scale.

Antoinette "Toni" Thomas is Microsoft's Chief Patient Experience Officer whose expertise is invaluable as we drive toward health systems truly being consumer centric.

John Doyle is Chief Technology Officer for Microsoft's worldwide health team. His ability to blend the technical side of AI with the practical challenges of deploying intelligent systems is invaluable in making AI real.

Kris Mendansky is Senior Editor at Taylor and Francis. She was the impetus behind getting my first book published and has been quietly persistent in getting me to write this book.

Note

1. Spencer Michels, What is biohacking and why should we care? Science, PBS, September 23, 2014, https://www.pbs.org/newshour/science/biohacking-care

About the Author

Tom Lawry serves as National Director of AI for Health & Life Sciences at Microsoft and previously served as Director of Worldwide Health. Tom works with providers, payers, and life science organizations in planning and implementing innovative solutions that improve the quality and efficiency of health services delivered around the globe.

Tom focuses on strategies for digital transformation applied to performance optimization including artificial intelligence (AI), machine learning (ML), and cognitive services. He previously served as Director of Organizational Performance for Microsoft's health incubator (Health Solutions Group).

Prior to Microsoft, Tom served as a Senior Director at GE Healthcare with global responsibilities for revenue cycle analytics and operational performance solutions.

Lawry was the founder and CEO of Verus, a healthcare software company named as one of the Top 100 Fastest Growing Washington Companies for three consecutive years and to the Deloitte Fast 500 Technologies list.

For 12 years, Lawry served in various executive management roles in hospitals and integrated delivery networks. He has published numerous articles and is a frequent conference speaker on using intelligent technology to innovate healthcare. His last book, *Artificial Intelligence in Healthcare: A Leader's Guide to Winning in the New Age of Intelligent Health Systems*, was published in seven languages and a global best seller.

Chapter 1

We Interrupt This Pandemic to Bring You Some Good News

Stop using your phones and laptops as toys and use them to start a revolution.

Van Jones

It arrived without warning. No announcements preceded it. No scientific papers were presented before it came crashing into our lives. The COVID-19 (COVID) pandemic was simply there when the day before it was not. We recognized it when our family, friends, and co-workers started getting sick and dying in numbers not seen since the beginning of the last century. Like something out of a bad science fiction novel, the humans versus virus battle was on.

We all have our stories. Mine was losing my healthy 94-year-old father. From diagnosis to death in three days.

Healthcare has always been steeped in emergency preparedness, but nothing prepared it for what was to come. ICUs were quickly overrun by critically ill patients. As COVID patients were highly infectious, treatments for other medical needs came to a grinding halt. The lack of common items such as ventilators and personal protective equipment (PPE) became a matter of life and death.

Frontline caregivers worked around the clock. When systems were pressed to the brink, resourceful people stepped in to bolster, bridge, and fix what wasn't working. Makeshift ICUs were created. Ventilators were MacGyvered back into service.

DOI: 10.4324/9781003286103-1

COVID-19 TIMELINE

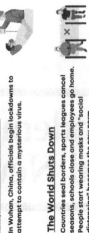

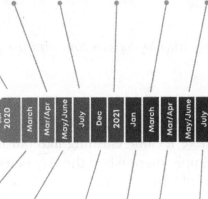

2020	
March	
Mar/Apr	
May/June	
July	
Dec	
2021	
Jan	
March	
Mar/Apr	
May/June	
July	
Dec	

A Mysterious New Illness

In Wuhan, China, officials begin lockdowns to attempt to contain a mysterious virus.

The World Shuts Down

Countries seal borders, sports leagues cancel seasons, schools close and employees go home. People start wearing masks and "social distancing" becomes the new norm.

Uptick in Mental Health Issues

People struggle with unemployment and/or working from home without child care and school. US breaks records for daily cases/deaths.

Light at the End of the Tunnel?

2021 begins with a race to vaccinate. Cases and deaths begin to fall. But the variants are still a threat, Vaccine rollout is uneven, and we are still wearing masks.

US Surpasses

100 million vaccinations administered.

After Upswing

CDC reinstates indoor mask mandate as Delta Variant explodes.

CDC Reports

Children who lost a parent or primary caregiver due to COVID-19 exceed 140,000.

The Virus Spreads, Cases Multiply

The Grand Princess cruise ship, docked outside of San Fran, has passengers with COVID-19; the Bay area is first in the US to announce it is overwhelmed; as cases grow; there is a nationwide shortage of PPE.

Flattening the Curve – For a While

After " Flattening the Curve," cases begin to skyrocket again as states "reopen" in different phases. Researchers race to identify treatments and make vaccines.

New Hope, New Mutations

The FDA authorizes two vaccines. Major variants begin to circulate which might impact vaccine effectiveness.

U.S COVID-19

Death toll surpasses 400,000.

Delta Variant

Becomes the dominant variant.

Hospitals Overwhelmed

New COVID-19 cases create staffing shortages as clinicians are pressed to the brink.

World Health Organization

WHO reports on Omicron, a new highly contagious variant.

Sources : ysm-res.cloudinary.com, Centers for Disease Control

Doctors and nurses displayed near superpowers. In the end, they were still human. What was already a problem of clinician burnout became an epidemic in its own right. It still is as I write this.

For some health providers, it was simply too much. Hospitals with no beds put critically ill COVID patients in planes, helicopters, and ambulances, sending them hundreds of miles away from family for treatment.[1] Refrigerator trucks served as makeshift morgues. People with other pressing medical conditions waited. And the sick and infected kept coming.

In the world of drug discovery, the race was on. As infection rates and death tolls climbed at a mind-blowing rate, we woke up to the fact that getting new drugs or a vaccine from the lab to the pharmacy historically took an average of 12 years at a cost of $2.6 billion.[2]

Almost overnight, consumers became legitimately fearful of premature death *en masse*. COVID cut to the core of what we universally care about the most. Our health. Our loved ones. Our jobs and financial security. In a matter of months, this singular issue forced everyone to change their daily living activities and see their life priorities in a different light.

The world was seemingly descending into darkness, never seen by those walking the planet today. Just when it felt like the bad news would never end, something happened. As humans always do, we learned. We adapted. We began to prevail.

People led the fight. The Intelligence Revolution gave them the tools to win.

AI to the Rescue

Early in the pandemic, health leaders discovered a body of knowledge on coronaviruses, but it was of little use as it was scattered around the world in disparate locations and formats. To solve this problem, the Allen Institute for AI, the National Institute of Health (NIH), and others leveraged something known as Natural Language Processing (NLP) and created the COVID-19 Open Research Dataset (CORD-19) that fused together 47,000 scholarly articles and studies in a matter of weeks.[3]

CORD-19 gave researchers, drug developers, and public health leaders open access to a unified body of knowledge that was fully searchable and readily sharable for collaborations worldwide, thus saving their precious time.

As pandemic pandemonium set in among citizens, Microsoft created a COVID bot and made it freely available to health organizations like the

Centers for Disease Control and Prevention (CDC). The bot walked anxious citizens through a series of questions and then provided guidance by intelligently mapping their specific situations to clinical guidelines. Forty million people used it to get accurate information and gain a sense of comfort.[4]

Because COVID was highly infectious, clinicians and health organizations turned to telehealth. Virtual visits became the centerpiece of adapting to keep consumers and providers connected. Before the pandemic, only 43% of health centers could provide telemedicine services. By the end of the first phase of the outbreak, 95% of health centers were using it. With this quick pivot, nearly one-third of all health visits in the summer of 2020 were conducted using telehealth.[5] At its peak, growth in telemedicine and virtual care shot up 38× from pre-pandemic levels.[6]

Telehealth facilitated patient triage and reconnected consumers to care providers. This reduced the effects of patient surges on care facilities. It also helped address limitations to healthcare access, conserved PPE, and reduced disease transmission.

Meanwhile, pharma and biotech companies faced impossible odds to compress the time to get a vaccine from the lab into the arms of consumers. AI evened those odds by improving the precision and speed of drug development while de-risking the process.

Intelligence tools were used to evaluate whether existing drugs could be repurposed for COVID. Researchers used AI to take ideas and progress them into actionable research accomplishing that in hours instead of months or years. It was used to interrogate massive datasets such as population-wide COVID infection rates and decades of accumulated research papers to spot valuable clues and trends for vaccine development.

AI expedited clinical trial simulations. As vaccines were approved and made available, AI tools ingested social determinants and other demographic data to identify and prioritize vulnerable and underserved populations to ensure equitable distribution.

Just as healthcare providers and pharma organizations were adapting through AI and digital technologies, so too were consumers in taking control of health issues that mattered most to them, using their smartphones, connected devices, and AI-driven apps to understand and manage their health and medical concerns.

In the first six months of the pandemic, downloads of mental health apps rose 200%. Diet and weight loss app usage climbed by 1,294%, while downloads to help manage diabetes jumped by 482%.[7] Mental health, diabetes, and cardiovascular disease apps account for almost half of disease-specific apps. Most are powered in some way by AI.[8]

In 2020 alone, more than 90,000 new consumer digital health apps hit the market. There are currently over 350,000 consumer health apps and that number is growing rapidly.[9]

Never Let a Good Crisis Go to Waste – Three Things We Learned

The pandemic challenged and changed all of us. It rearranged our priorities. It also taught us three valuable lessons:

■ When individuals and populations are healthy, everything works better. When they are not, the interconnectedness of health to the economy, job security and family safety become painfully and dangerously obvious.
■ Health systems and health leaders are capable of agile transformation when faced with a big challenge. An industry previously known for changing at glacial speed suddenly began moving at warp speed. If we can do this for COVID, we can do this to tackle other big challenges.
■ AI and intelligent health work. These tools and solutions deliver a rapid time-to-value for providers and consumers alike when properly curated and applied.

The speed and effectiveness of our response to COVID were made possible by strong leadership. Clinical, health, and business leaders led from the front. They assessed long-standing work methods and then quickly adapted to address the current problem before them.

And while humans fought the COVID battle, artificial intelligence (AI) allowed us to turn the tide in our favor quickly. It enabled and empowered clinicians and consumers alike to adapt at a much greater velocity.

Leveraging various intelligent tools, leaders rethought how to deliver care and services. Intelligent solutions were creatively put into service to make things smarter and faster. Without their use, the story would have been dramatically different.

Interconnected Digital and AI Technologies Used in the COVID-19 Response

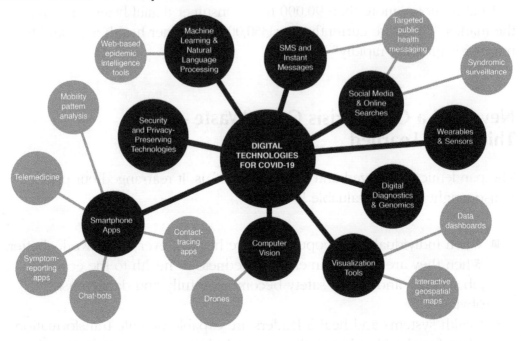

Source: Nature.com

In my last book, *AI in Health – A Leader's Guide to Winning in the New Age of Intelligent Health*, I put forward the concept of Intelligent Health Systems. Unlike Traditional Health Systems, Intelligent Health Systems are emerging as entities that leverage data, AI, the cloud, and digital tools to create strategic advantages and better outcomes. And while all health systems may lay claim to doing some of this, there is a difference in the approach taken by Traditional Health Systems compared to those on the path to becoming Intelligent Health Systems.

Both models recognize the inherent power of using data and AI to improve the delivery of health services. The approach of Traditional Health Systems is to use AI and digital tools to improve current service delivery models.

Intelligent Health Systems are taking this to the next level. They are using the Intelligent Health Revolution to rethink the entire delivery model. Their focus is on leveraging AI to efficiently provide health and medical services *across all touchpoints, experiences, and channels.*

Before the pandemic, we saw the slow but steady movement of traditional health providers and new entrants interested in becoming Intelligent Health Systems. The pandemic became a forcing function. It accelerated our thinking and willingness to change. It tested our ability to harness the power of the Intelligence Revolution to do good.

Satya Nadella, CEO of Microsoft, said it best at the beginning of the pandemic, *"We've seen two years' worth of digital transformation in two months."*[10]

Intelligent Health Systems are taking new approaches to overcome the age-old challenges of improving access, quality, and effectiveness, while lowering the costs of health services. In the future, they will become the health systems of choice as connected health consumers become the new norm.

This book is about understanding and applying what we learned from fighting a planetary health crisis. It's about using the Intelligence Revolution to tackle many other big challenges facing healthcare. Most importantly, it's about restoring power to clinicians and consumers alike by creating a system that is better aligned with our goals and balanced with available human and financial resources.

We had already started down the path of Intelligent Health Revolution. Nature came along and gave us the impetus to go faster. The days of slow progress are over. We know what can be done. It's time to apply our learnings and experiences to tackle healthcare's other significant challenges.

We have an unprecedented opportunity to take what we've learned and make healthcare better for all. To create a system that empowers citizens to be healthier while providing better ways to care for them when they are not. To harness the power of the most highly trained health workforce on the planet.

Thomas Jefferson said, *"Every generation needs a revolution."* Let the Intelligent Health Revolution be our charge to improve the health of our people, our nation, and the planet.

Making this happen starts with you.

Notes

1. Heather Hollingsworth, Jim Salter, With no beds, hospitals ship patients to far-off cities, AP News, August 18, 2021, https://apnews.com/article/health-coronavirus-pandemic-0ba6aa292483a89d52ab44b5f5434815.

2. FDA Drug Approval Process, Drug.com, April 13, 2020, https://www.drugs.com/fda-approval-process.html FDA.
3. Cliff Saran, Microsoft and Google join forces on Covid-19 dataset, Computer Weekly, March 17, 2020, https://www.computerweekly.com/news/252480156/Microsoft-and-Google-join-forces-on-Covid-19-dataset.
4. Delivering information and eliminating bottlenecks with CDC's COVID-19 assessment bot, March 20, 2020, Microsoft Official Blog. https://blogs.microsoft.com/blog/2020/03/20/delivering-information-and-eliminating-bottlenecks-with-cdcs-covid-19-assessment-bot/.
5. Trends in Use of Telehealth Among Health Centers During the COVID-19 Pandemic – United States, June 26–November 6, 2020, Centers for Disease Control, February 9, 2021, https://www.cdc.gov/mmwr/volumes/70/wr/mm7007a3.htm.
6. Oleg Bestsennyy, Greg Gilbert, Alex Harris, Jennifer Rost, Telehealth: A quarter trillion-dollar post COVID-19 reality? McKinsey and Company, 2021, https://www.mckinsey.com/industries/healthcare-systems-and-services/our-insights/telehealth-a-quarter-trillion-dollar-post-covid-19-reality.
7. COVID-19: Digital Health Trends and Opportunities for 2021, The Organization for the Review of Care and Health Applications (ORCHA), January 2021.
8. Chloe Kent, Digital health app market booming, finds IQVIA report, Medical Device Network, August 2021, https://www.medicaldevice-network.com/news/digital-health-apps/.
9. Chloe Kent, Digital health app market booming, finds IQVIA report, Medical Device Network, August 2021, https://www.medicaldevice-network.com/news/digital-health-apps/.
10. CIO.com, April 30, 2020. https://cio.economictimes.indiatimes.com/news/corporate-news/we-saw-2-years-of-digital-transformation-in-2-months-satya-nadella/75471759.

Chapter 2

Welcome to the Intelligent Health Revolution

rev·o·lu·tion | \ ˌre-və-ˈlü-shən
A: *a change of paradigm*
B: *a sudden, radical, or complete change*

Strap yourself in. We are about to blast off.

The smart folks at McKinsey & Company predict that we will experience more technological progress in the next decade than we have in the past 100 years.[1] Imagine that. Pop the hood on any of these up-and-coming tech attractions and you'll likely find AI driving things forward.

The first shots in the Intelligence Revolution were fired years ago. You benefit from them every time you go online, use a smart app, or get directions. The pandemic showed us that humans are better and faster in solving big problems in health and medicine because of them.

As a writer, conference speaker, and AI practitioner, I'm struck by how often I have lively conversations about AI and the Intelligence Revolution with others only to find we are talking about different things.

And so, before we go any further, let's define some of the key terms that are used throughout this book.

At a high level, the **Intelligence Revolution** is an example of what economists and historians who study scientific and technical progress call change that comes about due to a new *general-purpose technology*.

A **general-purpose technology** is one that has the power to continually transform itself, progressively branching out and boosting productivity and systemic change across all sectors and industries.[2] As this happens, a

DOI: 10.4324/9781003286103-2

general-purpose technology drastically alters societies through its impact on pre-existing economic and social structures.

Scientific and technical breakthroughs frequently change history. Systemic transformation brought about by a *general-purpose technology* is rare. Think steam engine, the electricity generator, and the printing press.

Let's use the steam engine to illustrate this point. It was originally designed to pump water out of mines. Over time others adopted and adapted this new technology. This gave rise to railroads, the transportation industry, and mass-production manufacturing. As this occurred, benefits began accruing to all sectors. Farmers, for example, adapted and used the steam engine for mechanical power which boosted production and improved crop yields. As agricultural output grew, they also now had a transportation network to deliver their goods from the country's interior to the coasts, facilitating trade with new markets.

Like the steam engine story, the Intelligence Revolution will produce exponential change based on the increasing sophistication of AI, virtually free data storage and communications that are combined with ever-increasing computational powers that now rival some human capabilities.

With the above in mind, we'll apply the following definitions to the content and discourse of this book:

Artificial Intelligence (AI) is a general-purpose technology. Simply put, it's *any system that can depict or mimic human brain functions.* We'll expand on this in Chapter 5.

The **Intelligence Revolution** is the pervasive change taking place as a result of the use of AI as a general-purpose technology that is being applied across all industries.

The **Intelligent Health Revolution** is a term used to characterize the pervasive change taking place now and in the future that comes from applying AI in the fields of health and medicine.

An **Intelligent Health System** is an entity that embraces the Intelligent Health Revolution by leveraging data and AI to create strategic advantages in providing health and medical services *across all touchpoints, experiences, and channels.*

Unlike Traditional Health Systems, Intelligent Health Systems use AI to drive *new approaches* to overcome the age-old challenges of improving access, quality, effectiveness, and costs of health services. They do this by being faster and better than similar but traditional organizations by using AI-enabling technologies, ubiquitous connectivity, and intelligent devices and systems.

An important nuance of these definitions is that AI *enables humans* to change how they live and work. It's up to humans to adopt AI technologies. In doing so, they must also be willing to adapt to the changes brought about by AI. More on this in Chapter 17.

Finally, while we are defining terms, let's look at the often-used phrase of **Digital Health.**

The Healthcare Information and Management Systems Society (HIMSS) is a global member association committed to transforming the health ecosystem. In a comprehensive review of healthcare transformation, HIMSS draws attention to the issue surrounding the use of this term:

> *"Digital health" has been discussed widely, yet an agreed upon definition of digital health remains elusive. A variety of terms and concepts are used interchangeably in reference to digital health, including "mHealth" (mobile health), "eHealth" (e.g., technology and digital applications to assist patients in their health), virtual care, and telehealth, to name just a few."[3]*

From the FDA to Wikipedia, many organizations offer their own definitions of digital health. A Google search on *"digital health"* turns up 4.2 billion results.

The Evolution of Health Information Technology (HIT)

1950–1960	1970–2000	2000–2020	2020+
Mainframe Computers	**Health IT**	**E-Health**	**Digital Health**
Mainframe computers are introduced into business sectors.	Health informatics as a discipline emerges. Problem oriented health record is implemented.	Growth in chronic illness rates, need for data given quality and safety challenges.	Analytics, AI, robotics, machine learning, Internet of Things, health apps, virtual reality.
Mainframe computers were agnostic to all sectors.	Personal computers on the market for consumers.	Consumerism emerges with use of personal computers and access to information via internet. Public funders invest in interoperability.	Pervasive use of ICT in "digital" societies.
Code written in machine and assembly in machine	Health IT departments in hospitals deploy IT enterprise systems.		Wellness focused.
Relatively limited impact on healthcare.		E-commerce emerges. Enterprise wide shared health record (EMR) implementation underway.	Consumers demand health services that are responsive when and where needed, digitally.
Focus: Limited focus on corporate support functions only.	Focus: Logistics and organizational functions a major focus, performance is prioritized. Management systems software focus.	Focus: Health IT focus on patient care delivery, digital technologies focus on provider directed and controlled care processes.	Focus: Consumer and person-centric – care that aligns with lifestyle. New data sources (e.g. wearables, sensors, social network data) connect to health systems.

Source: Digital Health – A Framework for Health Transformation, HIMSS

Whatever definition is used to define digital health, it's safe to assume that AI will be at the core of digital technology that is improving the way work and health processes are made better.

No matter what name you give it, our journey in using AI in health and medicine is just beginning. While no one has a perfect crystal ball in how the transformation will unfold, here are three trends that AI and the Intelligent Health Revolution are sure to drive.

From Reactive to Proactive

Today's traditional health systems are mainly reactive. Intelligent Health Systems are emerging that are proactive.

Consider something as basic as the "annual exam."

One in five adults in the United States gets a yearly physical in a physician's office.[4] In this face-to-face visit, a physician collects data using a stethoscope along with lab tests to provide a snapshot of a patient's health status at *that moment*. In doing so, it's really a "look back" at how your body and health have changed since the last time you had your annual checkup.

Should this "look-back" conclude that you have a medical condition, you're told to stop smoking, start eating healthy, curb your alcohol intake, get on a new drug regimen, have a corrective medical procedure, or a host of other things that are reacting to a medical issue you now have.

Like so many other aspects of how traditional health systems work, annual exams are the norm based on old thinking and past capabilities. Much of it keeps us in the realm of reactive healthcare.

In the world of intelligent health, let's consider an approach that proactively becomes a "perpetual exam." Your physician is still actively engaged. But instead of meeting in a physical location (medical office) at designated points in time (yearly) to essentially look in the rear-view mirror, a series of connected smart apps help to monitor, analyze, detect, and even predict future events before they happen. This is done on a continuous, real-time basis.

Innovative organizations, including the Mayo Clinic, University of California San Francisco, and Geisinger, are working to digitally transform the traditional, yearly physical visit into an ongoing virtual relationship.[5] With the new digital innovations, the physical will become a dynamic, proactive, and continuous process. This includes physicians having the ability to provide ongoing electronic reports and "nudges" to encourage consumers to take a more active role in managing their health.

Today, this is happening with intelligent devices that are external or wearable. In the future, smart sensors may be embedded under your skin, swallowed with your breakfast, or remain swimming in your bloodstream. They will constantly monitor your heart rate, respiration, temperature, skin secretions, and more.

Sound a little too Sci-Fi? Companies like Medtronic have already pioneered pacemakers and other intelligent implantable heart devices that connect to a patient's mobile device. In one situation, a patient with a connected heart implant felt dizzy while mowing the lawn with his phone in his pocket. In the time it took to go into the house and sit down, his phone was ringing. It was his clinic calling. His implanted device had already alerted a medical team and sent data related to the problem. This allowed them to assess and act in real-time.[6]

Research suggests patients with smart implants like this have higher overall survival rates, fewer emergency room visits, and shorter hospital stays.[7,8]

Beyond proactively monitoring and managing physical conditions such as chronic disease, AI is tackling a growing array of mental health issues. Companies like Kintsugi are using AI to develop voice biomarker solutions that predict and assess things like clinical depression and anxiety.[9] They do this by analyzing snippets of free-form speech. There is a wealth of information about our health encoded in our speech. In applying AI to voice recognition, solutions are being created that can extend and improve telehealth platforms and patient monitoring applications.[10]

Consumers increasingly expect to play a more significant role in their care and health. The shift to proactive services will improve overall health status. AI will also help make healthcare more proactive by removing traditional barriers and improving access for more citizens.

From "Health Systems" to "Systems of Health"

In shifting from reactive to proactive, Intelligent Health Systems will go beyond making us better at what we do today by moving away from the current "health systems" model and moving us toward "systems of health."

The predominant focus of "health systems" today is managing medical conditions as or after they arise. Intelligent Health Systems will move us toward "systems of health" that focus on using our wisdom and technology to empower citizens to live more healthy and optimized lives which ultimately may prevent medical conditions like Type 2 diabetes from occurring in the first place.

Stop and think about that for a moment. Imagine a time in the future where very few people die prematurely of *preventable disease.* Today, 30 million people die every year from conditions that are reversible if caught early.[11]

Cardiovascular conditions, diabetes, and chronic obstructive pulmonary disorder (COPD) are the top three preventable and manageable chronic conditions in the United States. Beyond the premature loss of life, these conditions alone have a combined economic burden of $590 billion a year.[12]

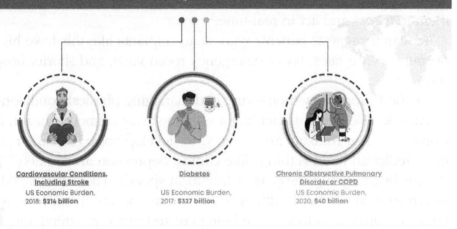

Top 3 Preventable and Manageable Chronic Conditions in US

Cardiovascular Conditions, Including Stroke
US Economic Burden, 2018: $214 billion

Diabetes
US Economic Burden, 2017: $327 billion

Chronic Obstructive Pulmonary Disorder or COPD
US Economic Burden, 2020: $40 billion

Source: Centers for Disease Control and Prevention, World Health Organization

The pandemic highlighted the need for the health system to focus on *whole-person health.* This means addressing behavioral, social, and economic vulnerabilities.

Intelligent health consumerism is emerging rapidly as individuals empower themselves with smart apps to guide health decisions and lifestyle choices. As this happens, there is a significant disconnect between the health and wellness tools consumers are using and traditional healthcare systems.

This "disconnect" has evolved for two reasons. First, traditional health systems focus primarily on managing illness and disease using prescribed care pathways rather than focusing on individual health and wellness goals.[13]

Second, most digital tools and platforms available to consumers are not connected to the information infrastructures of traditional health systems.

This makes it nearly impossible for consumers and health providers to connect and collaborate.[14]

The emergence of AI will provide a dual benefit. It is already improving the current disease management focus of health systems today. More importantly, when smart consumer health apps are connected to traditional health data systems, they will empower new proactive and predictive strategies that focus on keeping people healthy and caring more effectively for them when they are not.

Making Personalized Health Real

Beyond being reactive, traditional health largely follows a one-size-fits-all approach. In reality, no two consumers are ever the same, even if they have a common chronic illness. Each of us has a unique set of characteristics, including our genetic makeup, microbiome, age, gender, and many other variables that affect our health.

One of the benefits of the growing array of AI solutions is accessing and analyzing enormous amounts of data from medical records, personal diagnostic devices, research studies, and other sources like social determinant data. When these capabilities are paired with clinicians' wisdom, experience, and training, the results include more accurate predictions, diagnoses, and treatments that are custom-tailored to the individual.

What Traditional Health Systems often miss in prioritizing the health and wellness of people or populations is an understanding of the motivations and goals of those turning to them. Consumers are increasingly demanding care that is personalized to their unique values, needs, and life circumstances.[15]

The Intelligent Health Revolution will provide health practitioners with the tools they need to personalize care, shifting the focus to the patient, not the disease or illness.

As we look ahead at the possibilities for improving health and medical services by enlisting the help of AI, I'm reminded of what's known as Amara's law (credited to many but originally coined by Roy Amara, Past President of the Institute of the Future). It states:

> "We tend to overestimate the effect of a technology in the short run and underestimate the effect in the long run."
>
> **- Amara's Law**

We are in the early stages of the emergence of the Intelligence Revolution in health. The best is ahead.

Notes

1. Sean Fleming, Top 10 Tech Trends That Will Shape the Coming Decade, According to McKinsey, World Economic Forum, October 12, 2021, https://www.weforum.org/agenda/2021/10/technology-trends-2021-mckinsey/.
2. Martin Mühleisen, The Long and Short of The Digital Revolution, International Monetary Fund, June 2018. https://www.imf.org/external/pubs/ft/fandd/2018/06/impact-of-digital-technology-on-economic-growth/muhleisen.htm.
3. Digital Health: A Framework for Healthcare Transformation White Paper, HIMSS, April 13, 2021, https://www.himss.org/resources/digital-health-framework-healthcare-transformation-white-paper.
4. Jackie Drees, 'We're in the Messy Adolescence of this Experience': How the Annual Physical Visit Is Shifting to Virtual, Becker's IT Review, September 7, 2021, https://www.beckershospitalreview.com/digital-transformation/we-re-in-the-messy-adolescence-of-this-experience-how-the-annual-physical-visit-is-shifting-to-virtual.html.
5. RON WINSLOW, Tech Advances Put the Annual Doctor Visit on the Critical List, Wall Street Journal, September 6, 2021, https://www.wsj.com/articles/tech-advances-put-the-annual-doctor-visit-on-the-critical-list-11630933201?mod=tech_lead_pos5.
6. https://news.medtronic.com/connected-heart-devices-named-top-innovation
7. Saxon LA, Hayes DL, Gilliam FR, et al. Long-term outcome after ICD and CRT implantation and influence of remote device follow-up: the ALTITUDE survival study. Circulation. December 7, 2010;122(23):2359–2367.
8. Crossley GH, Boyle A, Vitense H, Chang Y, Mead RH; CONNECT Investigators. The CONNECT (Clinical Evaluation of Remote Notification to Reduce Time to Clinical Decision) trial: the value of wireless remote monitoring with automatic clinician alerts. J Am Coll Cardiol. March 8, 2011;57(10):1181–1189.
9. https://kintsugihello.com/.
10. https://kintsugihello.com/.
11. Sergey Young, The Science and Technology of Growing Young, 2021.
12. US Chronic Disease Management Growth, Frost & Sullivan, October 2021.
13. Snowdon A, Schnarr K, Alessi C. "It's All About Me": The Personalization of Health Systems, 2014. Retrieved from: https://www.ivey.uwo.ca/cmsmedia/3467873/its-all-about-me-the-personalizationof-health-systems.pdf.
14. Ibid.
15. Dr. Anne Snowdon and Hugh MacLeod, Let's Get Personalized!, Researchgate, 2014, https://www.researchgate.net/publication/281287557_Lets_Get_Personalized.

Chapter 3

The Coming Care Calamity

Some people don't like change, but you need to embrace change if the alternative is disaster.

Elon Musk

Let's get the good news out of the way first.

If you are going to get sick and have great insurance or lots of money, there is no better place to do so than in the United States. We excel at taking care of really sick people.

Medical miracles are performed daily by an amazing pool of talented clinicians who have access to the best technology, facilities, and pharmaceuticals.

In this regard, we are the envy of the rest of the world.

But there remains a most vexing question: *Why do we invest more in healthcare than any country on the planet only to come in last compared to other countries in health success measures?*

Simply put, America's investment in health services does not correlate to better overall health.

The Commonwealth Fund is a private foundation started in 1918 by one of America's first female philanthropists, Anna Harkness. Its mission is to research and promote high-performing healthcare systems to achieve better access, improved quality, and greater efficiency, particularly for society's most vulnerable citizens.

According to data from the Commonwealth Fund, the United States healthcare system is the most expensive in the world. Despite enormous investments, it ranks last in overall health including access to care, administrative efficiency, equity, and healthcare outcomes.[1]

DOI: 10.4324/9781003286103-3

HEALTH CARE SYSTEM PERFORMANCE RANKINGS

	AUS	CAN	FRA	GER	NETH	NZ	NOR	SWE	SWIZ	UK	US
OVERALL RANKING	3	10	8	5	2	6	1	7	9	4	11
Access to Care	8	9	7	3	1	5	2	6	10	4	11
Care Process	8	9	7	3	1	5	2	6	10	4	11
Administrative Efficiency	8	9	7	3	1	5	2	6	10	4	11
Equity	8	9	7	3	1	5	2	6	10	4	11
Health Care Outcomes	8	9	7	3	1	5	2	6	10	4	11

Data: Commonwealth Fund analyzis.
Source: Eric C. Schneider et al., *Mirror, Mirror 2021 – Reflecting Poorly: Health Care in the U.S. Compared to Other High-Income Countrues* (Commonwealth Fund, Aug. 2021). https://doi.org/10.26099/01DV-H208

Before the onset of COVID, average annual healthcare spending for people with employer-sponsored insurance rose 2.9% to $6001 per person in 2019. Between 2015 and 2019, overall spending increased by 21.8% or $1074 per person.[2] Meanwhile, Medicare's total per-enrollee spending in 2019 weighed in at $14,151.[3]

Many studies have looked at why America is first in spending and last in results. Most conclude that a causal factor is the reactive nature of the US health system. Characteristics of a reactive model include:[4]

■ Most expenditures support a "break-fix" model of care delivery
■ Minimal investments in health improvements (as a percentage of total healthcare spend)
■ A significant number of citizens faced with access issues
■ A de-emphasis on public health

It's important to note that America's poor comparative performance is not an indictment of the talented, dedicated people who work in health, nor is it a reflection of the worthiness of the mission of health organizations or the science behind all of it.

When it comes to taking what we have learned from the pandemic to create a better system, the first question to be addressed is a simple one – *How do we best apply our incredible people and considerable resources to keep individuals and populations healthy and productive?* However, you answer that question, the Intelligent Health Revolution will play a vital role in the future.

Healthcare's Perfect Storm

Even if you believe the current system is worth perpetuating, a closer look at demographic and economic trends strongly suggests that a care calamity is coming. We've never experienced the likes of what may be ahead. We did, however, get a glimpse of what the future might look like in the summer of 2021.

At the time, we seemingly had COVID on the run. Vaccinations were underway. ICU beds were emptying, and infection rates were going down. Public events were starting up. People felt safe scheduling weddings earlier delayed, birthday parties were happening, and neighborhood BBQs and car vacations were being planned. Just as we began to shake off "COVID fatigue," a new wave of the Delta Variant hit.

One health system in the South saw a 1000% increase in COVID admissions in a week. In Texas, 6,500 travel nurses were needed to keep up with new COVID cases.[5] In Oregon, things got so bad so fast that the Governor mobilized the National Guard to help staff and keep hospitals open.[6]

COVID had already stretched the health system to its limits in the first phase of the pandemic. It was not equipped to handle this new wave. While more experienced and better prepared this time around, the breaking point came down to a people crisis.

We went into the pandemic with a shortage of qualified clinicians and caregivers. When the first wave of COVID hit, we pushed our frontline workers to the brink.

Then the next wave washed over us. We had depleted the resilience of the very people we counted on who were already in short supply. They were worn out physically, mentally, and emotionally. They labored under heavy workloads, long hours, and the stress of treating critically ill and dying COVID patients, while patients with serious non-COVID diseases like cancer often struggled to access care.

Many clinicians and frontline staff had nothing else to give as they were pressed back into service. As a result, we turned our frontline workers into a different type of COVID casualty. The words of a frontline nurse from Denver spoke for many:

> *Coping with this (Delta variant) wave has made me feel the most helpless, sad, and angry since the beginning of the pandemic. The burnout and PTSD used to feel like a temporary chapter. I see no end now. If you get sick, I hope there are healthcare workers left to take care of you. We stopped feeling like heroes long ago.*[7]

A longitudinal study by the Association of Nurse Leaders highlights the problem of putting the health workforce in such an impossible position. Emotional health declined. Twenty-five percent of nurse leaders reported being not emotionally healthy. This leads to more nurses deciding to leave the profession early. Staffing shortages and retention are a growing concern, with 90% of nurse leaders anticipating significant shortages in the future.[8]

Putting good people in bad situations negatively affects their well-being. It also diminishes the quality of care. Provider burnout doubles the odd of adverse patient safety events.[9]

Today, one-third of healthcare workers agree with the statement *"the American healthcare system is on the verge of collapse."* One quarter say they are likely to leave the field in the near future.[10]

The summer of 2021 was an episodic experience. Omicron's appearance in the fall of 2021 and winter of 2022 only exacerbated the strain on our health system. Without significant change, we risk having this situation become a perpetual state for caregivers and consumers in the not-too-distant future.

A Case of Supply and Demand

Healthcare is already the largest employment field in the United States, representing one out of every eight jobs. It employs 16 million workers and is expected to generate one-third of all new jobs in this decade. It surpasses manufacturing and retail in the total number of employees.[11,12]

And while these numbers are impressive, we are nowhere close to having enough qualified health workers to keep up with today's demand, let alone for what is coming.[13] At least not the way the health system operates today.

While the reasons for a potential care calamity are complex, the challenge is a straightforward case of supply and demand. A healthcare worker shortage has been predicted for 15–20 years. It's coming to fruition at a time when baby boomers are getting older and have more healthcare needs.

The short story goes like this: As the population ages, the need for health services increases. Older people have multiple diagnoses and comorbidities. They are surviving longer. Thanks to modern medicine, many diseases that were once terminal are now survivable, but treating these long-term illnesses is costly and strains the workforce. Detail on the challenges and opportunities to leverage Intelligent Health to serve our aging population can be found in Chapter 9.

Adding to this burden is that many of the most experienced caregivers we count on today are retiring. Let's look at nurses. Annual retirements from the nursing workforce a decade ago were 20,000. In this decade, it is estimated that we'll lose nearly 80,000 nurses a year due to retirement.[14]

According to a study by Mercer, based on the growth of the aging population alone, the United States will need to hire 2.3 million new healthcare workers by 2025 to keep up with the demand for services.[15] Provider organizations already struggle to find and retain healthcare workers; thousands of positions go unfilled due to a lack of qualified workers.

There is significant demand for not just clinicians but also a range of occupations. This includes community health workers, home health aides, personal-care aides, and nursing assistants.

The United States has experienced healthcare worker shortages periodically since the early 1900s. From world wars to economic recessions, many factors have driven such shortages. But the magnitude of future shortages is more significant than we have ever seen.[16]

The Intelligent Health Revolution to the Rescue

Done right, the Intelligent Health Revolution will help solve one of the most significant challenges facing healthcare – The shortage of human capital.

It will do this by using artificial intelligence (AI) to automate many repetitive work tasks. One of its greatest values in transforming health services is its ability to augment the experiences and skills of knowledge workers to help them be better at what they do.

AI holds the promise of freeing health practitioners from many of the repetitive administrative tasks that soak up their time and make them less effective as caregivers. A time is coming where AI-assisted analytics, simulation, and hypothesis testing can help humans drive decision making, strategy, and innovation across all care settings (as we saw with its use in managing the pandemic).

Beyond empowering and extending the skills of clinicians, the ultimate goal of applying the Intelligence Revolution to health is to provide a more efficient and personalized experience for patients and consumers.

Whether supporting clinicians to work to their highest capabilities or ensuring health organizations have sufficient human resources to keep up with the demand for services, AI can solve many of the human capital problems facing healthcare today.

Consider This Example

Before the pandemic, more than 40% of physicians were experiencing at least one sign of burnout, according to a study by the Joint Commission Journal on Quality and Patient Safety.[17] It noted that a leading contributor to physician burnout is the overwhelming load of varied tasks that must be performed daily in their practice. It concluded that for each 10% drop in task load, the risk of physician burnout dropped by one-third.

Another study by McKinsey & Company concluded that using AI and intelligent solutions in healthcare could reduce repetitive activities performed by clinicians by 36%.[18]

Imagine eliminating a third of lower-value, repetitive activities that doctors, nurses, and others deal with every day.

Today, one-third of doctors spend 20 or more hours per week doing paperwork.[19] The electronic health record (EHR) creates a virtual 24/7 work environment for physicians. The impact of such "desktop medicine" on their wellness is a challenge for clinicians and organizations alike.

Doctors currently spend more time entering data into an EHR than they spend with their patients.[20] Time spent by physicians on the EHR has been linked to their reduced satisfaction with work.[21] More than 70% say the use of antiquated EHRs has increased the number of hours worked and contributes to physician burnout.[22]

Done right, the introduction and use of AI in health and medicine enables both cost-cutting automation of routine work and value-adding augmentation of human capabilities. Improving the performance of the health system today while planning to address the challenges of the future requires *everyone to think differently*.

Doctors Spend More Time in Electronic Health Record (EHR) Than With Patients

12 Min

Interacting with **patients** during visit

8 Min

Interacting with **EHR** during visit

11 Min

Interacting with **EHR** outisde visit

Source: Stanford Medicine and The Harris Poll - How Doctors Feel About Electronic Health Record

31 minutes spent on behalf of each patient; **19** of which spent in **EHR**

As AI becomes pervasive in health and medicine, a new intelligent health system will emerge. It will facilitate systems that improve health while delivering greater value. It will provide a more personalized experience for consumers and patients. It will liberate clinicians and restore them to be the caregivers they want to be rather than the data entry clerks we're turning them into by forcing them to use systems and processes conceived decades ago.

Such is the hope and opportunity to apply AI to solve healthcare's biggest challenges.

CREATING A SMARTER EHR WITH AI

Electronic health records (EHRs) have been widely adopted with the hope they would save time and improve the quality of patient care. And while the benefits of EHRs are well documented, so too are the burdens they create for doctors, nurses, and others who use them in the course of providing care.

EHR systems are often viewed as monolithic, inflexible, difficult to use and costly to configure. They are almost always obtained from commercial vendors and require considerable time, money, and consulting assistance to implement, support and optimize.[23]

Many practicing clinicians find these systems complex and difficult to navigate. The challenge of making these systems help rather than hinder is increasing. For example, the additional complexity from regulated billing and revenue cycle requirements further reduces the time clinicians have to engage with patients.

Today enterprising organizations are working to reinvent EHRs by focusing first on how they best benefit clinicians' needs and uses. In making such systems more user-friendly and effective, AI is a critical part of rethinking and redesigning EHRs.

Researchers at MIT and the Beth Israel Deaconess Medical Center are combining machine learning and human-computer interaction to create a better EHR. They developed MedKnowts, a system that unifies processes to look up medical records and documenting patient information into a single, interactive interface.[24]

Driven by AI, this "smart" EHR automatically displays customized, patient-specific medical records when a clinician needs them. The system

(Continued)

also provides autocomplete for clinical terms and auto-populates fields with patient information to help doctors work more efficiently.

Other features include a note-taking editor with a side panel that displays relevant information from the patient's medical history. That historical information appears in the form of cards that are focused on particular problems or concepts.

For instance, if the system identifies the clinical term "diabetes" in the text as a clinician types, the system can automatically display a "diabetes card" containing medications, lab values, and snippets from past records that are relevant to diabetes treatment.

Most old-style EHRs store historical information on separate pages and list medications or lab values alphabetically or chronologically, forcing the clinician to search through data to find the information they need. The MIT-developed system only displays information relevant to the particular disease or conditions the clinician is entering into the record.

Next steps for researchers include improving the machine learning algorithms that drive the EHR so the system can more effectively highlight the most relevant parts of the medical record. They also are looking at how best to meet the needs of medical users. An emergency department physician seeing a patient for the first time is likely to need different information different than a primary care physician who knows their patients better.

Other areas where AI is being used to improve EHRs include:

Data extraction from free text: AI is being used to review provider notes and pull-out structured data. This helps EHR users recognize key terms and uncover insights, increasing their productivity.

Diagnostic and/or predictive algorithms: Algorithms are being deployed within EHRs to warn clinicians of high risk conditions such as sepsis and heart failure. AI is in use to identify patients most at risk as well as those most likely to respond to treatment protocols.

Clinical documentation and data entry: Capturing clinical notes with natural language processing allows clinicians to focus on their patients rather than keyboards and screens.

Clinical decision support: In the past, decision support, which recommends treatment strategies, was generic and rule-based. Machine-learning solutions are emerging today that learn based on new data and enable more personalized care.

(Continued)

While AI in EHR systems is being applied principally to improve data discovery and extraction and personalize treatment recommendations, it has great potential to make EHRs more user friendly. In the future, AI and machine learning will help EHRs continuously adapt to users' preferences, improving both clinical outcomes and clinicians' quality of life.

Future EHRs will also make use of AI to effectively integrate other systems like telehealth technologies. As the advent of "care anywhere" occurs it will help integrate devices such as glucometers and blood pressure cuffs to automatically measure and send results from the patient's home to the EHR.

Notes

1. Mirror, Mirror 2021: Reflecting Poorly, Commonwealth Fund, https://www.commonwealthfund.org/publications/fund-reports/2021/aug/mirror-mirror-2021-reflecting-poorly.
2. Health Care Cost and Utilization Report (HCCUR), Healthcare Cost Institute, 2020, https://healthcostinstitute.org/health-care-cost-and-utilization-report/annual-reports.
3. How much does the average Medicare beneficiary pay out of pocket for medical expenses?, Medicare Resources.org, https://www.medicareresources.org/faqs/how-much-does-the-average-medicare-beneficiary-pay-out-of-pocket-for-medical-expenses/#:~:text=Medicare%E2%80%99s%20total%20per-enrollee%20spending%20rose%20from%20%2411%2C902%20in,188%20of%20the%20Medicare%20Trustees%20Report%20for%202020.
4. Ibid.
5. Kelsey Thompson, The worst that we've seen it in Texas': 6,500 travel nurses needed as COVID cases surge. KXAN. August 10, 2021, https://www.kxan.com/news/coronavirus/the-worst-that-weve-seen-it-in-texas-6500-travel-nurses-needed-as-covid-cases-surge/.
6. Kristian Foden-Vencil, Oregon National Guard troops to help hospitals struggling with COVID patients, OPB, August 14, 2021. https://www.opb.org/article/2021/08/13/oregon-covid-19-cases-governor-kate-brown-national-guard-delta-variant/.
7. Gabrielle Mason, Horrific working conditions' & 'no end' in sight: 3 nurses tell NYT what working this surge is like. Beckers Hospital Review, August 26, 2021. https://www.beckershospitalreview.com/nursing/horrific-working-conditions-no-end-in-sight-3-nurses-tell-nyt-what-working-this-surge-is-like.html?utm_campaign=bhr&utm_source=website&utm_content=latestarticles.
8. Nurse Leaders' Top Challenges, Emotional Health, and Areas of Needed Support July 2020 to August 2021, Association of Nurse Leaders, August 2021. https://www.aonl.org/resources/nursing-leadership-covid-19-survey.

9. Panagioti M, Geraghty K, Johnson J, et al. Association Between Physician Burnout and Patient Safety, Professionalism, and Patient Satisfaction: A Systematic Review and Meta-analysis. *JAMA Intern Med.* 2018;178(10):1317–1331. doi:10.1001/jamainternmed.2018.3713.

10. Chris Jackson, American Healthcare Workers Persevering, but Remain Stressed, Ipsos, February 22, 2022, https://www.ipsos.com/en-us/news-polls/usa-today-ipsos-healthcare-workers-covid19-poll-022222

11. Derek Thomson, Health Care Just Became the U.S.'s Largest Employer, The Atlantic, 2018, https://www.theatlantic.com/business/archive/2018/01/health-care-america-jobs/550079/.

12. Ibid.

13. Ibid.

14. Auerbach, David I.; Buerhaus, Peter I.; Staiger, Douglas O.. Will the RN Workforce Weather the Retirement of the Baby Boomers?, Medical Care: October 2015 - Volume 53 - Issue 10 - p 850-856 doi: 10.1097/MLR.0000000000000415.

15. Mathew Stevenson, Demand for Healthcare Workers Will outpace Supply by 2025-An Analysis of the US Healthcare Labor Market, Mercer HPA, 2018, https://www.mercer.us/our-thinking/career/workforce-for-the-future/demand-for-healthcare-workers-will-outpace-supply-by-2025.html.

16. Linda Workman, "Confronting the Nursing Shortage," Nurse Key: https://nursekey.com/confronting-the-nursing-shortage/.

17. Correlation between physician task load and risk of burnout, *The Joint Commission Journal on Quality and Patient Safety, February, 2021.* https://www.jcrinc.com/about-us/news/2021/01/correlation-between-physician-task-load-and-risk-of-burnout/.

18. Michael Chui, Where Machines Could Replace Humans-And where They Can't, McKinsey & Company, 2017, https://www.mckinsey.com/business-functions/digital-mckinsey/our-insights/where-machines-could-replace-humans-and-where-they-cant-yet.

19. The Medscape Physician Compensation Report, Medscape, 2021, https://www.medscape.com/sites/public/physician-comp/2018.

20. How Doctors Feel About Electronic Health Records National Physician Poll, Stanford University and the Harris Poll. 2018.

21. Tai-Seale M, Olson CW, Li J, Chan AS, Morikawa C, Durbin M, et al. Electronic health record logs indicate that physicians split time evenly between seeing patients and desktop medicine. Health Aff (Millwood). 2017;36(4):655–62. Go to the article, Google Scholar.

22. How Doctors Feel About Electronic Health Records National Physician Poll, Stanford University and the Harris Poll. 2018.

23. Thomas H. Davenport, Tonya M. Hongsermeier, and Kimberly Alba Mc Cord, Using AI to Improve Electronic Health Records, Harvard Business Review, December 13, 2018, https://hbr.org/2018/12/using-ai-to-improve-electronic-health-records.

24. Adam Zewe, Toward a smarter electronic health record, MIT News, September 23, 2021, https://news.mit.edu/2021/medknowts-electronic-health-record-0923.

Chapter 4

The Future of Everything

When we look back in 2041, we will likely see healthcare as the industry most transformed by AI.

Kai-Fu Lee

Co-chair, Artificial Intelligence Council, World Economic Forum

The pandemic showed us what happens when things go wrong in the world of health. Public health leaders and economists have always stressed the interconnectedness of health, economic well-being, and security. COVID made this connection painfully real for the rest of us.

COVID will graduate from a pandemic to become another endemic disease, like chicken pox and malaria. As this occurs, the big question for all of us is this:

How Will We Apply What We Learned?

What we do with our newfound wisdom and experience is at the heart of how our health system will work and serve us in the future.

The pandemic revealed many holes in the healthcare safety net. It also accelerated the use of AI in ways that are already reshaping the future of healthcare.

It is not a stretch to predict that AI and the Intelligent Health Revolution will define the trajectory of healthcare in the twenty-first century. The journey may not be linear, but we've reached a tipping point, and there's no turning back.

In preparing for the post-COVID era, successful clinical and health leaders will use their *"pandemic learnings"* to rethink how health and medical organizations work. They'll look more closely at who they serve and why they even exist.

DOI: 10.4324/9781003286103-4

In the end, the pandemic gave clinicians and consumers alike a new lens to look through in reimagining how health and medicine will serve our needs in the future.

The pandemic showed us the power of AI in helping humans rapidly respond and win against one of the most significant health challenges of the last century.

What we learned should become our North Star in applying AI to tackle the many other BIG challenges we face. There are plenty to go around.

Opioids

Before the COVID crisis, there was the opioid crisis. As the pandemic grabbed headlines, the opioid crisis quietly grew to become a full-fledged epidemic.

Today, Americans continue to die of opioids at eye-watering rates. Fatal opioid overdoses are rocketing upward among people of color. Meanwhile, there is a growing availability of much more dangerous synthetic opioids like fentanyl.[1]

Not surprisingly, new research correlates increased death rates from opioid overdoses to economic instability such as job losses.[2]

Chronic Disease

If you are one of the millions of people managing a chronic health condition, you know it's a daily challenge. Chronic diseases remain the leading cause of death and disability in the United States. Sixty percent of Americans have at least one chronic condition. Forty-two percent have multiple chronic conditions. Healthcare costs associated with these diseases are astronomical, accounting for 86% of America's annual healthcare expenditures.[3]

New data suggests that people who develop chronic conditions are becoming sick and increasingly sicker earlier in life.[4] Look closely at our traditional approach to chronic conditions and you see why: We spend resources reactively to treat chronic conditions rather than investing in proactively preventing or slowing the progression of things like diabetes and heart disease.

Mental Health

Even before COVID hit, life expectancy for Americans had been trending downward since 2014, while other developed nations have been steadily increasing the lifespan of their citizens.[5]

This is happening, in part, due to a dramatic uptick in "deaths of despair." There has been a 900% increase in drug-related deaths alone in the past few years.[6] Suicide rates have been rising and are especially prevalent and tragic among our young and middle-aged citizens.

Consumer Unrest

Looking beyond how we manage health and medical conditions, there are significant issues in how we treat people when they need help. When people are already feeling vulnerable because they are ill or injured, we often put them through a labyrinth of archaic processes, making them feel confused and unvalued.

A study of health consumers by Change Healthcare and The Harris Poll reports that more than two-thirds say every step of seeking healthcare is a chore. Finding, accessing, and paying for healthcare in America requires so much work that half of the consumers surveyed said they avoid seeking care altogether. It also notes that nearly all want to see healthcare offer a fully connected digital experience.[7] More information on this is available in Chapter 8.

Half of consumers have avoided seeking care because:

They weren't sure what the cost would be (53%)

They weren't sure where to start (48%)
67% millennials I 59% High Deductible

59% have gone into an appointment before without being sure if they could afford it
72% millennials I 71% High Deductible

Source: The 2020 Healthcare Consumer Experience Index.
www.changehealthcare.com/insights/healthcare-consumer-experience-index

Access and Equity

Access to needed health and medical services is an issue for millions of Americans today. Barriers to access include where they live, how much money they make, and the color of their skin. According to a study by UCLA, health equity has shown no improvement in the last 25 years. Health disparities by income are actually increasing.[8]

Geography is also an impediment. Many people with heart disease live in low-resource settings.[9] They live in rural areas far from available clinics or hospitals. Digital connectivity and intelligent telehealth services are often lacking in these remote areas, even though the option to be seen, diagnosed, and treated without the need for an in-person visit is more important than ever in rural locations.

It took a pandemic to emphasize the critical role of AI and digital solutions to bolster and augment the work of humans. As we saw with the pandemic, they can sometimes mean the difference between life and death.

The Time for Intelligent Health Systems Is Now

COVID raced into our lives and rightfully became the front and center priority. The list of health and medical issues facing us before the pandemic has not gone away and many of these challenges have gotten bigger or closer.

When you look at the almost endless list of health challenges and consider what we've learned, you don't need this book to know that fixing the inadequacy of today's healthcare system is the most significant economic and social issue of our time.

Whether you are sick or not, it's affecting your life as you read the words on this page. If you never set foot in a doctor's office or hospital, the system will still profoundly impact your life.

The pandemic taught us much about ourselves and what we expect. It reinforced the importance of healthy citizens and healthy nations. It demonstrated our capacity to change. It also solidified the role AI plays in making things better. These learnings are at the heart of our collective ability to rethink and reboot a system that, without change, is not likely sustainable.

We can create a better future state for health. The Intelligent Health Revolution is just getting started. As technological capabilities increase and we master the human-machine symbiosis, the results will profoundly reshape health services and systems.

Done right, it's a revolution that empowers both clinicians and consumers. It frees us from the shackles of the past. It exponentially increases our ability to gather and use data to do good. It not only raises the bar to increase health status but also helps to make the best use of our finite resources.

It could not have come at a better time.

Notes

1. THE COVID-19 PANDEMIC IS FUELING THE OPIOID CRISIS!, National Institute of Environmental Health Sciences.
2. American Medical Association, Issue brief: Reports of increases in opioid-related overdose and other concerns during COVID pandemic, https://www.ama-assn.org/system/fles/2020-06/issue-brief-increases-in-opioid-related-overdose.pdf.
3. Christine Buttorff, Teague Ruder, and Melissa Bauman, Multiple Chronic Conditions in the United States, 2017. https://www.rand.org/pubs/tools/TL221.html.
4. Alan R. Weil and Rachel Dolan, REDUCING THE BURDEN OF CHRONIC DISEASE A Report of the Aspen Health Strategy Group, 2019. https://www.aspeninstitute.org/wp-content/uploads/2019/02/AHSG-Chronic-Disease-Report-2019.pdf.
5. Steven H. Woolf; Heidi Schoomaker, Life Expectancy and Mortality Rates in the United States, 1959-2017, JAMA Network, November 26, 2019. https://jamanetwork.com/journals/jama/article-abstract/2756187?guestaccesskey=c1202c42-e6b9-4c99-a936-0976a270551f&utm_source=for_the_media&utm_medium=referral&utm_campaign=ftm_links&utm_content=tfl&utm_term=112619&alert=article.
6. Sean Fleming, US life expectancy is falling – here's why, World Economic Forum, January 2020, https://www.weforum.org/agenda/2020/01/us-life-expectancy-decline/.
7. 2020 Change Healthcare – Harris Poll Consumer Experience Index, July 2020, https://analyze.changehealthcare.com/healthcare-consumer-experience-research.
8. Zimmerman FJ, Anderson NW. Trends in Health Equity in the United States by Race/Ethnicity, Sex, and Income, 1993–2017. JAMA Netw Open. 2019;2(6): e196386. doi:10.1001/jamanetworkopen.2019.6386.
9. Jean-Luc Eiselé, How digital equality could boost heart health, World Economic Forum, September 29, 2021, https://www.weforum.org/agenda/2021/09/how-digital-equality-can-boost-heart-health/.

Chapter 5

AI Comes of Age: A Primer

What we want is a machine that can learn from experience.

Alan Turing

As a young Assistant Math Professor at Dartmouth, 1956 was shaping up to be a good year for John McCarthy. He had just scored a grant from the Rockefeller Foundation to underwrite a gathering to explore concepts for imbuing machines with intelligence. Pretty far-out stuff for the 1950s.

And so, that summer, a ragtag collection of mathematicians and scientists sequestered themselves on the top floor of the Dartmouth Math Department for what today would be considered a rolling two-month nerd-fest.

From this gathering came the term "Artificial Intelligence," along with many concepts of how machines could use language, form abstractions, and begin to solve problems previously reserved for humans. Many of the concepts from this mid-century idea fest remain relevant today, including concepts that formed the basis for machine learning (ML) and natural language processing (NLP).

AI Is One Thing and Many Things

Let's clarify something right away. As a clinician, health executive, or consumer, it is not necessary to know how artificial intelligence (AI) actually works (though such knowledge never hurts). What is important to understand is what capabilities exist and how to put them to work in service of your mission and goals.

DOI: 10.4324/9781003286103-5

When it comes to defining AI, there is generally broad agreement on what it is, but little or no standardization when it comes to organizing the components or building blocks of AI into a universally accepted taxonomy.

With this in mind, this chapter provides a working definition of AI as well as a nontechnical framework for understanding and applying these "AI building blocks." This book, and this chapter, is not designed as technical resources for AI. Many great resources are available for those interested in going deeper into technical definitions and capabilities.

Today, AI gives intelligent machines (be they computers, imaging devices, clinical decision support tools, supply chain systems, or intelligent consumer health apps, and devices) the ability to mimic capabilities previously reserved for humans.

The terms "Artificial Intelligence" and "AI" are often bandied about as if there is a singular definition that is universally understood. In reality, AI is not one technology.

AI is an umbrella term that includes multiple concepts and technologies used individually and in combination to add intelligence to computers and machines. For example, it's commonplace for the terms AI and ML to be used interchangeably. In reality, they are not the same. This misperception often causes confusion (as you will learn in this chapter, ML is usually classified as a subset of AI).

Equally important to understand is that the set of capabilities that fits within the term AI is evolving. As a clinical or health leader, it is not imperative to be an expert in AI. It is, however, useful to understand the basics on which intelligent systems are built. To effectively plan and lead your organization's AI strategy, it's essential to have a general understanding of what it is. This includes having a framework for how the "components" and "capabilities" are used to define, build, and manage intelligent systems.

Defining Artificial Intelligence – General

Let's start with a simple but functional definition of AI:

> Artificial Intelligence (AI) is an area of computer science that emphasizes the creation of machines that work and react like humans. This means systems that can depict or mimic human brain functions, including learning, speech (recognition and generation), problem-solving, vision, and knowledge generation.

AI is a constellation of technologies that allows computers and machines to sense, comprehend, act and learn. Unlike IT systems of the past that merely generated or stored data, the value of AI systems is that they can increasingly learn, adapt, and complete tasks in ways similar to a human being. In this regard, AI imbues machines with intelligence. To understand and test this concept, one can turn to what was posited by Alan Turing more than 60 years ago as a simple but effective definition of whether a machine is intelligent. The "Turing test" states that a machine can be considered "intelligent" if a human cannot distinguish the responses of a machine compared to responses from a human.[1]

AI Building Blocks

The general definition offered above is a descriptor for what AI *is*. The components of AI described below are the "*how*" part of the equation. These are the functional capabilities provided by AI.

The remainder of this chapter is designed to create a framework for understanding AI capabilities. We'll do this by taking the broad definition noted above and breaking it down further into AI building blocks. A building block is an explicit component of AI that mimics a capability found in humans. We'll further separate the definition into two types of building blocks: ML and cognitive services.

Machine Learning (ML)

Ask anyone today what type of AI project they are working on, and the most likely answer will be something they want to predict. The ability to predict things comes from machine learning (ML) which is a subset of AI. ML provides software, machines, devices, and robots with the ability to learn without human intervention or assistance or static program instructions.

ML evolved from the study of pattern recognition and computational learning theory. The term was coined by AI pioneer Arthur Lee Samuel in 1959, who defined it as a "*field of study that gives computers the ability to learn without being explicitly programmed.*[2]"

Interestingly, Samuel is best known for his work with AI and computer gaming. If you think your kids spend too much time gaming, you can thank Samuel; he is credited with creating the world's first computer game. Known as the Samuel Checkers-playing Program, it was among the first self-learning programs that demonstrated the fundamental concept of AI.

Other things that were to come decades later, such as the use of IBM Watson to beat the best players at chess or the game show Jeopardy, have their origins rooted in Samuel's groundbreaking work.

Today, ML is at the forefront of making AI real in healthcare. It's at the heart of our ability to predict things we care about. It's used to identify the root cause of quality problems, recommend treatment options to clinicians, drive smartphone apps for consumers, improve operational efficiencies, and more.

ML-enabled processes rely on developing and using computerized algorithms that "learn" from data sets rather than strictly following rule-based preprogramed logic. An algorithm is a mathematical model based on sample data, known as "training data."

ML uses algorithms to identify patterns in the data and then make predictions from those patterns with a degree of certainty. Based on input data, ML can improve its accuracy over time through a feedback loop and modify the approach it takes in the future – hence the term "learning."

It's important to understand that the "*learning*" part of "*machine learning*" is purely mathematical and has little to do with understanding what the algorithm has learned. This is different from when humans analyze data to build an actual understanding of the data to a certain extent. In the next chapter, we'll go deeper into understanding and applying the differences in what AI is good at versus humans.

Despite lacking deliberate understanding and being a mathematical process, ML can be helpful in many tasks. It provides many AI applications the power to mimic rational thinking given a certain context when learning occurs by using the correct data.

Within the general category of ML are various models used to create different types of algorithms. For example, supervised learning algorithms are ML that involves direct human supervision and use labeled data to predict future outcomes after being trained based on past data. Unsupervised learning focuses on using data in an unguided fashion that has not been labeled, classified, or categorized to complete a cluster analysis that looks for relevant patterns or trends within the data.

Reinforcement learning is the training of ML models to make a sequence of decisions by identifying patterns and making decisions with minimal human intervention. It focuses on developing a self-sustained system that improves itself based on the combination of labeled data and interactions with new data throughout contiguous sequences of trials and errors.

Even within these three models are many terms you may hear about. For example, neural networks are a form of supervised learning consisting of interconnected units (like neurons) that process information by responding to external inputs, relaying information between each unit. The process requires multiple passes at the data to find connections and derive meaning from undefined data.

Deep learning uses large neural networks with many layers of processing units, taking advantage of advances in computing power and improved training techniques to learn complex patterns in large amounts of data. Typical applications include image and speech recognition.

With ML, AI is increasingly good at sensing and predicting things we care about like which patients are at high risk of readmissions, falls, or unexpected deterioration. It can help with predictions of which treatments may produce the best outcomes. It's already making diagnostic images more "intelligent."

There are many outstanding technical books and resources available to describe the various types and forms of ML algorithms that can take (Linear regression, logic regression, decision tree, and decision forests) as well as the various languages and methodologies used to create them (R, Python, Lisp to name a few). Unless you are a budding data scientist, it is sufficient to recognize that there are various types of ML models and algorithms. This diversity of languages and models allows data scientists and developers to design an approach using various models and languages that best fit the type of problem to be solved.

Cognitive Services

Beyond the power of making predictions through ML, there are a growing number of applications or solutions that can be categorized as cognitive services. As the title implies, these AI building blocks mimic specific human functions, including perception (e.g., seeing, hearing), language, thinking, and learning.

Such functionality is available today and most often deployed through the use of an "**Application Programming Interface or API**." An API is a preset group of computer commands and protocols used by programers to create software or interact with external systems. APIs allow developers to efficiently perform common operations without writing code from scratch.

While the list of Cognitive Services is constantly evolving, here are the most common types of applications.

Computer Vision: This is a field of computer science that enables computers to see, identify and process images in the same way that human vision does. It then provides appropriate output to complete a task. Computer vision is a form of AI, as the computer must interpret what it sees and then perform appropriate analysis.

Vision services allow humans to gain insights from images, pictures, and videos. These capabilities include detecting faces in photos, automated image analysis, text or video moderation, and person recognition. Computer vision's goal is not only to see but also to process and provide useful results based on the observation. For example, the application of computer vision in healthcare ranges from detecting faces to aid in things like member verification and patient registration to clinical applications, including auto-detecting abnormalities in diagnostic and pathology images.

Knowledge Extraction: This allows for identifying, organizing, and extracting specific information and knowledge from large amounts of preexisting data and information. As the amount of data and information increases in healthcare, extracting and mining this data to acquire new knowledge becomes vitally important.

Knowledge extraction allows us to use massive quantities of data and information to look for patterns that humans simply don't have the ability or time to see.

Speech: The speech component of AI is getting a lot of uptake in healthcare today. It provides the ability to implement speech translation and recognition features into applications and workflows to make an automated process more human (understand what a human is saying). This area also involves converting text to speech and vice versa on the go to understand user intent and interact with patients and consumers.

Speech recognition has been around a while, but AI-enhanced capabilities have brought the capabilities of machines to be on par with humans' speech and language capabilities.

Language Understanding: This allows a computer application to understand what a person is saying and wants in their own words.

Natural Language Processing (NLP): NLP enables computers to derive computable and actionable data from text, mainly when text is recorded in the form of natural human language (i.e., phrases, sentences, paragraphs). This technology allows humans to record information in the most natural method of human communication (narrative text) and then enables computers to extract actionable information from that text. NLP can also analyze the often-non-standard grammatical constructions common in medical terminology. Natural language understanding (NLU) is a subset of NLP that uses reasoning, inference, and semantic searching to help clinicians make decisions and take action.[3]

Text Analytics: Provides NLP over raw text for sentiment analysis, key phrase extraction, and language detection.

Search: Search is one of the most essential services for nearly every application or solution nowadays. It is critical for a search service to provide the best possible results.

Applying AI Building Blocks

The AI "building blocks" described above are often combined and deployed with other technologies (like sensors) to drive value in automating or augmenting work previously done by humans.

AI is sometimes classified by the level of sophistication or type of use. For example, **Narrow AI** (Artificial Narrow Intelligence or ANI) is good at performing a single task, such as predicting which patient is likely to be a no-show for an appointment. AI components like ML, computer vision, and NLP are currently in this stage. Narrow AI excels at one particular type of task within a limited context but cannot take on tasks beyond what it was designed to do. Even when pushing the boundaries of today's AI, almost everything being done is through Narrow AI. For example, self-driving car technology is still considered narrow AI, or more precisely, a coordination of several narrow AIs.[4]

Understanding that almost all AI deployed today is considered "narrow AI" is something we'll build on in the next chapter, as creating value is heavily dependent on understanding how to leverage and balance the capabilities of AI with the unique capabilities of humans.

General AI (also known as Artificial General AI or AGI) is the type of AI that can understand and reason across its environment as a human would. General AI has always been elusive. This category of AI is where many organizations aspire to be someday, but any true form of this is not likely in the short- to medium-term horizon.

As you will learn in the next chapter, humans might not process data as fast as computers, but they can think abstractly and plan and solve problems based on their experience and creativity. These factors, which are vitally important in delivering health services, are not found in the realm of what computers can replicate today nor likely anytime soon.

Finally, another category known as Super Intelligence (Artificial Super Intelligence or ASI) is a level of computer sophistication where machines become more intelligent than the humans that create them. This is the stuff that becomes fodder for science fiction movies. It's also the type of AI you occasionally hear people like Elon Musk waxing over as they ponder the dangers to humanity should we reach this level of AI capability.

For now, recognize that pretty much everything being done today falls into the Narrow AI category. Investments are being made in the tech industry to move systems closer to the General AI category.[5]

Here are some of the common ways AI is packaged and deployed today:

AI Apps: Web or mobile applications are infused with AI capabilities, such as vision, language, or ML. For example, AI is pervasive in our daily lives. From anonymized data from smartphones and other data, AI analyzes the speed and movement of traffic at any given time to predict when you will reach your destination and the best route to do so. As you make an online transaction with your credit card, AI is running in the background to monitor and predict whether the charge is fraudulent. When it comes to health, thousands of consumer health apps help monitor body functions, provide alerts for various health indicators, and guide recommendations on everything from nutrition to maintaining emotional and mental wellness.

Bots and Conversational AI: A bot is an automated application used to perform simple and repetitive tasks that are often time-consuming for a human to perform. Conversational AI makes use of speech and language building blocks to automate communications and create personalized customer experiences that are scalable.

With consumers increasingly looking to access information on demand, bots and conversational AI provide short and high-value interactions with customers and staff through task automation and automated workflows. The goal of Bots and Conversational AI is to improve the customer experience while reducing the need for lower-value human interactions.

In one survey of consumers, nearly 70% saw chatbots as the best way to get instant answers to their questions, and over one-fifth (21%) saw chatbots as the easiest way to contact a company.[6]

Intelligent IoT

The IoT is a network of internet-connected devices that communicate embedded sensor data to the cloud for centralized processing. These sensors can be embedded in everyday items such as cell phones, digital weight scales, wearable health, medical devices, or components of larger machines and systems such as medical imaging or lab systems.

The introduction of intelligence with IoT enables health organizations to reimagine existing services or create new types of services that cut across historical care settings. Intelligent IoT also improves operational efficiencies in areas that include intelligent remote patient monitoring or improved predictive maintenance of equipment and facilities.

Intelligent Robots

According to a study by Accenture, robot-assisted surgery is estimated to produce $40 billion in near-term value to health organizations.[7] With the help of AI, robots can use data from past operations to guide surgeons to improve existing surgical techniques and reduce the invasive nature of some surgeries. One study of smart robotics in orthopedic surgeries resulted in five times fewer complications.[8]

Ambient Intelligence

Just as ambient music plays in the background to enhance an environment, ambient intelligence is AI embedded in a user's immediate environment through a range of sensors, cameras, and listening devices. The goal is to have various components of AI in play but mainly invisible. Today ambient intelligence is used in patient exam rooms to automate repetitive activities such as clinical notes. This saves time for the clinician and allows more time to interact with patients. Ambient intelligence also holds promise for improving independent and assisted living.

FROM GODS TO GEEKS – A BRIEF HISTORY OF AI

While AI is a hot topic today, its history can be traced as far back as Greek mythology. Here's a brief look at how it started leading up to its use today.

(Continued)

Basic concepts for what AI is today can be traced back to Greek mythology. The story of Hephaestus, the god of smiths, is about a blacksmith who manufactured mechanical servants. The story of Talos introduces and incorporates the idea of intelligent robots. Interestingly, the term "robot" would not be coined until 1925 when it was first used by Czech writer Karel Čapek in his play Rossum's Universal Robots.

In the 1500s the beloved son of King Philip II of Spain became ill and near to death. Upon his unexpected recovery the King commissioned the development of a mechanical Monk so that he might automate the offering of continuous prayers. This might be considered an early "chatbot".

In the 1600s philosopher Rene Descartes pondered the possibility that machines would one day think and make decisions. He also identified a division between machines that might learn about performing one specific task and those that might be able to adapt to any job. Today, this categorization is known as Narrow AI and General AI.[9]

In the 1700s Thomas Bayes, an English nonconformist theologian and mathematician became the first to use probability inductively and established a mathematical basis for probability inference. Known as Bayesian inference, this framework for reasoning about the probability of events is still in use today.

In the 1800s Ada Lovelace, the daughter of Lord Byron, became well known as an English mathematician and writer. As a teenager, she was befriended by Charles Babbage who was a preeminent mathematician, philosopher, and inventor who originated the concept of a digital programmable computer.[10] Based on her experiences with Babbage, Lovelace was the first to recognize and write about how computing machines had application beyond pure calculation noting that machines in the future "*might compose elaborate and scientific pieces of music of any degree of complexity or extent.*"[11]

She went on to write and publish the first algorithm intended to be use on the mechanical computer that Babbage had designed thereby making her possibly the first known computer programmer.

In the 1900s AI was given a face and began moving into the mainstream of science and society.

In the summer of 1914 and a great deal of excitement was generated when an autonomous machine capable of playing chess made its debut at the University of Paris. Considered by some to be the world's first

(Continued)

computer game, El Ajedrecista (the chess player), was a fully automated machine able to play chess without any human guidance.

In 1935, at Cambridge University, Alan Turing conceived the principle of the modern computer. He described an abstract digital computing machine consisting of a limitless memory and a scanner that moves back and forth through the memory, symbol by symbol, reading what it finds, and writing further symbols.[12]

In the 1940s scientists from a variety of fields (mathematics, psychology, engineering, economics, and political science) began to imagine and research the possibility of imbuing machines with intelligence. It was World War II that brought forth the value of such an idea. The Allied forces had been intercepting and manually decoding encrypted messages from the German forces when, at some point, messages being intercepted were encoded with a totally different method that could not be cracked.

The need to decipher this vital intelligence as rapidly as possible led to the creating of the first fully functioning digital computer in 1943. It wasn't until the 1970s that details came to light about how electronic computations had been successfully used to help win the war. Historians for the British government estimated that the war in Europe was shortened by at least two years as a result of this early intelligence initiative.[13]

Early concepts in conceptualizing intelligent machines actually came from clinical research. For example, during the 1930s and 1940s research in the area of neurology showed that the brain was a network of neurons. Walter Pitts and Warren McCulloch were MIT professors and early AI pioneers who took key concepts from clinical research to speculate on how "artificial neurons" might be allow machines to perform simple logical functions. In 1943 the duo published a seminal paper in scientific history, titled "A Logical Calculus of Ideas Immanent in Nervous Activity".[14] This paper proposed the first mathematical model of a neural network.

Today, neural networks form the basis of what is known as deep learning and is a means of doing ML where a computer learns to perform tasks by analyzing training examples. Many of the image recognition systems used in healthcare and other industries today make use of neural networks.

It was 1956 and as people were shuffling back to work from their Christmas and New Year's holidays swapping stories of their time off, Herbert A. Simon and Allen Newell had a Christmas break story to top

(Continued)

them all. "Over the Christmas holiday," Dr. Simon famously blurted to one of his classes at Carnegie Institute of Technology, "Al Newell and I invented a thinking machine."[15]

While the idea of a digital computer was still in its infancy, researchers, philosophers, and others were talking about developing a crude device as an "electronic brain". As others mused over such concepts, these two young Carnegie Tech scientists used their holiday to work through their own version of a thinking machine and put it in a form that could be programmed into a computer.

Later, that year a summer conference organized by John McCarthy brought together top minds at Dartmouth College to specifically focus on the idea of imbuing machines with intelligence. The proposal for the conference included the assertion that *"every aspect of learning or any other feature of intelligence can be so precisely described that a machine can be made to simulate it."*[16] It was from this gathering that AI gained its name and mission and is considered by many as the official "birth of AI" as it legitimized the field as a formal scientific discipline. Those who attended would become the leaders of AI research for decades.

In the period between the late 1950s and the early 1960s came a torrent of theories and experiments that both moved AI forward and brought it into the public and government spotlight.

In 1959 Arthur Samuel, considered as a pioneer in the gaming world, coined the term "machine learning," in a journal article outlining how a computer could be programmed to play a better game of checkers than the person who wrote the program demonstrating that the computers could be able to master a process of learning.[17]

By 1961 early forms of AI were making their way into commercial use. In this year, the first industrial robot called Unimate began working on an assembly line in a General Motors plant in New Jersey.[18] At the same time, the space race was getting underway, which meant that major investments were being made to universities and private labs to expand the capabilities and reach of this new science.

In 1964 ELIZA, the world's first chatbot, was created at the MIT Artificial Intelligence Lab to demonstrate basic communications between humans and machines.

As the 1970s came around AI was about to go into the phase described as the "Trough of Disillusionment." Criticism was growing about how AI

(Continued)

researchers had overpromised and under delivered solutions that would have real-world impact. With enthusiasm for AI having spiraled out of control for the past two decades what followed in the 1980s was a period of greatly reduced funding and interest in AI research.

Until a resurgence of interest and investing beginning in the mid-2000s, many top computer scientists and software engineers were deliberate in avoiding the term "artificial intelligence" for fear of being viewed as "wide-eyed dreamers."[19] In order to receive funding, advances continued during this period, but many initiatives were packaged under different names such as informatics or data science.

While it was roughly a decade ago that the AI resurgence began, the impetus for a new awakening came in 1991 when CERN researcher Tim Berners-Lee put the world's first website online and published the workings of the hypertext transfer protocol (HTTP). Although computers had been connecting to share data for decades, it occurred mainly at educational institutions and large businesses.

The arrival of the worldwide web was the catalyst for society at large to plug itself into the online world. As millions of people from every part of the world began getting connected, new types of data were being developed and shared at a previously inconceivable rate and a new chapter in AI growth began.

In 2007, a team from Princeton University successfully assembled ImageNet, a large database of annotated images designed to be used in visual recognition software.[20] An annual competition known as the ImageNet Challenge, pitted researchers from around the world in developing algorithms that can recognize and describe a library of 1000 images. Since ImageNet launched in 2010 the accuracy rate of the winning algorithm jumped from 71.8% to 97.3%. In 2015 judges declared that computers could identify objects in visual data more accurately than humans.[21]

In 2009, Google started a secret project to develop a driverless car. In 2014, it became the first autonomous vehicle to pass a US state self-driving test in the United States. In the same year, computer scientists at Northwestern University developed a program that wrote sport news stories without human intervention.

In 2011, IBM enlisted Watson, its cognitive computing platform, to compete in the popular television show Jeopardy! Watson defeated two

(Continued)

former Jeopardy! champions. IBM used this public relations event to launch Watson as a major move to bring AI to healthcare.[22]

Not to be outdone, Google showcased its AI prowess by training an algorithm designed to beat what is known as the world's most complex game; Go. Google's algorithm, called AlphaGo, first beat the European Go champion in 2015, then the Korean Go champion in 2016, and finally the World Go champion in 2017.[23]

In 2016, Microsoft made a major breakthrough in speech recognition, demonstrating for the first time that a computer could recognize the words in a conversation as well as a person does.[24]

In 2017, the AI Now Institute was launched at New York University (NYU) to research and study the social implications of AI. Its work focuses on four core domains including rights and liberties, labor and automation, bias and inclusion, and safety and critical infrastructure.

Today we are inundated with news of new breakthroughs and capabilities that are moving from the lab and research centers into everyday use. As we look ahead to the possibilities and applications in our professional and personal lives its worth reflecting how we are standing on the shoulders of those who came before us.

Notes

1. Stuart J. Russell, Peter Norvig (2009). *Artificial Intelligence: A Modern Approach* (3rd ed.). Upper Saddle River, NJ: Prentice Hall. ISBN 978-0-13-604259-4.
2. J.A.N. Lee, Arthur Lee Samuel, Computer Piooneers, IEEE Computer Society, https://history.computer.org/pioneers/samuel.html.
3. *Laura Bryan*, With Natural Language Processing You Can Have Your Cake and Eat It Too, HIMSS, 2019, https://www.himss.org/news/natural-language-processing-you-can-have-your-cake-and-eat-it-too.
4. Ben Dickson, What is Narrow, General and Super Artificial Intelligence, TEchTalks, 2017, https://bdtechtalks.com/2017/05/12/what-is-narrow-general-and-super-artificial-intelligence/.
5. Dean Van Nguyen, Elon Musk Calls Artificial Intelligence 'our biggest existential threat', Silicon Republic, 2014, https://www.siliconrepublic.com/machines/elon-musk-calls-artificial-intelligence-our-biggest-existential-threat.
6. 2017 Chatbot Survey, Ubisend, 2017, https://www.ubisend.com/insights/2017-chatbot-report.

7. Matt Collier, Artificial Intelligences-Healthcare's New Nervous system, Accenture, 2017.

8. Brian Kalis, Matt Collier, Richard Fu, 10 Promising AI Applications in Health Care, Harvard Business Review, 2018, https://hbr.org/2018/05/10-promising-ai-applications-in-health-care.

9. Bernard Marr, The Most Amazing Artificial Intelligence Milestones So Far, Forbes, 2018, https://www.forbes.com/sites/bernardmarr/2018/12/31/the-most-amazing-artificial-intelligence-milestones-so-far/#35fe52ef7753.

10. B. Jack Copeland (18 December 2000). "The Modern History of Computing". *The Modern History of Computing (Stanford Encyclopedia of Philosophy)*. *Stanford Encyclopedia of Philosophy*. Metaphysics Research Lab, Stanford University. Retrieved 1 March 2017.

11. Ada Lovelace, Wikipedia, Accessed 2019, https://en.wikipedia.org/wiki/Ada_Lovelace.

12. Jack Copeland, A Brief History of Computing, AlanTuring.net, Accessed 2019, http://www.alanturing.net/turing_archive/pages/Reference%20Articles/BriefHistofComp.html.

13. Ibid.

14. A Logical Calculus of the Ideas Immanent in Nervous Activity, Bulletin of Mathematical Biology, 1990, https://www.sciencedirect.com/science/article/pii/S0092824005800060.

15. Byron Spice, Over the Holidays 50 Years Ago, Two Scientists Hatched Artificial Intelligence, Post-Gazette.com, 2006, http://old.post-gazette.com/pg/06002/631149-96.stm Read more: http://old.post-gazette.com/pg/06002/631149-96.stm#ixzz5yZBgKjhm.

16. John McCarthy, Marvin Minsky, Nathan Rochester, Claude Shannon (31 August 1955). *A Proposal for the Dartmouth Summer Research Project on Artificial Intelligence*, retrieved 16 October 2008.

17. Gil Press, A Very Short History Of Artificial Intelligence (AI), Forbes, 2016, https://www.forbes.com/sites/gilpress/2016/12/30/a-very-short-history-of-artificial-intelligence-ai/#4ab002866fba.

18. Ibid.

19. John Markoff Behind Artificial Intelligence, A Squadron of Bright Real People, The New York Times, 2005, https://www.nytimes.com/2005/10/14/technology/behind-artificial-intelligence-a-squadron-of-bright-real-people.html.

20. ImageNet, Wikipedia, Accessed 2019, https://en.wikipedia.org/wiki/ImageNet.

21. Bernard Marr, The Most Amazing Artificial Intelligence Milestones So Far, Forbes, 2018, https://www.forbes.com/sites/bernardmarr/2018/12/31/the-most-amazing-artificial-intelligence-milestones-so-far/#35fe52ef7753.

22. Jo Best, IBM Watson: The Inside Story of How the Jeopardy-Winning Supercomputer Was Born, and What It Wants to Do Next, Tech Republic, 2013, https://www.techrepublic.com/article/ibm-watson-the-inside-story-of-how-the-jeopardy-winning-supercomputer-was-born-and-what-it-wants-to-do-next/.

23. ANIRUDH VK, 10 Breakthroughs In Artificial Intelligence That Skyrocketed Its Popularity This Decade, Analytics India Magazine, 2019, https://www.analyticsindiamag.com/10-breakthroughs-in-artificial-intelligence-that-skyrocketed-its-popularity-this-decade/.
24. Allison Linn, Historic Achievement: Microsoft Researchers Reach Human Parity in Conversational Speech Recognition, Microsoft AI Blog, 2016, https://blogs.microsoft.com/ai/historic-achievement-microsoft-researchers-reach-human-parity-conversational-speech-recognition/.

Chapter 6

Artificial Intelligence (AI) vs. Natural Human Intelligence (NHI)

It's ridiculous to live 100 years and only be able to remember 30 million bytes. You know, less than a compact disc.

Marvin Minsky
Cofounder of MIT AI Laboratory

There are many outstanding books written on neuroscience and neurophysiology. One of my favorites is *A Thousand Brains* by Jeff Hawkins. It's a great read about how our brains work and new theories of intelligence.

But if you want to skip these treatises, let me net out what you should know: The human brain is a pretty awesome organ. Weighing an average of 3 pounds, it has 100 billion neurons and 100,000 miles of capillaries.[1] It's what lifted homo-sapiens to the top of the food chain.

You're probably not conscious of how your brain is working right now:

As soon as you saw this page something started happening inside your cranium. Electrical transmissions from your eyes triggered neuro-responders in your brain. These signals stimulated your brain to begin recognizing patterns known to you as letters, words and punctuation.

Based on other cognitive capabilities, these words encapsulate, and trigger retained knowledge from previous patterning that is

DOI: 10.4324/9781003286103-6

unlocked based on the unique sequence of patterns on the pages of this book.

The human brain is so smart that it invented ways to outsource certain human intelligence capabilities to machines. We call this artificial intelligence or AI.

Not only was AI developed by humans, but it's also delivered through human-made elements such as silicon, plastics, and code.

Natural human intelligence (NHI) on the other hand is very different. It's delivered through a blob of protoplasm that AI pioneer Alan Turing once described as an organ *"having the consistency of cold porridge."*

And so, why is this important?

To use AI to transform anything, especially healthcare, one must first understand the capability differences between AI and NHI. Once understood, this becomes your superpower. You now have the ability to pair the unique characteristics of each to drive change.

Before we go any further, let's clear up something. What exactly is intelligence?

The modern study of intelligence is often credited to Charles Spearman, an English psychologist known for his work in statistics and as a pioneer of factor analysis. He also developed early models for human intelligence that became the foundation for intelligence testing.[2] He proposed that intelligence could be understood in terms of a general ability that pervaded all intellectual tasks, and specific abilities that were unique to each particular intellectual task.[3]

That's a bit incomprehensible. For the sake of this book, let's use a simpler definition from the American Psychological Association:

> *Intelligence is the ability to derive information, learn from experience, adapt to the environment, understand, and correctly utilize thought and reason.*[4]

AI capabilities have reached human parity for things like vision, speech recognition, reading, translation, speech synthesis, and language understanding. This means they are equal to the ability of humans.

Beyond reaching parity, some AI capabilities now exceed those of its creators.

For example, *knowledge extraction* allows for the identification, organization, and extraction of specific information and knowledge from large amounts of pre-existing data and information. As the amount of healthcare data and information increases the ability to easily extract and mine this data to acquire new knowledge becomes vitally important.

To illustrate this point, researchers from the Lawrence Berkeley National Laboratory used AI to reveal new scientific knowledge hidden in old research papers. Using just the language in millions of old scientific papers, a deep learning algorithm was able to make new scientific discoveries by sifting through scientific papers for connections humans had missed. And while the experiment was focused on new discoveries in material science, the process could just as easily be applied to other disciplines such as medical research and drug discovery.[5]

AI allows us to leverage massive quantities of data and information to look for patterns that humans simply don't have the ability or time to see. AI is good at finding and predicting things we care about, such as identifying patients at high risk of readmissions, falls, or unexpected deterioration. It can help predict which treatments may produce the best outcomes. It's already making diagnostic images more "intelligent" by identifying patterns relevant to making a diagnosis.

In considering the capabilities and benefits of AI, it's important to also recognize its limitations.

Let's use something known as "deep learning" to illustrate this point. It's a recent AI breakthrough that gets a lot of attention because it has produced the most successful results within the field of machine learning. The first academic papers describing deep learning go back to the 1960s. It took almost 50 years for this technology to work and produce results. But as powerful as it is, deep learning is fragile and messy. To work, it requires massive amounts of relevant data, a narrow focus, and a concrete objective function to optimize.[6]

By contrast, while humans lack deep learning's ability to analyze huge numbers of data points at the same time, we have the unique ability to draw on experience, abstract concepts, and common sense to make decisions.

As "smart" as AI is becoming at certain things, no one has figured out how to imbue machines with qualities that are essential in the world of health like wisdom, reasoning, judgment, imagination, critical thinking, common sense, and empathy. Such attributes remain as uniquely human characteristics that are essential to the provision of health services.

A smart machine can sense or predict temperature variation but doesn't know how a patient feels when they have a fever. Measuring spikes in blood pressure might correlate to a person feeling anxious but a smart machine can't understand what anxiety feels like for a patient or family member and what to do about it.

Strengths and Weakness of AI vs NHI

	Human Brain	AI Brain (Deep Learning)
Data required to learn	Few data points	Huge amount of data
Quantitative optimizing and matching (picking a face out of a million)	Hard	Easy
Customizing for each situation (showing each user a different product to maximize purchasing)	Hard	Easy
Abstract concepts, analytical reasoning, inferences, common sense, and insight	Easy	Hard
Creativity	Easy	Hard

Source: AI 2041, Kai-Fu Lee, p. 27.

The key to creating value is knowing the differences in what AI versus humans do best. Value comes when you understand and apply the smart machine-human symbiosis to change how work is done and services are provided.

Correlation versus Causation

Whether in research or caring for patients, a critical part of many processes in medical science is identifying patterns and measuring relationships between two or more factors. This is at the heart of things like drug development and making diagnoses and treatment recommendations.

In this regard, AI is a great enabler to help clinicians and researchers. It works well when you understand and apply its unique capabilities. It does not work so well when you don't.

As we learned in the last chapter, AI is good at identifying patterns and making predictions based on the relationship or correlation of various points of data. But there is more to using AI than making correlational predictions.

Issues arise when the limits of AI are not understood. An issue well-known among clinicians and data scientists is the distinction between *Correlation and Causation.*

Correlation is when two events can be logically connected to each other *without actually directly* influencing one another. AI excels at finding *correlations* between two or more things.

Much more difficult to find and understand is evidence that one variable *actually causes another variable to change.* If adequate proof is provided, we can claim that event A causes event B to take place. This is causation.

The most important thing to understand is that correlation is *not* the same as causation – sometimes two things can share a relationship without one causing the other.

In this regard, AI has the ability to find and correlate variables. Humans are better at determining causation. This is done through our use of reasoning, wisdom, experience, and common sense.

With the right tools, AI can sift through data to find many interesting correlations. For example, with the right data, there is an almost perfect correlation between per capita cheese consumption and the number of people who die each year by becoming tangled in their bedsheets (correlation: 94.71% r = .947091).[7] Does this mean that we can save lives if step away from the cheese platter at the neighborhood party? Probably not.

Per capita cheese consumption
correlates with
Number of people who died by becoming tangled in their bedsheets
Correlation: 94.71% (r=0.947091)

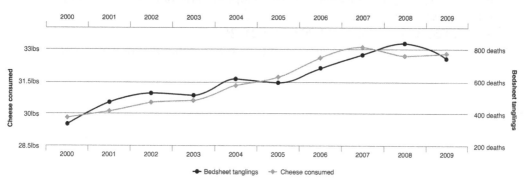

Source: Spurious Correlations, Tyler Vigen

In this situation, correlation is merely a mathematical relationship in which two variables are associated but not causally related, due to either coincidence or the presence of some unseen factor.

As you set off to plan and execute your organization's AI strategy, a key factor in leveraging its power to improve things that clinicians, and consumers care about is to understand what AI is great at and what it's not so good at. AI works best when it is to support, bolster, and augment the unique skills and capabilities of humans.

By taking advantage of the growing array of capabilities defined in the previous chapter, AI holds great promise. As it changes the nature of work, innovative leaders will define and execute AI plans that create performance loops where humans and smart machines collaborate. This unique partnership will allow us to get the best from each to improve the quality and effectiveness of health services delivered around the globe.

Notes

1. Emma Scott, How much does the human brain weigh? Med Health Daily, https://www.medhealthdaily.com/how-much-does-the-human-brain-weigh/.
2. Charles Spearman, Wikipedia, https://en.wikipedia.org/wiki/Charles_Spearman.
3. Spearman C. *The Abilities of Man. New York, NY: Macmillan.* 1927.
4. APA Dictionary of Psychology. https://dictionary.apa.org/intelligence.
5. Vahe Tshitoyan, Unsupervised Word Embeddings Capture Latent Knowledge from Materials Science Literature, Nature, 2019, https://www.nature.com/articles/s41586-019-1335-8.epdf?referrer_access_token=gjs4tfb7-T50BFnuqtYx5N RgN0jAjWel9jnR3ZoTv0P9QxlcO86f_GXZRxwYijrqa11Mx55SgniZXv55YKOR_ sn816NK2x0O46Vim16XrS-SjyP9GMXeDQinUN75ES6enlxK__J5UabR6J dgR19bZSVLL5ZsK8146qMcipEbItW65C8aSk29Q_BfrKz4Gb5-kjz3m7dIaoRxs3e 1I6qW4022QZ6aZMaOPxlATK7OOqj8lrhj-yufvROMPdStMZjAEK-efja6SfW5n-6xhZuV3zQTFR_u132mC6hkt8Zqp29_su0pmsC0jrneuemHnqg8&tracking_ referrer=www.vice.com.
6. Kai-Fu Lee, Chen Qiufan, AI 2041. PP 24–26.
7. Tyler Vigen, Spurious Correlations. https://tylervigen.com/spurious-correlations.

Chapter 7

Creating Value Today with AI

AI is a tool. The choice about how it gets deployed is ours.

Oren Etzioni
CEO, Allen Institute for Artificial Intelligence

Imagine a time where healthcare can seamlessly tailor itself to fit the needs of each patient and the clinicians who serve them. It's a world where practitioners and researchers are freed from repetitive administrative tasks. Clinicians leverage all data to serve patients and consumers better. Consumers are empowered to choose and actively supported to map out intelligent health and lifestyle plans unique to them.

AI will increasingly move us toward such personalized and on-demand experiences. We are not there yet, but AI is already reshaping healthcare in multiple ways.

The rise of Intelligent Health Systems will come in stages. We are already seeing AI enhance existing processes and practices. Over time AI will redefine how we assess, monitor, diagnose, and manage health.

AI is different from other tech trends you've experienced. New generations of health and medical systems will benefit from the continuous learning nature of AI. Just as humans do, AI-infused systems will learn and adjust from past experiences based on patient and doctor responses and system outcomes over time.

With this in mind, your AI strategy should include a broad vision for change and a clear and pragmatic view of where and how AI is used in health today. This includes deciding the areas in which you initially invest your time, attention, and resources. Let's look at what's happening now in the practical adoption and use of AI today and in the near term. We'll look ahead to more futuristic use cases that build on today's efforts in Chapter 21.

DOI: 10.4324/9781003286103-7

AI Is About Change and Value

Healthcare innovation is occurring at an unprecedented pace.

AI in health is opening up new possibilities for creating value. This could not come at a better time. A study in the Journal of the American Medical Association (JAMA) concludes that 20–25% of American healthcare spending is wasteful.[1] It's a startling number but not a new finding. AI is being effectively deployed today to reduce clinical variability and waste. It's enabling more precise and efficient diagnostics and ensuring tighter adherence to established and personalized treatment protocols.

As we move toward a post-pandemic world, AI will come of age as a driving force in solving domain-specific challenges. Benefits will accrue, including improved quality, increased productivity, and better use of knowledge workers' time and expertise.

Healthcare innovation is occurring at an unprecedented pace. The use of AI in support of other enabling technologies can generate over $400 billion in value in health by 2025, according to a study by McKinsey and Company.[2]

Today's key question is how AI will be used to generate greater value.

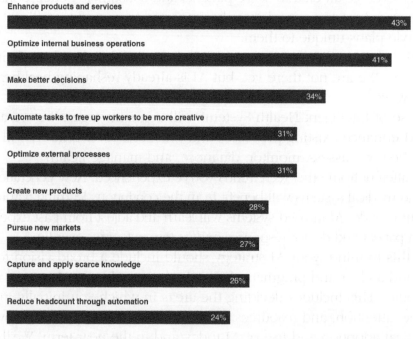

AI benefits include improving operations and decision-making, as well as freeing up workers to concentrate on less-mundane tasks

Rating each a top-three primary benefit of AI technology for their company

Enhance products and services	43%
Optimize internal business operations	41%
Make better decisions	34%
Automate tasks to free up workers to be more creative	31%
Optimize external processes	31%
Create new products	28%
Pursue new markets	27%
Capture and apply scarce knowledge	26%
Reduce headcount through automation	24%

Source: Deloitte analysis based on Deloitte's AI in the Enterprise, 2nd Edition survey of 1,900 AI early adopters in seven countries. Talent and workforce effects in the age of AI, Deloitte.

Here are examples of current use cases driving value today.

Enhanced Clinical Productivity and Care Effectiveness

Data suggests that the healthcare industry lags other industries in its ability to *"do more for less."*[3] Using AI to improve clinical productivity in clinical settings promises to improve process efficiencies while lowering the number of repetitive, lower value activities. Such change also helps to improve outcomes and reduce the risk of clinician burnout.

Clinical decision support (CDS) is seeing rapid growth as the application of AI and machine learning automates the processes of evidence-based clinical and scientific decision-making. General areas where this is being used include population health management, precision medicine, and predictive analytics at the Point of Care (POC).

Example: Yale-New Haven (Conn.) Health uses AI to predict sepsis, acute kidney injury, congestive heart failure, deterioration, and one-year mortality rates.[4]

Improving the use and effectiveness of EHRs is an area where AI can improve usability and save time. Most EHRs are built on older underlying technologies that are complex and difficult to navigate. As a result, clinicians often struggle matching EHRs with how they practice.

AI is being used to make existing EHR systems more flexible and intelligent. This includes using intelligent text mining to improve data extraction from free text such as provider notes, diagnostic, or predictive algorithms to warn clinicians of high-risk conditions and automating clinical documentation and data entry with natural language processing.[5]

Example: Researchers at MIT and the Beth Israel Deaconess Medical Center are creating a better electronic health record by combining machine learning and human-computer interactions. The system they have developed unifies looking up medical records and documenting patient information into a single, interactive interface. Driven by AI, this "smart" EHR automatically displays customized, patient-specific medical records when a clinician needs them. It also provides autocomplete for clinical terms and auto-populates fields with patient information to help doctors work more efficiently.[6]

Medical imaging and diagnostics use AI solutions by enabling radiologists to interpret hidden disease patterns from clinical images and drive more personalized diagnosis at a greater speed and scale. Focus areas include general imaging, cardiovascular, breast imaging, and image-guided therapies.

Examples: A new type of deep-learning model can predict from a mammogram if a patient is likely to develop breast cancer as far as five years in the future. Developed by a team from MIT's Computer Science and Artificial Intelligence Laboratory (CSAIL) and Massachusetts General Hospital (MGH), the model focuses on learning the subtle patterns in breast tissue that are precursors to malignant tumors.[7]

In another use case, the University of Pennsylvania Health System and Brown University-affiliated hospitals made use of AI with chest X-rays to improve the ability to predict the risk of progression to critical illness in patients with COVID-19.

Additionally, various studies, including one from NYU Langone Health, found that using AI with certain types of images to flag specific anomalies quickly and accurately for a radiologist's review was up to 97% faster than a panel of radiologists. Such results open the door to giving radiologists more time to focus on deeper interpretations or consultations.[8]

Recent developments in robotics, artificial intelligence, and machine learning have put us on the cusp of a new automation age. Robots and computers can not only perform a range of routine physical work activities better and more cheaply than humans, but they are also increasingly capable of accomplishing activities that include cognitive capabilities once considered too difficult to automate successfully, such as making tacit judgments, sensing emotion, or even driving.

AI-assisted surgery improves surgical outcomes by helping surgeons perform better and reducing surgeon variation.

While robotic-assisted surgeries have been around for some time, new developments in robotics, artificial intelligence, and machine learning have put us on the cusp of a new automation age. A new generation of surgical robotics is helping surgeons determine what is happening during complex surgical procedures by providing real-time data points about the surgeon's movements during the procedure. Additionally, AI is being used to provide real-time predictions that assist anesthesiologists during surgery to improve compliance and machine learning for modeling surgical workflow. Robots enabled with artificial intelligence are increasingly helping the microsurgical procedures to reduce surgeon variations that could negatively affect patient recovery.

Example: A study of orthopedic patients across nine surgical sites found that an AI-assisted robotic techniques resulted in a five-fold reduction in surgical complications compared to cases in which surgeons operated unassisted.[9]

Predictive insights and risk analytics using AI-powered tools to manage payers' and providers' clinical risks are seeing strong uptake in the market. Current focus areas include predicting and reducing medical errors, preventable inpatient readmissions, hospital-acquired infections, and adverse drug reactions.

Example: Atlantic Health is improving outcomes and performance by using AI to predict which patients are likely to develop adverse events such as congestive heart failure or be readmitted and by forecasting appointment no-shows.[10]

Augmenting staff with virtual nursing assistants could reduce unnecessary hospital visits and lessen the burden on medical professionals. In one study, 64% of patients reported that they would be comfortable with AI virtual nurse assistants, citing the benefits of 24/7 access to answers and support, round-the-clock monitoring, and the ability to get quick answers to questions about medications.[11]

Identifying care gaps and clinical opportunities in patient populations is where AI can prevent expensive and disruptive hospitalizations, readmissions, and emergency department visits. Many organizations cannot quickly identify patients with certain diagnoses, let alone flag individuals with rising risks that may lead to a diagnosis in the future.

AI tools that comb through EHR, lab data, pharmacy, and hospital utilization information will predict which individuals living with chronic conditions are headed for a crisis event that can be avoided.

Identifying and addressing the social determinants of health will benefit from the power of intelligent tools that use clinical data and nonclinical data to identify environmental factors impacting health status and treatment outcomes.

Chronic condition management is an area where AI can assist clinicians in providing better intuitive care management. AI solutions can transform the status quo, which is characterized by data non-interoperability, provider burnout, and care leakages. Integration of lifestyle data with AI platforms can provide compelling near-term benefits for preventive care practice. General focus areas include population health risk stratification, predictive analytics for preventative care, and guidance for optimal disease management.

Improving Nonclinical Efficiency

The estimated yearly cost of waste in the US healthcare system ranges from $760 billion to $935 billion. The largest single source of waste is in nonclinical administrative costs, totaling $266 billion a year.[12]

AI-Driven operational command centers leverage massive amounts of information generated by health organizations to find and fix operational inefficiencies in real-time. AI command centers equipped with predictive tools pull together data from multiple IT systems to help prioritize need-based activity in specific sections of the hospital. This allows the hospital to assign beds faster, discharge patients more quickly, and accept more complex and time-consuming cases.

Example: AI-powered obstetrics command centers are being used to assist clinicians in visualizing trends in the fetal heart rate patterns, maternal vital signs, and the progression of labor. SCL Health uses a system that condenses and consolidates many hours' worth of monitoring data and provides caregivers with a virtual "second set of eyes to actively monitor maternal and fetal conditions."[13]

Operations-focused AI is also helping improve efficiencies by optimizing scheduling for clinical departments with a high volume of procedures such as Surgery, Cath, and GI labs. By predicting how much time each procedure will take, these AI-driven scheduling apps reduce the amount of time high-volume procedure rooms go empty, reduce wait times, and maximize the use of operating rooms and lab facilities.

Example: AI is being used to improve patient flow, the discharge process, and triage ancillary services. UnityPoint Health uses a system that reduces the number of back-and-forth calls to coordinate patient discharges, getting hospital staff on the same page during discharge rounds, and shift handoffs.[14]

Creating better consumer experiences and higher satisfaction will be done by making better use of data to provide a more personalized approach. From streamlining frustrating billing and scheduling processes to reducing clinic wait times, data-driven insights can help providers create smoother experiences that keep patients feeling cared for and engaged.

Predicting and preventing poor customer experience issues is made possible through the power of AI to parse through large bodies of data to spot patterns that otherwise might not be seen. The use of AI as part of customer journey analytics can find every single relationship in the existing data *without expressly being told to look for it*. It can predict the likelihood of future behaviors with high accuracy.

Example: AI-backed financing solutions for patients are improving collections and customer satisfaction. Geisinger Health uses an algorithm that looks at more than 30,000 data points to analyze a patient's ability to pay, resulting in a 23% improvement in payment adherence.[15]

Reducing appointment no-shows and cancellations is occurring due to predictive analytics to identify which patients are likely to skip an appointment without advance notice. Using past patient data, patient demographics, locations, and environmental factors, algorithms can predict who will show up late, cancel, or be a no-show. The average cost of a no-show is $200 per patient.[16] AI gives providers the chance to send additional reminders, offer transportation, or other services to increase the likelihood of patients making appointments.

Example: While Beth Israel Deaconess Medical Center has garnered attention for an AI-enabled cancer screen, its first foray into AI was more prosaic: using it to reduce hospital readmission rates and identify possible no-shows. Using machine learning, technologists at Beth Israel Medical Center developed an application to predict which patients are likely to be no-shows or lapse on treatment so they can intervene ahead of time.[17]

Fraud detection and prevention is an expensive problem for healthcare organizations and insurers. Fraud detection has traditionally relied on a combination of computerized (rules-based) and manual reviews of medical claims. It's a time-consuming process that hinges on being able to spot anomalies after the incident occurs to intervene quickly. Health insurers are experimenting with AI-supported data mining, coupled with AI-based neural networks (which mimic the processes of the human brain, but much more rapidly) to search Medicare claims for patterns associated with medical reimbursement fraud.

Today, more than 75% of insurers report using machine-learning algorithms to flag fraud cases.[18] It is estimated that AI could create $17 billion in annual savings by improving the speed and accuracy of fraud detection in Medicare claims alone.[19]

Patient throughput is increasingly benefitting from predictive tools that forecast the flow of patients to improve the management of human and material resources in areas where there are high patient volumes and variance in demand for services. Areas of focus include predicting patient flow and utilization and improved ability to forecast staffing, expenses, and revenue.

Example: Seattle Children's Hospital uses AI to predict census and the capacity needed to support it. They also use AI to predict ED demand to optimize staffing and capacity.[20]

Optimizing staffing is being done with the help of AI with a specialized focus on predicting and better managing resource matching to address fluctuations based on future patient volumes, flow, and acuity. Using AI to predict patterns in utilization helps to ensure optimal staffing levels and contributes to reduced wait times and improved patient satisfaction.

Billing errors and claims denials can be improved with the use of AI. According to the American Medical Association research, the health industry could save $15.5 billion each year if claims were processed correctly the first time.[21] Such errors drive up costs and slow down revenue. Today, health organizations are applying machine learning to prospectively rate and predict which claims are at risk of being denied and then proactively resolving issues that automatically expedite claims and payments.

Prior authorization is being improved with computer vision and machine learning in combination to automate the highly repetitive nature of the prior authorizations process.

Consumer-Focused Care Optimization

The use of AI and other technological breakthroughs will erase historical boundaries for how and where care is provided. This move will enable greater healthcare innovations for all health consumers and patients.

Telehealth and Virtual Visits came into the spotlight during the pandemic. While driven by clinicians, AI plays a role in improving and making the experience better for the physician and the consumer.

Care anywhere is becoming a reality thanks to AI and the Cloud, which facilitates opportunities to serve patients and consumers across a seamless continuum of care settings.

Lifestyle management and monitoring benefits from AI-powered analytics. When applied to the increasing burden of lifestyle-driven chronic health conditions, AI-powered platforms can help patients and their families make healthier decisions. AI provides compelling applications across health reward and motivation platforms to achieve desired health and wellness goals. From remote monitoring and smartphone apps, to wearable devices, focus areas include chronic disease monitoring, treatment adherence, and preventive care programs.

Personalized responses to consumers are now possible with the use of Conversational AI. Chatbots are AI-based conversation agents used in various consumer-engagement scenarios to simulate human interactions and provide immediate, personalized responses. Conversational AI goes beyond traditional automated response systems to provide cognitive responses that mimic humans and eliminate frustrating delays and errors in customer service, particularly for handling customer complaints.

The application of conversational AI allows for more efficient and regular communication between patients and care providers to support administrative tasks, including referrals, patient satisfaction surveys, appointment scheduling, billing, and insurance verification.

Personalizing consumer engagement activities, whether for an individual or a broad population, are enabled by AI and becoming a vital service for both providers and insurance companies looking to build loyalty, promote wellness, and reduce long-term spending. The application of intelligent analytics tools to create consumer profiles allows health organizations to provide tailored messaging, improve customer retention, and keep patients engaged with their financial and clinical responsibilities.

Barriers to Adoption

While many powerful use cases produce value today, challenges remain in health organizations' enterprise-wide adoption and use of AI.

The successful adoption of AI requires an alignment among people, processes, and technology. From a tactical perspective, building and ensuring trust, upskilling-talent, clearly defining an AI strategy, along with ways to measure ROI, are among the top challenges that hinder successful AI adoption.

A survey of the current thinking by health system executives indicates that the most common challenge in their AI journey is defining the right uses cases and the need for clarity in measuring ROI.

Here are some of the most common barriers to mobilizing an effective plan to harness the power of AI in health organizations today:

Lack of Executive Support

Beyond the skepticism noted above, clinical and business leaders often don't understand AI technology and how it can help them achieve desired outcomes. As a result, they fail to champion AI initiatives and have been known to sabotage AI planning and investments. A survey by IDC found that 49% of enterprises deploying AI technology experienced challenges with stakeholder buy-in.[22]

Employee Resistance and Job Security

In a survey of 1000 managers, 42% believe AI will eliminate jobs, and 40% believe that employees lack the skills needed for AI adoption. Overcoming employee resistance is also a critical factor in the success of any AI initiative.

Lack of Data and Expertise

With the increasing demand for AI adoption across all industries and a limited talent pool, healthcare organizations find it challenging to initiate AI-based projects due to the lack of resources. At the same time, there is an almost overwhelming set of needs to build and support a data estate foundation for data preparation, exploration, and use. The degree of difficulty is often compounded by data availability and quality issues.

Developing a clear IT and data staffing plan that supports creating and managing your organization's data estate will help overcome these issues (Chapter 13).

Lack of Interoperability

Interoperability plays a significant role in supporting data sharing, which is at the heart of what powers almost all AI applications. Without access to comprehensive data from various sources, healthcare will not be able to fully benefit from all that AI has to offer.

AI Budget Availability

In a survey of health leaders by the Society of Actuaries, the lack of funding for AI initiatives was cited as the biggest challenge to implementation within their organization even though most leaders surveyed believed AI would provide measurable financial benefit within five years.[23]

Lack of Cloud Adoption

While AI can be done with on-premise solutions, much of its power and usefulness comes from having data and applications in the cloud. Unfortunately, some healthcare organizations are still hesitant to move data to the cloud. This results in some organizations abandoning cloud-based AI applications in healthcare and resorting to on-premises solutions that may have limited capabilities and potentially more complexity due to the IT environment requirements. Details on the role of the cloud in AI are provided in Chapter 19.

Notes

1. Shrank WH, Rogstad TL, Parekh N. Waste in the US Health Care System: Estimated Costs and Potential for Savings. JAMA. 2019;322(15):1501–1509. doi:10.1001/jama.2019.13978.

2. Shubham Singhal and Stephanie Carlton, The era of exponential improvement in healthcare? McKinsey & Company, May 14, 2019, https://www.mckinsey.com/industries/healthcare-systems-and-services/our-insights/the-era-of-exponential-improvement-in-healthcare.

3. Singhal S, Coe E. The Next Imperatives for US Healthcare. McKinsey White Paper. November 2016.

4. 'The Ferrari of data science': 7 Hospital Execs Share how they Use Predictive Analytics, Becker's Hospital Review, October 8, 2021, https://www.beckershospitalreview.com/innovation/the-ferrari-of-data-science-7-hospital-execs-share-how-they-use-predictive-analytics.html.

5. Thomas H. Davenport, Tonya M. Hongsermeier, Kimberly Alba Mc Cord, Using AI to Improve Electronic Health Records, Harvard Business Review, 2018, https://hbr.org/2018/12/using-ai-to-improve-electronic-health-records.

6. Zewe A. Toward a Smarter Electronic Health Record, MIT News, September 23, 2021, https://news.mit.edu/2021/medknowts-electronic-health-record-0923.

7. Adam Conner-Simons and Rachel Gordon, Using AI to Predict Breast Cancer and Personalize Care, MIT News, May 7, 2019, https://news.mit.edu/2019/using-ai-predict-breast-cancer-and-personalize-care-0507.

8. Koo CW, Anand V, Girvin F, Wickstrom ML, Fantauzzi JP, Bogoni L, Babb JS, Ko JP. Improved Efficiency of CT Interpretation Using an Automated Lung Nodule Matching Program, American Journal of Roengentology, 2012, https://www.ajronline.org/doi/pdf/10.2214/AJR.11.7522.

9. Schroerlucke SR, Wang MY, Cannestra AF, Lim J, Hsu VW, Zahrawi F, Complication Rate in Robotic-Guided vs Fluoro-Guided Minimally Invasive Spinal Fusion Surgery: Report from MIS Refresh Prospective Comparative Study, The Spine Journal, October 1, 2017, https://www.thespinejournalonline.com/article/S1529-9430(17)30851-3/fulltext#relatedArticles.

10. 'The Ferrari of data science': 7 Hospital Execs Share how they Use Predictive Analytics, Becker's Hospital Review, October 8, 2021, https://www.beckershospitalreview.com/innovation/the-ferrari-of-data-science-7-hospital-execs-share-how-they-use-predictive-analytics.html.

11. Zaidi D. The 3 Most Valuable Applications of AI in Health Care, VentureBeat, 2018, https://venturebeat.com/2018/04/22/the-3-most-valuable-applications-of-ai-in-health-care/.

12. Frakt A. The Huge Waste in the U.S. Health System, The New York Times, October 9, 2019, https://www.nytimes.com/2019/10/07/upshot/health-care-waste-study.html.

13. SCL Health to Deploy System-Wide OB Hub Powered by PeriWatch Command Center PR Newswire, October 26, 2021. https://www.prnewswire.com/news-releases/scl-health-to-deploy-system-wide-ob-hub-powered-by-periwatch-command-center-301408284.html.

14. UnityPoint Health inks AI partnership to accelerate discharges, triage hospital services, Becker's Healthcare IT. July 26, 2021, https://www.beckershospitalreview.com/healthcare-information-technology/unitypoint-health-inks-ai-partnership-to-accelerate-discharges-triage-hospital-services.html.

15. Geisinger Ups Payment Adherence 23% with AI-Backed Payment Solution, Becker's Health IT, October 18, 2021. https://www.beckershospitalreview.com/digital-transformation/geisinger-ups-payment-adherence-23-with-ai-backed-payment-solution.html.
16. Kheirkhah P, Feng Q, Travis LM, Tavakoli-Tabasi S, Sharafkhaneh A, Prevalence, Predictors and Economic Consequences of No-Shows, US National Library of Medicine National Institutes of Health, 2016, https://www.ncbi.nlm.nih.gov/pmc/articles/PMC4714455/.
17. Kalis B, Collier M, and Fu R. 10 Promising AI Applications in Health Care, Harvard Business Review, May 10, 2018, https://hbr.org/2018/05/10-promising-ai-applications-in-health-care.
18. The State of Insurance Fraud Technology, Coalition Against Insurance Fraud, 2016, http://www.insurancefraud.org/downloads/State_of_Insurance_Fraud_Technology2016.pdf.
19. Kalis B, Collier M, and Fu R. 10 Promising AI Applications in Health Care, Harvard Business Review, May 10, 2018, https://hbr.org/2018/05/10-promising-ai-applications-in-health-care.
20. 'The Ferrari of data science': 7 Hospital Execs Share How They Use Predictive Analytics, Becker's Hospital Review, October 8, 2021, https://www.beckershospitalreview.com/innovation/the-ferrari-of-data-science-7-hospital-execs-share-how-they-use-predictive-analytics.html.
21. Stern A, US Doctors Say 1 in 5 Insurance Claims Mishandled, Reuters, 2010, https://www.reuters.com/article/doctors-insurers/corrected-us-doctors-say-1-in-5-insurance-claims-mishandled-idUSN1422071220100615.
22. Staying Ahead of the Game with Artificial Intelligence, IDC, 2018, https://blog.datarobot.com/infographic-staying-ahead-game-artificial-intelligence.
23. 2017 Predictive Analytics in Healthcare Trend Forecast, Society of Actuaries, 2017, https://www.soa.org/globalassets/assets/Files/programs/predictive-analytics/2017-health-care-trend.pdf.

Chapter 8

The Patient Will See You Now

In 2013, the movie *Her* won the Oscar for Best Original Screenplay. The genius of this sci-fi romance was that it took place in the not-too-distant future when the world would be dominated by millennials (those born between 1982 and 1997). The movie's main character, Theodore Twombly (played by Joaquin Phoenix), falls in love with an intelligent operating system named Samantha. We catch glimpses throughout the movie of a future where the millennials' love of intelligent technology is ingrained into every aspect of society.

Fast-forward to the present day. One out of every three adults in America *is* a millennial. They have more spending power than any other generation. By 2025 millennials will make up 75% of the workforce. With each passing year, they will increasingly dominate the nation's workplaces, corporate cultures, politics, and lifestyle trends.[1]

And for the record, there are in fact reported cases of humans ending up in therapy because they fell in love with their virtual assistants.[2]

Millennials have a love affair with smart technologies. After all, they are the first generation to be "digital natives." This means that they do not remember a time when the internet, social media, and smart apps didn't exist. As a result, they communicate, shop, and manage all aspects of their lives differently than the generations before them.

When it comes to healthcare, their expectations are no different. They want to schedule and complete a medical consultation from the same place they order dinner – their couch. They want answers now. They don't just want it to be easy; they want it to be fast, enjoyable, and accurate. If it's not, they are more likely to make their dissatisfaction known (also by going online).[3]

DOI: 10.4324/9781003286103-8

Millennials see health as important. They are more proactive and health conscious than their parents and grandparents. They're also more willing to spend money on fitness, healthy food, and self-care.[4] Not surprisingly, they (and Gen Zers, those born in 1997 or later) have the highest levels of dissatisfaction with traditional health systems when it comes to the services offered and how they are treated. They give the lowest marks for treatment effectiveness and convenience. They are also less satisfied with transparency and operational effectiveness.[5]

The millennials highlight both the problems and the opportunities faced by healthcare when it comes to giving people what they want. Every generation is different. How we currently serve them is not. This is where intelligent health will shine.

All Generations Are Ready for Change

One only needs to review any number of surveys and reports on the satisfaction of health consumers to understand why all generations are ready for change.

One such study is the Change Healthcare Consumer Experience Index. It was completed by the Harris Poll organization to quantify consumer perceptions on how easy or hard it is to find, access, and pay for healthcare.[6] It also examines the impact such efforts have on consumer behavior.

The study paints a bleak picture of what traditional health systems put consumers through. It reports that:

- Two-thirds of consumers said that the effort required to find, access, and pay for care is excessive and a burden. Half said it is such a hassle that they avoid seeking needed care
- Not one healthcare activity was described by consumers as effortless
- Three out of four believe that telehealth is the future of medicine
- Sixty-seven percent would like to be able to shop for healthcare entirely online
- Fifty-eight percent are looking for a tech company to deliver a new type of healthcare experience

Consumers were already feeling worn down by inefficient and disjointed processes before the pandemic. When COVID hit, consumers used their *"lockdown"* time *to find in-home alternatives* to manage *out-of-home activities*. Healthcare rose to the top of the list. This process elevated the problems faced by consumers and accelerated their desires for something better. They found it in telehealth and other digital services.

A snapshot of 2020 from Rock Health shows how quickly consumers pivoted to new ways of getting their health needs met, with 43% reporting that they had a virtual visit. Use of wearables was up. Self-management of chronic conditions drove this uptick. Sixty-six percent of those who started using a wearable for the first time did so to manage a diagnosed health condition.[7]

Health consumers escalated their use of smart apps and technology to monitor conditions, measure fitness, schedule appointments, and order prescription drug refills. More than three-quarters of those who track their health say it's changing their behavior at least moderately.[8]

Many shifts in consumer attitudes and actions are expected to stick after the pandemic.[9]

Getting Personal Means Getting Generational

Traditional health systems largely follow a one-size-fits-all approach to those they serve. In reality, no two consumers are alike, even if they have a common chronic illness. Each has a unique set of characteristics that affect their health.

While many health organizations aspire to deliver "patient-centered care," most rely on standardized care pathways and care models. Such things help produce better quality in clinical outcomes but do not go far enough when it comes to consistently providing the personalized and frictionless experience desired by consumers.

The days of providing the same experience to all patients and health consumers are ending. AI is a driving force in making healthcare personal. In the future, more intelligent health consumers will vote with their feet and wallets in seeking out the services that best meet their health and convenience needs.

Gearing up to shape future health services starts by understanding and embracing the tenet that optimal health experiences are generational.

Satisfaction with traditional health system varies by generation. Younger generations have the highest level of dissatisfaction with how traditional health operates.[10]

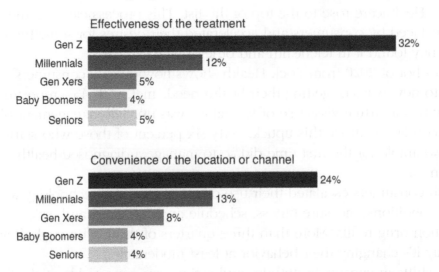

Younger generations dissatisfied with traditional care

Effectiveness of the treatment

Generation	Percent
Gen Z	32%
Millennials	12%
Gen Xers	5%
Baby Boomers	4%
Seniors	5%

Convenience of the location or channel

Generation	Percent
Gen Z	24%
Millennials	13%
Gen Xers	8%
Baby Boomers	4%
Seniors	4%

Source: Accenture 2019. www.accenture.com/us-en/insights/health/todays-consumers-reveal-future-healthcare

Beyond general satisfaction levels, it's important to recognize, plan for, and accommodate generational patterns and preferences. This means better matching the consumer's needs with their experiences when interacting with the system.

Let's look at something as basic as having a designated primary care physician (PCP). Why is this important? Many health plans and provider organizations still use PCPs as gatekeepers. This means that to access specialty care, a consumer must go through a process of getting a referral from their PCP.

As noted in the chart below, seniors and baby boomers have a higher likelihood of having a designated PCP. Older generations grew up believing that all things passed through a "family doctor." When care is needed, they make an appointment to see their PCP who helps them navigate the system. In some ways, the PCP and their staff serve as this generation's "app."

Millennials and Gen Zers, on the other hand, grew up in a time of online services, urgent care clinics, and retail health. They are less likely to use a system that requires being tethered to a PCP: 74% would rather see a doctor through telemedicine. And when a situation calls for more than a video chat, they want to avoid a primary care doctor and go straight to specialists and alternative solutions. In seeking out specialty care, they are more likely to turn to former patients and seek out reviews online to quickly rule out doctors they don't want to see.[11]

And so, the traditional process for accessing specialty care works for those who have and rely on a PCP but creates a friction point for those who don't.

Health Preferences Differ by Generation

	Gen Z (Born 1997 or later)	Millennials (Born 1982–1997)	Gen X (Born 1965–1981)	Baby boomers (Born 1946–1964)	Seniors (Born 1900–1945)
Have a primary care physician (PCP)	55%	67%	76%	84%	85%
Prefer virtual visit over in-person care	41%	33%	22%	9%	7%
Trust tech companies for health & wellness services	26%	43%	32%	20%	14%
Openness to receiving virtual care from retail brands	34%	30%	26%	20%	28%

Sources: 2021 Global Health Care Outlook – Accelerating Industry Change, Deloitte
How can Leaders Make Recent Digital Health Gains Last? Accenture

Providing the same patient experience across the board no longer works. As consumer expectations change, intelligent health systems will use data to understand what different generations want and will use AI and digital solutions to provide it.

There are many factors to consider when it comes to optimizing experiences.

While most consumers today still want in-person visits, younger generations prefer virtual over in-person care when given a choice. Among Gen Zers, 41% prefer a virtual or digital experience with a doctor or other medical professional, along with 33% of millennials.[12]

And although consumers are willing to receive virtual services from traditional care providers, they are increasingly open to virtual services being provided by new entrants to the health market. Twenty-seven percent are open to receiving virtual care from technology or social media companies like Google and Microsoft. Almost half of all millennials say they would trust big tech companies for health and wellness services.[13]

There is also a growing openness to receiving virtual care from retail brands. Twenty-five percent of consumers are open to seeking and receiving care from brands such as Walmart and CVS. One in five is open to having care provided by medical start-ups. Even among seniors, more than one in four would consider receiving virtual care from these new purveyors of health services.[14]

Spurred by the pandemic, the health consumer movement will continue to unfold. Successful organizations will offer services better geared towards the lifestyles, preferences, and values of those being served.

AI to the Rescue

Preferences vary by generation, but the overarching trend among all health consumers is the growing use of data, AI, and digital solutions to manage health services on their terms. Organizations and practitioners seeking to serve these consumers will embrace the changes and know how to pivot, adapt, and innovate quickly.

More than ever, consumers expect intelligent technologies to make health services more effective and personalized. Their preferences are driving the development of AI-enabled, seamlessly connected clinician-patient interactions.

To be clear, providing for those who are sick or injured remains a priority for consumers and health organizations alike. At the same time, consumers are also demanding a focus shift from just healthcare when they are sick to health and well-being when they are not. This means more resources (time, money, and attention) will be re-allocated from the end of the healthcare value chain (treatment and aftercare) to the beginning.[15] This includes greater focus and investment in promoting healthy lifestyles, vitality and wellness, primary and secondary prevention, and early diagnosis. This is where the use of AI shines.

Intelligent health services will connect and empower people and populations to manage health and wellness based on the needs and preferences of each person served. Technology and AI will not replace but rather augment accessible and supportive provider teams who can work within more flexible and digitally-enabled care environments to transform the care delivered. This means that the care experience will be more seamless across all care settings. Innovative health organizations are responding with new options like virtual-first health plans and digital front doors (more on this in Chapter 11).

As we enlist the power of data and intelligent systems to better understand and manage each individual's health, we can personalize the experience to better fit the unique values, needs, and life circumstances of individuals and populations.

A new value chain is emerging around health data that goes beyond the typical data captured and used by traditional health systems. Individuals themselves are experiencing a data explosion through a wide variety of devices and technologies, including social networks, wearables, telemonitoring, genomics analysis (both private and public sector), and health applications that can be personalized to capture outcomes to track health and wellness.

In the future, consumers will have more access to and control over their data through intelligent digital technologies. As this occurs, the historical dynamics that have benefited traditional health systems will give way to a growing population of informed and empowered health consumers.

As people are empowered by owning and controlling access to their health data, new health service delivery models will emerge. No longer bound by the processes and methods used by long-standing healthcare system incumbents, consumers will create their own personal health management "ecosystems" quite literally in the palms of their hands. They will do this by using cloud-based tools based on their own preferences. This includes clinical preferences such as how they wish to monitor and manage their health and healthcare. It will also allow them to personalize how they manage their health benefits and payments.

As this movement grows, two realities are likely. One is that the change taking place will be driven or facilitated by better use of a variety of data to power intelligent apps and experiences. The second is that fundamental shifts in the current balance of power will occur.

Successful provider and payer organizations will embrace and leverage this change. They'll make better use of data, first to understand what different generations and consumers want and then use AI to deliver personalized experiences. Who knows, there may come a time where *"delighted"* becomes a category on a digital health satisfaction survey.

Notes

1. Beth Jones Sanborn, 'Digital natives' will lead the healthcare consumer revolution, HealthcareIT News, March 26, 2018, https://www.healthcareitnews.com/news/digital-natives-will-lead-healthcare-consumer-revolution
2. XiaoIce robot users have ended up in therapy for falling in love with their Artificial Intelligence, Entrepreneur, August 26, 2021, https://www.entrepreneur.com/article/381966
3. Beth Jones Sanborn, 'Digital natives' will lead the healthcare consumer revolution, HealthcareIT News, March 26, 2018, https://www.healthcareitnews.com/news/digital-natives-will-lead-healthcare-consumer-revolution
4. Millennials and Healthcare Benefits, Harvard Pilgrim Healthcare, https://www.harvardpilgrim.org/hapiguide/millennials-health-benefits/
5. Today's consumers reveal the future of healthcare, Accenture, February 12, 2019, https://www.accenture.com/us-en/insights/health/todays-consumers-reveal-future-healthcare

6. The 2020 Healthcare Consumer Experience Index. Change Healthcare & The Harris Poll Organization, www.changehealthcare.com/insights/healthcare-consumer-experience-index

7. Digital Health Consumer Adoption Report 2020 How COVID-19 accelerated digital health beyond its years, Rock Health/Stanford Medicine Center for Digital Health.

8. Source: David Betts and Leslie Korenda, A consumer-centered future of health, Deloitte Insights, 2019; Deloitte Insights, Meeting consumers' changing needs: Moving towards the future of health.

9. Jenny Cordina, Eric Levin, Andrew Ramish, and Nikhil Seshan, How COVID-19 has changed the way US consumers think about healthcare, McKinsey and Company.

10. Today's consumers reveal the future of healthcare, Accenture, February 12, 2019, https://www.accenture.com/us-en/insights/health/todays-consumers-reveal-future-healthcare.

11. What Millennials Want When It Comes To Healthcare, MediaPost, December 23, 2016, https://www.mediapost.com/publications/article/291796/what-millennials-want-when-it-comes-to-healthcare.html.

12. How can Health Leaders Make Digital Health Gains Last?, Accenture, https://www.accenture.com/_acnmedia/PDF-130/Accenture-2020-Digital-Health-Consumer-Survey-US.pdf.

13. Ibid.

14. Ibid.

15. John Luijs, Mathieu van Bergen, and Lucien Engelen, The health(care) future of the Netherlands, Deloitte, 2020.

Chapter 9

Intelligent Aging Is Healthcare's Moonshot

It's not how old you are, it's how you are old.

Jules Renard

Have you ever had a perfect workday? I did a while back. I was riding out the pandemic in a fixer-upper farmhouse near Monterey, California, when I was invited to meet with America's foremost gerontologist and aging expert Ken Dychtwald, Ph.D.

After an amazing drive down the coastal highway, I arrived at the Esalen Institute in Big Sur. Having spent endless hours trapped in my home office doing virtual meetings, it was a delight to spend the day sitting in Adirondack chairs on a cliff by the ocean talking with Dychtwald about the challenges and opportunities of using AI to rethink how to empower older Americans to be healthy and well.

With 19 prescient books to his credit, Ken is one of my intellectual heroes. For three decades, he has been the leading harbinger of truth for the medical, political, social, and financial realities that come with the aging of the baby boomers.

His 1989 book *Age Wave* accurately foresaw and predicted the impact of the boomers. These predictions are now becoming realities in how the aging of this generation is affecting all generations.

Nowhere will this be felt more strongly than in healthcare.

DOI: 10.4324/9781003286103-9

Keeping Promises Made

It was the summer of 1965 when Medicare was signed into law, guaranteeing that the federal government would manage the provision and cost of medical care for all seniors. In doing so, President Lyndon Johnson proudly declared, *"No longer will older Americans be denied the healing miracle of modern medicine. No longer will illness crush and destroy the savings that they have so carefully put away over a lifetime."*[1]

As the country's then 19 million seniors celebrated, little note was taken of the 76 million children who were part of a generation that would come to be known as the "baby boomers."[2, 3]

A nation of people once very young is today growing older by the minute. As noted by Dychtwald,

> *"The diaper business prospered when the baby boomers arrived. When they took their first steps, the shoe and photo industries skyrocketed. When a few thousand people share an opinion, buy a product, or back a candidate, it's a movement. When 76 million people do so, it's a revolution. Those born between 1946 and 1964 have always been a force by any measure."*[4]

And like every stage of their time on this planet, the generation that coined the phrase *"hell no, we won't go"* is not entering into the later stages of life quietly.

Dychtwald likens this to *"a pig moving through a python"* as the sheer mass of this generation will always dominate the social, political, and financial landscape.

The boomers are about to disrupt everyone's lives, starting with how healthcare works. No one, including corporations and other generations, will be untouched by what Dychtwald calls the "Age Wave."

Today, two-thirds of all the people who have ever lived past the age of 65 in the entire history of the world are alive today.[5] Equally important, for the first time in America's history, we will soon have more older Americans than we have children.[6]

Just as AI supported managing the pandemic, the Intelligence Revolution will play a critical role in creating new models for ensuring the health and well-being of this vital population.

The Countdown Has Started

Every 15 seconds, another baby boomer turns 65. This will continue for the next ten years. Medicare covers 62 million beneficiaries today. This will swell to over 80 million beneficiaries by 2030.[7,8] As this tectonic demographic shift happens, there is another essential fact to consider: On average, those 65 and older consume 5 times more health resources than those under 65.[9]

Medicare already accounts for 17% of all US health expenditures, one-eighth of the federal budget, and 2% of gross domestic product.[10] It is the federal government's third-largest commitment after social security and defense spending.[11] And, costs will only increase ... if Medicare survives.

There are many challenges to Medicare. One is the sheer cost and results of how it works. Another is the declining number of workers who are taxed to pay for it.

Caring for aging boomers will stress the economic well-being of the working-age population. The number of taxpaying workers per Medicare beneficiary has declined from 4.6 during the program's early years to 2.9 today. By 2030, this number is projected to be 2.3.[12]

Given this trend, Medicare is already causing intergenerational strife as costs go up and the number of workers bearing the burden goes down.

Additionally, Medicare relies heavily on general revenues. This reliance is projected to increase, which means the current system will cannibalize funding for other things like education, transportation, and the environment.[13]

Change in the Medicare Population and the Number of Workers per Beneficiary

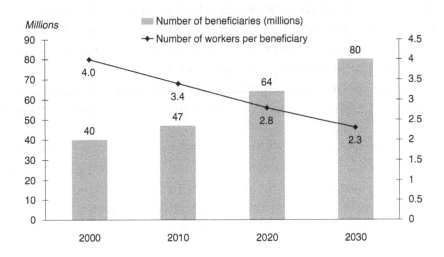

Source: 2021 Medicare Trustee Report,
www.cms.gov/Research-Statistics-Data-and-Systems/Statistics-Trends-and-Reports/ReportsTrustFunds

In its current form, Medicare is unsustainable to deliver what it promised to seniors without changes to how these promises are delivered, and what they cost.

The hypergrowth of Medicare beneficiaries multiplied by a 5× consumption factor is problematic. Add medical inflation, an expected staffing shortfall, and a decreasing number of workers to pay for it, and you grasp the magnitude of the problem.

Changing Outcomes by Changing the Model

Despite the benefits of the existing health system, a paradigm shift is needed to better manage older citizens' needs and curb rising costs. The use of AI and a move toward intelligent health will help address the following:

Reactive to proactive: As discussed in Chapter 2, traditional health systems are reactive. Delivery of, and payment for, health and medical services are based on a "break-fix" model. Intelligent Health Systems will proactively focus more on prevention and the overall holistic health of populations rather than episodic and transaction-based treatments. They will balance investments in "care anywhere" services with desired outcomes. One of the top beneficiaries of this model will be the boomers and their families.

Compared to previous generations who became Medicare beneficiaries, the baby-boom generation has longer life expectancies and lower smoking rates. This generation also has higher rates of obesity and other chronic conditions. At the same time, they are more motivated than previous generations to control certain health conditions.[14] Such dynamics bode well for intelligent health serving a population that is ready and desirous of change.

When it comes to the health and well-being of older people, much of what needs to be done comes down to preventing and better managing chronic conditions. As noted in the chart below, those aged 65 and over need help with health conditions that can be proactively monitored and managed with intelligent lifestyle and community-based services.

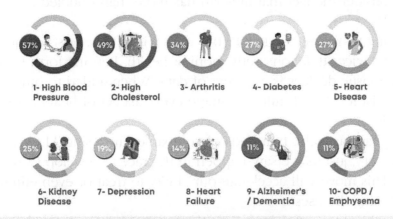

Top 10 Chronic Conditions Among Medicare Beneficiaries

57%	49%	34%	27%	27%
1- High Blood Pressure	2- High Cholesterol	3- Arthritis	4- Diabetes	5- Heart Disease

25%	19%	14%	11%	11%
6- Kidney Disease	7- Depression	8- Heart Failure	9- Alzheimer's / Dementia	10- COPD / Emphysema

Source : Medicare Beneficiaries At-A-Glance, CMS

Beyond chronic conditions, helping new generations of older Americans be healthy, safe, and independent includes providing non-medical solutions that have a significant impact on health and well-being.

Here's an example. Try to guess what health challenge I'm referring to:

■ This "hidden epidemic" is pervasive and deadly among older Americans.
■ It puts an older citizen in an Emergency Department every 13 seconds.
■ It takes a life every 20 minutes.
■ It costs $34 billion in direct medical costs each year, but little is invested in prevention.

What are we talking about? The answer is falls. They are the leading cause of death from unintentional injuries among older Americans today.[15]

AI devices that predict and prevent falls are available today. Smart walkers and sensors in the home can determine when someone has fallen or has encountered other accidents and can notify family members or emergency services for assistance.

Matching Healthspan to Lifespan

There is growing evidence that the Intelligent Health Revolution will give rise to a Longevity Revolution. In his book, *The Science and Technology of Growing Young*, Sergey Young foresees a time when the average citizen can be expected to live well into their 100s. In case you think this sounds far-fetched, consider the fact that lifespan has more than doubled in the last 100 years.[16]

According to Young, the key to this shift will be low-cost, ubiquitous, connected devices that constantly monitor health. Pouring forth from these digital diagnostic devices is a torrent of data. When added to other data, it becomes grist for the AI mill to reshape every aspect of healthcare as we know it.

In the pharma world, hundreds of companies are using AI to reshape drug discovery, just as we saw happen in the race to develop COVID-19 vaccines. This move will accelerate our ability to treat or even eliminate life-threatening diseases.

As we extend the amount of time the average human lives, the real issue is not lifespan but healthspan. Lifespan is the total number of years we live. Healthspan is how many of those years we have an acceptable level of health and well-being.

Rather than worrying about dying too young, many people today worry about living too long without sufficient quality of life. In the United States, the difference between life expectancy, or lifespan, and healthy life expectancy, or healthspan, is almost ten years.[17]

When it comes to their health, what do Boomers say they want? According to Dychtwald, it's *"To take charge of their health because they don't trust the system to take care of them. To prevent or manage their chronic conditions to live the active lifestyles they want. To avoid cognitive decline. And to stay healthy and look and feel their best without breaking the bank."*

"Do they want to live to be 100 or more? It's an intriguing prospect, but only 22% of Americans say yes. Among those already 65 and older, twice as many say no (35%) as yes (17%). The most common response, of course, is... "it depends on the quality of life."[18]

The use of AI is a critical factor in bridging this gap.

Raising the Outcomes Bar: The Happiness Factor

As the Intelligent Health Revolution closes the gap between healthspan and lifespan, it will open the door to a new opportunity that may come to be known as the "happiness factor." Think of this as more people moving toward living in the upper quadrant of a "well-being" continuum.

Consider this: When asked to define the goals of today's health system, the answer most often given is to achieve some level of *health and well-being.*

In the current break-fix model, the *"health"* part of this answer typically focuses on restoring something to a former or original state. If it's a joint replacement, it means returning to a normal range of movement. If it's cancer, it means the absence of cancer cells for a period of time. For many serious medical conditions, achieving such outcomes is nothing short of a modern miracle that significantly impacts the quality of life.

For now, let's think of the "health" portion of the system's goal as essential, as well as seeing it as a base upon which to build.

Traditional Health Systems tend to be overweighted in focusing on restoring or maintaining health and underweighted in helping people achieve and maintain a state of well-being.

Merriam Webster defines well-being as "the *state of being happy, healthy, or prosperous.*"[19] Think about your experience with the pandemic; chances are you've had your own firsthand experience with the interrelatedness of happiness, health, and prosperity.

The Intelligent Health Revolution gives us a chance to rebalance the health *and* well-being equation. It provides the opportunity to reimagine outcomes and raise the bar on what we get in the future.

Let's use the prevailing view of mental health services as an example. Everyone understands that the health system must be geared toward providing services for mental health (though it is a lightning rod for what services are actually covered). Most often, the current definition and expectations focus on the provision of services that mitigate or eliminate the presence of mental illness. And while this is a precursor to achieving well-being, it falls short of actually delivering that goal.

Let's define the happiness factor as the ability to leverage and deploy new tech-supported health models that help move everyone, especially older citizens, higher on the scale of well-being. It changes our expectations from the absence of medical and mental conditions that impede our health, to an approach and mindset that helps people thrive in well-being and achieve their best potential at all stages of life including while living with those medical and mental health conditions. It helps close the gap between healthspan and lifespan by raising expectations in what we get out of the health system to achieve higher levels of individual and collective well-being.

AI gives us the ability to not only extend the length of life but improve its quality as well.

Intelligent Aging Opportunities

Over the next 15 years, the number of people 65 and older in the United States will grow by over 50%.[20]

This generational shift will be accompanied by a change in technology acceptance among older people. Someone who is 70 today may have first experienced some form of personalized IT in middle age or later, while a 50-year-old today is far more technology-friendly and savvy. As a result, there will be a growing interest and market for already available and maturing intelligent technologies to support physical, emotional, social, and mental health as we age.

Here are a few likely examples:

Ambient Intelligence will become commonplace. This is where AI is embedded in a user's immediate environment through sensors, cameras, and listening devices that are mainly invisible. As this happens, continuous "anywhere" monitoring will provide new and ongoing opportunities to assess and manage the health and wellness of older citizens. Whether through wearables, sensing devices in the home, or embedded in things we have regular contact with like car seats and mattresses, smart devices will gather data that is analyzed by healthcare professionals and/or presented back to the consumer.

These continuous sensing services will support better management of a range of health issues, including chronic diseases.

The FDA has already approved a remote monitoring platform for chronically ill people with ICU-level accuracy in tracking a wide range of vital signs. This AI-powered platform works with a small sensor worn on a person's upper arm.[21]

Beyond physiological monitoring, the use of voice AI allows for analyzing speech patterns to assess mental health status, including the prediction of things like depression, anxiety, and propensity for dementia.

Automating virtual visits through intelligence will improve and extend telemedicine and virtual care experiences. The use of AI for virtual visits is growing in capability and popularity.

In the pre-visit phase, AI will facilitate self-administered steps to collect data such as weight, temperature, blood pressure, and blood oxygen content. Conversational AI can ask questions to determine an initial diagnosis. Then, through a virtual visit with a live provider, the patient can verify the information and discuss a treatment plan. As this interaction is happening, AI can automatically assess things like the risk of depression. During the virtual visit, AI is being used in the background relieving the clinician of the burden of writing clinical visit notes, suggesting the appropriate diagnostic code, and automating much of the administrative work that comes with each patient encounter.

AI virtual assistants will be used between human visits to keep people healthy. They will assess and provide individuals with ongoing and real-time intelligent advice. Manually managing and recording daily activities such as nutrition and fitness has always been tedious and difficult. AI virtual assistants will automate the acquisition of deep knowledge of an individual's diet, exercise, medications, and emotional state.

Using existing AI capabilities, including computer vision, natural language understanding, and machine learning, will enable individuals to easily "show" or "talk to" their AI virtual assistant about what they're doing. These devices will also be able to "know" what is transpiring via motion detection, infrared cameras, and sensors.

Such devices will automate many routine inquiries while also serving as a means of effectively triaging when a human caregiver is involved.

AI will help automate the collection of valuable, personalized data. Doing so will guide both clinicians and consumers to encourage and support the pursuit of a healthy lifestyle.

AI will reduce social isolation for many older Americans and create new healthy connections among friends, family members, and the community. AI chatbots at home will keep people on top of things like taking medications, reminding them of doctors' appointments, and even scheduling transportation.

Social robots will provide intelligent companionship that will reduce loneliness while increasing intellectual and emotional stimulation. As smart devices, social robots will use continuous learning to tailor responses to the individual. This will allow them to nudge humans toward personalized, healthy, and self-caring behaviors. This might include letting their human companions know about upcoming social activities in their neighborhood.

AI will also help keep older people connected to friends and families. Using mobile applications or web-based platforms, family members and volunteer caregivers will get easy access to information regarding things like daily activities, compliance with medications, and alerts on a variety of measures. These systems will be especially valuable for family members who don't live nearby or cannot visit frequently.

New intelligent medical devices and applications will focus on improving the daily living needs of older women and men. AI-powered hearing aids and visual assistive devices will mitigate the effects of hearing and vision loss, enhancing safety and social connection. Physical assistive devices such as intelligent walkers, wheelchairs, and exoskeletons will extend the range of activities for those needing assistance. Mobile applications that monitor movement and activities, coupled with social platforms, will make recommendations to maintain mental and physical health.

An explosion of low-cost sensing technologies will increase capabilities for older citizens to remain healthy and independent longer. These innovations will also introduce questions regarding privacy within various circles, including friends, family, and caregivers, and create new challenges to accommodate a more active and engaged population.

A Bright Future for Older Consumers

As we consider the health, medical, and economic challenges of serving this important population, let's start first by acknowledging and celebrating our successes. Things like public health and medical breakthroughs are allowing more people to live longer than at any point in history. As we celebrate this accomplishment, let us recognize that this success creates new challenges that the existing healthcare system was never designed to address.

The societal inevitability of this population shift will affect every aspect of our culture, including social and personal relationships, financial and political power.

Creating a new approach starts with moving away from our traditional views and beliefs regarding aging. Nowhere will this be more important than how we approach the provision of services to manage the health and well-being of older citizens.

There is growing recognition that to better manage the needs of older citizens and curb rising costs, we need a better ecosystem that focuses more on prevention and the overall holistic health of populations rather than today's model of episodic reaction and transaction-based medical treatments.

The Intelligent Health Revolution is the vehicle by which this will happen.

GET READY FOR THE AGETECH REVOLUTION

AgeTech is a growing category of technology solutions designed to meet the needs of the 50+ audience. This $8.3 trillion-dollar market sits at the intersection of longevity and technology. AgeTech includes products, services, and experiences across industries that contribute to longer, healthier lives, and empower people to choose how they live as they age.[22]

While many players are coming into this space, some of the most promising opportunities are being championed by an organization many people know and trust – the American Association of Retired Persons, commonly known as AARP. AARP has a long history of providing personal technology resources, including digital literacy initiatives, practical guidebooks, and advocacy on technology issues for the 50+ crowd.

AARP recently created the AgeTech Collaborative. Its mission is to discover, support, and scale ideas that will help empower millions of people to choose how they live as they age. The initiative brings together leading startups, forward-thinking investors, industry leaders, and creative testbeds to innovate and introduce innovative solutions for older Americans.

Andy Miller is Senior Vice President for Innovation and Product Development. A former co-founder and tech exec in the startup space, Miller is leveraging his background and experience to help AARP incubate and enable new models for tech solutions that support intelligent aging.

This includes providing startups that are accepted into the collaborative with access to funding, services, and piloting opportunities. The goal is to incubate meaningful new models for industry leaders to adopt.

"The Age Tech space is often misunderstood. It's not just about older people. It's designed to serve all of us. We are all aging every day. The question is, how do we age more gracefully? How do we age to be happier, healthier, and live longer lives? We should be able to age the way we want and be empowered to choose how we live as we age. Technology has an important role to play in our approach to answering these questions," says Miller.

(Continued)

While not known as a technology-related organization, AARP's mission, brand, and following make it unique in the AgeTech space.

> *"Others have tried to accomplish what we are doing. We've seen initiatives run by for-profit companies focused on Elder Tech or Senior Tech. They talk about addressing the needs of the "silver tsunami." Few have been successful in the space for several reasons. This includes being profit-driven rather than mission-driven, being focused on a narrow definition of health and a lack of understanding the market to be served."*

> *"In many ways, AARP is well suited to this space. A key asset we bring to the table is our convening power. So, when you tie our convening power to the fact that we are a social mission-driven organization, AgeTech becomes a vehicle to deliver on our mission of empowering people to choose how they live as they age,"* says Miller.

AARP's AgeTech initiative is a collaborative effort that brings together start-ups and other organizations to develop or deploy technology and services that support intelligent aging.

Organizations that join the collaborative are provided with a variety of services. Discovery services help startups and investors find each other. Participants have access to various experts and workshops to hone their skills on things like human-centered design or how to bring products to market. These knowledge exchange processes are supported with practical tools, including digital "sandboxes" to help startups test and validate new solutions.

One aspect of the program that is particularly compelling is its holistic approach to health and well-being. It includes technology solutions that focus on digital health and housing, caregiver support, financial resilience, and social connections.

> *"Housing is a big opportunity. It includes a diverse set of opportunities in how we approach everything from remote monitoring to how we create options for placing a smart ADU in the backyard as an alternative to putting your aged mom or dad*

(Continued)

in a care facility. Intelligent caregiving is another area ripe for change. Think about the situation where there is an older person with adult children. There are ten million Millennial caregivers in the United States today looking for better ways to take care of their aging parents."

"Often overlooked is the area of intergenerational engagement and maintaining social connections. We see our work encompassing the facilitation of generational engagement, which includes passing knowledge down to younger generations. Grandparents find great joy in helping their grandchildren learn or do something. This brings them happiness which has a direct correlation to their health," says Miller.

A wide range of AI solutions and use cases that support intelligent aging is part of AgeTech's portfolio.

"Virtual reality (VR) and augmented reality (AR) are really interesting, with some great use cases coming forward. When older adults try VR or AR, we see that they absolutely love it, which means it can be applied in many ways. It has application as part of therapeutic processes. It's also being used for things like reminiscence therapy. For those who are isolated or have mobility issues, this technology can be used to take people on virtual safaris or give them other travel experiences," says Miller.

While COVID has had a dramatic impact on the health and well-being of older Americans, it also produced benefits in moving more people to try online services.

"Many of those in the 60 and 70+ age range used digital services before the pandemic, but much of this was used for 'nice to have' things like seeing pictures of grandkids on Facebook. When COVID hit, it changed the habits of many. They still wanted to use it to stay connected to family and loved ones, but they still needed to see a doctor. They still had bills to pay

(Continued)

and did not want to venture out to do such things. And so, they began doing things online that they previously were reluctant to try or do. Now that they've tried it, many think it's great and are looking at doing more online," says Miller.

In the end, Miller and the AgeTech Collaborative are aiming at changing how technology will support all generations to age well.

"AARP and the AgeTech Collaborative are bringing together a diverse set of leaders and organizations who are working to introduce smart solutions that drive meaningful new models for intelligent aging. In the end, all of our efforts come back to our mission which is to discover, support, and scale ideas that help empower millions of people to choose how they live as they age," says Miller.

Notes

1. What Did Medicare Do (And Was It Worth It)?. Amy Finkelstein, Robin McKnight. NBER Working Paper No. 11609. April 2006. http://www.nber.org/papers/w11609.
2. Older Americans 2016: Key Indicators of Well-Being http://www.seniorcare.com/featured/aging-america/.
3. U.S. Census Bureau, *Current Population Reports*. https://www.childstats.gov/AMERICASCHILDREN/tables/pop1.asp.
4. Ken Dychtwald, Age Wave. St. Martin's Press, 1989.
5. Ken Dychtwald, Will the "Age Wave" Make or Break America? The Questions That Trump, Clinton and Sanders Must Answer, Huffington Post, May 19, 2017. https://www.huffpost.com/entry/will-the-age-wave-make-or_b_9998384.
6. Maya Meinert, Seniors will soon outnumber children, but the U.S. isn't ready, USC News, June 21, 2018. https://news.usc.edu/143675/aging-u-s-population-unique-health-challenges/.
7. The Next Generation of Medicare Beneficiaries, MedPac Report to the Congress: Medicare and the Health Care Delivery System. 2015 http://www.medpac.gov/docs/default-source/reports/chapter-2-the-next-generation-of-medicare-beneficiaries-june-2015-report-.pdf#:~:text=The%20number%20of%20taxpaying%20workers%20per%20Medicare%20beneficiary,projected%20by%20the%20Medicare%20Trustees%20to%20be%202.3.
8. 2021 Medicare Beneficiaries at a Glance, CMS. https://www.cms.gov/Research-Statistics-Data-and-Systems/Statistics-Trends-and-Reports/Beneficiary-Snapshot/Bene_Snapshot.

9. *Lubitz J, Greenberg LG, Gorina Y et al. Three decades of health care use by the elderly, 1965–1998. Health Aff (Millwood) 2001;20:19–32.*

10. Medicare and Its Impact, National Bureau of Economic Research, April, 2006. https://www.nber.org/digest/apr06/medicare-and-its-impact.

11. Pew Research Center. Baby boomers retire. Pew Research Center Web site. http://pewresearch.org/databank/dailynumber/?NumberID=1150.

12. Medicare 2021 Trustee Report, CMS, https://www.cms.gov/Research-Statistics-Data-and-Systems/Statistics-Trends-and-Reports/ReportsTrustFunds.

13. The Next Generation of Medicare Beneficiaries, MedPac Report to the Congress: Medicare and the Health Care Delivery System. 2015 http://www.medpac.gov/docs/default-source/reports/chapter-2-the-next-generation-of-medicare-beneficiaries-june-2015-report-.pdf#:~:text=The%20number%20of%20taxpaying%20workers%20per%20Medicare%20beneficiary,projected%20by%20the%20Medicare%20Trustees%20to%20be%202.3.

14. The Next Generation of Medicare Beneficiaries, MedPac Report to the Congress: Medicare and the Health Care Delivery System. 2015 http://www.medpac.gov/docs/default-source/reports/chapter-2-the-next-generation-of-medicare-beneficiaries-june-2015-report-.

15. CDC's National Center for Injury Prevention and Control. https://www.cdc.gov/mmwr/volumes/65/wr/mm6537a2.htm

16. Max Roser, Twice as long – life expectancy around the world, Our World in Data, October 8, 2018. https://ourworldindata.org/life-expectancy-globally

17. Ken Dychtwald, Lifespan versus Healthspan, September 2, 2021, LinkedIn. https://www.linkedin.com/pulse/lifespan-versus-healthspan-ken-dychtwald/.

18. Ibid.

19. Merriam Webster online dictionary, https://www.merriam-webster.com/dictionary/well-being.

20. Jennifer M. Ortman, Victoria A. Velkoff, and Howard Hogan, "An Aging Nation: The Older Population in the United States: Population Estimates and Projections," Current Population Reports, U.S Census Bureau (May 2014), accessed August 1, 2016, https://www.census.gov/prod/2014pubs/p25-1140.pdf.

21. *Anicka Slachta, FDA clears AI-powered platform for remote patient monitoring, Cardiovascular Business, April 26, 2019.* https://www.cardiovascularbusiness.com/topics/practice-management/fda-clears-platform-remote-patient-monitoring.

22. AgeTech Collaborative website, https://agetechcollaborative.org/about/.

Chapter 10

Telehealth Comes of Age

If you have always done it that way, it is probably wrong.

Charles Kettering

Somewhere along the way, healthcare developed an *"edifice complex."* This condition is marked by the belief that *real* health and medical care means going to a brick-and-mortar location like a hospital or doctor's office to be seen face-to-face by a clinician.

Telehealth has been around for three decades. It took a pandemic to move it from the shadows into the spotlight for everyone to see and use. Those who tried it found that health and medical services are effective, efficient, and convenient when humans connect through intelligent and secure technologies.

For example, Medicare fee-for-service (FFS) beneficiary telehealth visits increased 63-fold in 2020, from approximately 840,000 in 2019 to nearly 52.7 million in 2020.[1] Equally important, 95% of Medicare beneficiaries were satisfied with their telehealth experience.[2]

Today utilization of telehealth is stabilizing at levels that are 38× higher than before the pandemic. Forty percent of consumers want to continue using it – up from 11% before COVID. Connected health consumers are also looking ahead to other online experiences like virtual-first health plans.[3]

Telehealth will be a defining force for health management and care delivery in the next century. Its success comes from the confluence of what intelligent connectivity and technology provides and what a large and growing percentage of the population wants: Personalized care delivered anywhere on their terms.

DOI: 10.4324/9781003286103-10

The value proposition for telehealth is straightforward: It effectively connects individuals and healthcare providers when in-person services are not necessary, possible, or desired. Beyond being a medium to bring consumers and providers together, it's a superhighway for a host of interconnected services and content. It creates an almost infinite number of possibilities for clinicians to provide and consumers to receive health and medical services.

With telehealth bursting onto the scene due to COVID, we are awash in jargon. Telehealth, telemedicine, virtual care, remote monitoring, wearables, and hospital-at-home are just a few terms used to describe what is being done outside the walls of traditional health organizations.

Soon we'll drop such descriptors. Telehealth will simply become health. Virtual care will be seen as care. Like other services we use to streamline and manage our lives, telehealth will seamlessly blend into the way health systems work. We'll know we've reached this destination when consumers can seek out information, have meaningful consultations, and get complex diagnoses across a seamless continuum of secure virtual and physical locations. We are not there yet, but this is clearly the market's direction.

Telehealth Is Defining 21st Century Care

The term "telehealth" refers to a broad umbrella of services that allows consumers to receive care, consult with a provider, get information about a condition or treatment, arrange for prescriptions, receive a diagnosis, or get help in managing an episodic or chronic health condition.

The American Telemedicine Association (ATA) provides a useful taxonomy to describe today's most commonly used approaches in telehealth. They include:[4]

Virtual Visits: Live, synchronous, and interactive encounters between a patient and a healthcare provider via video, telephone, or live chat.

Chat-based Interactions: Asynchronous online or mobile app communications to transmit a patient's health data, vital signs, and other physiological data or diagnostic images to a healthcare provider to review and deliver a consultation, diagnosis, or treatment plan at a later time.

Remote Patient Monitoring: The collection, transmission, evaluation, and communication of individual health data from a patient to their healthcare provider or extended care team from outside a hospital or clinical office (i.e., the patient's home) using personal health technologies including wireless devices, wearable sensors, implanted health monitors, smartphones, and mobile apps. Remote patient monitoring supports ongoing condition monitoring and chronic disease management and can be synchronous or asynchronous, depending upon the patient's needs. The application of emerging technologies, including artificial intelligence (AI) and machine learning, can enable better disease surveillance and early detection, allow for improved diagnoses, and support personalized medicine.

Technology-Enabled Modalities: Telehealth and virtual care solutions also provide for physician-to-physician consultation, patient education, data transmission, data interpretation, digital diagnostics (algorithm-enabled diagnostic support), and digital therapeutics (the use of personal health devices and sensors, either alone or in combination with conventional drug therapies, for disease prevention and management).

Telehealth vs. Telemedicine

At times the terms telehealth and telemedicine are used interchangeably. Telemedicine typically refers to a narrow range of clinical services. Telehealth refers to a broad scope of remote healthcare services.

The ATA offers the following definitions:

Telemedicine is the use of medical information exchanged from one site to another via electronic communications to improve patients' health status.

Telehealth is closely associated with telemedicine but encompasses a broader definition of remote healthcare that does not always involve clinical services.

The Centers for Medicare and Medicaid Services (CMS) defines telehealth as:

The use of telecommunications and information technology to provide access to health assessment, diagnosis, intervention, consultation, supervision, and information across distance.

Telehealth includes such technologies as telephones, facsimile machines, electronic mail systems, and remote patient monitoring devices, which are used to collect and transmit data for monitoring and interpretation.[5]

Telehealth Benefits

In the 30 plus years that telehealth has been in use, it has consistently shown to be a safe and valuable care modality. It is a convenient option for both patients and clinicians that provides a secure environment for collecting and transmitting personal health information. In combination, these attributes extend where and how care is delivered.

Telehealth increases access to care for rural communities. It also can be used to expand access to underserved and vulnerable populations. It increases access to care for individuals unable to secure in-person care, ensuring that more people have access when and where they need it. For example, telehealth supports access to high-quality, safe, and convenient care for older adults, allowing them to "age-in-place" while connecting with a provider regularly. Telehealth also improves efficiencies, helps to reduce costs, and enables healthcare providers and hospital systems to do more good for more people.[6]

Here are some of the benefits of telehealth:

Improved Access: Since its inception, telehealth has been used to bring healthcare services to consumers in rural and distant locations. It can provide millions of people in rural and urban areas access to safe, effective, and appropriate care when and where it is needed.

Telehealth improves consumer access and extends the geographic reach and expertise of physicians and health facilities. Given provider shortages and a growing crisis with clinician burnout, telehealth extends the expertise of caregivers while supporting them in their own personal well-being.

Cost Efficiencies: Reducing or containing healthcare costs is one of the strongest motivators to adopt virtual care technologies. Telehealth reduces the cost of healthcare and increases efficiency with better management of chronic diseases, shared health professional staffing, reduced travel times, and fewer or shorter hospital stays.

McKinsey and Company estimates that up to $250 billion of current US healthcare spending could potentially be virtualized.[7]

**A significant portion of Medicare & Medicaid Services
and spend could potentially be virtualized**

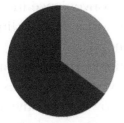  

35% of Home Health
Services virtualized

24% of Office Visits and
Outpatient Encounters
Department visits
virtualized

20% of Emergency
Department visits diverted
to virtual visits

Source: Telehealth: A quarter-trillion-dollar post-COVID-19 reality?, McKinsey & Company, 2021

Improved Quality: Studies have consistently shown that the quality of telehealth services to be as good as those delivered in traditional in-person settings. In some specialties, such as mental health, telehealth delivers effective service options with better outcomes and consumer satisfaction.

Consumer Demand: The most significant impact of telehealth is on the consumer, their family, and their community. Telehealth technologies reduce travel time and related stresses for the consumer. Over the past 15 years, multiple studies have documented consumer satisfaction and support for telehealth services that give consumers access to providers who might not be available otherwise, and without the need to travel long distances.

Consumers interested in virtual care – From basic to specialty services

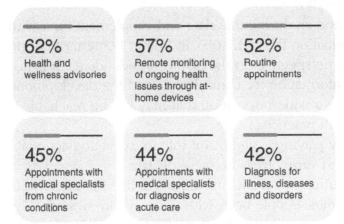

Source: How Can Leaders make Recent Digital Health Gains Last? – Reexamining the
Accenture 2020 Digital Health Consumer Survey. Accenture

The Role of AI in Telehealth

AI leads to improvements in quality, effectiveness, and convenience in telehealth services the same way it does when used in hospitals and clinics.

It enables and empowers clinicians to make real-time, data-enabled decisions to produce better outcomes and improve patient experiences along the way. It does not replace but rather enhances and leverages the skills and wisdom of human experts. It automates repetitive, low-value activities to allow physicians to do other things, reducing burnout. One study by MIT, for example, notes that four out of five health organizations using AI say it proactively helps avert workplace burnout.[8]

AI and telehealth work as partners in providing better healthcare services. Telehealth already incorporates technology in the form of wireless tools, smartphones, and other telecommunications devices and a host of intelligent clinical and health management apps. Integrating AI further enhances the usability of these devices. Some of the benefits of AI in telemedicine include:

Providing Better Diagnoses: As we saw during the pandemic, remote diagnosis is possible through telehealth. Doctors can monitor, diagnose, and treat diseases remotely with the help of telemedicine. The use of AI augments and extends providers' skills in various ways, including tools and apps that prescreen for certain types of conditions.

Almost all consumers have access to devices with sensors to collect valuable data about their health. From smartphones and watches with step trackers to wearables that can track heartbeat and other vitals around the clock, a growing proportion of health-related data is generated on the go in real time.

Collecting and analyzing this data and supplementing it with patient-provided information through apps and other home monitoring devices can offer a unique perspective on the health of individuals. It is also invaluable in collecting information for clinical trials and the development of new therapies across a wide population that may not be reachable through traditional health practices.

AI is already playing a significant role in extracting actionable insights from a large and varied treasure trove of data.

We are beginning to see its use in things like the identification of rare genetic syndromes. People born with these syndromes often have specific facial features that serve as indicators of the existence of a potential problem. AI-based methods are leveraging facial analysis to identify rare genetic syndromes based on the physical manifestation of these syndromes. This process is called next-generation phenotyping (NGP).[9]

Without AI, the challenge facing clinicians and their patients is that there are thousands of possible syndromes, making it nearly impossible to make a positive diagnosis. This is where AI-based technology comes in – to support clinicians in reaching a proper diagnosis by paring down the number of potential syndromes to only a handful of possibilities.

Currently, patients with rare genetic disorders, on average, require seven doctors before a correct diagnosis of the disease can be made. With AI and telemedicine, the number of visits can be reduced.

Recommending Treatments: The next step after diagnosis is providing the best treatment recommendations. AI can help deliver better treatment recommendations with less human effort by analyzing massive amounts of diverse data. This significantly reduces the time doctors spend going through medical histories. In searching greater amounts of data in a shorter amount of time, AI helps physicians prescribe the best treatment options more quickly.

Improving Quality and Treatment Compliance: There are many ways in which AI can be used to improve compliance with recommended care paths which, in turn, increase the quality and desired outcomes.

Improving self-administered medication compliance is one such area. From swallowing pills to injecting insulin, patients frequently administer their own medications. But they don't always get it right. Improper adherence to doctors' orders is commonplace. This lack of compliance accounts for thousands of deaths and billions of dollars in medical costs annually.[10]

New systems using AI can detect errors in a consumer's self-medication administration which is especially important for those with chronic conditions. For example, research suggests that up to 70% of diabetic patients do not take their insulin as prescribed. One such system developed at MIT uses AI to scour sensor data. When it detects an error in the patient's self-administration of insulin, it can alert the patient, provider, or family member.[11]

Improved Health Monitoring and Predictions: Patient monitoring is one of the first and most common telehealth applications that utilize AI. The objective is to provide monitoring services that are automatic and continuous. This improves accessibility and efficiency and reduces monitoring costs compared to face-to-face or in-person patient monitoring.

Telehealth applications allow clinicians to remotely monitor ECG, heartbeat, blood pressure, temperature, and other vital signs. This, combined with AI, can alert the patient and physician to potential health conditions. Treatments can then be tailored to the unique needs of patients through predictive analytics and monitoring thresholds. This holds promise to enhance the quality of care while helping physicians access more data automatically and allowing them to be proactive in managing care.

Enabling Telehealth Beyond the Pandemic

While telehealth provides benefits across the continuum of care, changes are needed in how it is managed and paid for by public and private payers.

A challenge for telehealth will be establishing reimbursement policies that create payment parity between telehealth and in-clinic care. Without addressing payment parity over the long term, it will be more difficult for clinicians and health organizations to provide services, despite numerous studies suggesting clinicians and consumers are broadly supportive about its use.[12]

Telehealth has also been historically limited by geographic rules governing medical licensing. Some states are creating interstate medical licensing agreements to enable physicians to practice across state lines via telehealth. Such moves will expand the reach of telehealth providers making services more broadly available.[13]

Other challenges to scaling telehealth include better data integration and improved data flow among the various players in the health ecosystem. Creating best practices for integrating virtual health into day-to-day workflows of clinicians, and the shift from fee-for-service to value-based care, will improve the prospects for telehealth going forward.

For a broader discussion of these issues, see Chapter 20.

Telehealth Is Here to Stay

Supported by AI, telehealth is already reshaping the healthcare experience. From rural clinics to national hospital systems and school-based health centers, telehealth is bringing focused clinical expertise to patients who might otherwise go untreated. It's also creating new options for consumers who want to have an active role in managing their health and well-being.

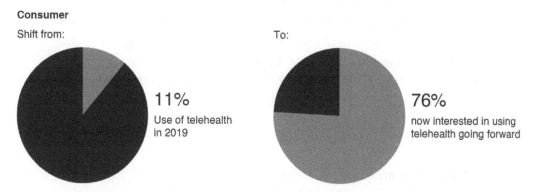

How has COVID-19 changed the outlook for telehealth?

Consumer

Shift from:

11%
Use of telehealth
in 2019

To:

76%
now interested in using
telehealth going forward

While the surge in telehealth has been driven by the immediate goal to avoid exposure to COVID-19, with more than 70 percent of in-person visits cancelled, 76 percent of survey respondents indicated they were highly or moderately likely to use telehealth going forward, and 74 percent of telehealth users reported high satisfaction.

Source: Telehealth: A quarter-trillion-dollar post-COVID-19 reality?, McKinsey & Company, 2021

Policy experts predict US health expenditures will climb to $6.2 trillion by 2028. Healthcare leaders are turning to telehealth to expand care options, personalize the health consumer experience while generating significant cost savings. In the future, patients and health consumers will not only desire telehealth options but they will also expect and demand them.

AN INTERVIEW WITH ANN MOND JOHNSON, CEO, AMERICAN TELEMEDICINE ASSOCIATION

When it comes to understanding and championing telehealth, few organizations have as much history and experience as the ATA and its CEO, Ann Mond Johnson. Long before telehealth was making headlines, the ATA's mission has been to ensure that people can get care where and when they need it while enabling clinicians to do more good for more people.

"When the pandemic began, we faced a huge problem we knew little about and had a scared populace. Health leaders stepped up and quickly drove an astonishing amount of change

(Continued)

and innovation. They set aside their competitive interests to work collaboratively to keep people healthy. Combined with the waivers associated with the public health emergency, the pandemic gave us a better understanding of what happens when we remove outdated regulatory and legal restrictions from telehealth," says Mond Johnson.

A big part of the change was the accelerated use of telehealth.

"The pandemic drove a rapid and dramatic uptick in the use of telehealth services that had actually been broadly available for some time. Telehealth made a huge difference in our ability to continue seeing patients and delivering care, while helping to reduce the risk of infection for frontline healthcare providers, patients and our communities by delivering quality care virtually. As more people used telehealth, many were pleasantly surprised at the increased efficiencies and quality patient-provider interactions that could be achieved," says Mond Johnson.

When faced with having to change the way they delivered care, we saw that the use of telehealth was an easier sell than anybody thought it would be for both clinicians and consumers.

As telehealth adoption increased, clinicians' and health organizations' views on virtual care delivery began to shift.

"There are some clinical interactions that can't be done with telehealth, but there is so much providers can do to assess, triage or care for their patients that does not require a face-to-face meeting. One of our top challenges is changing the industry's longstanding, historical bias towards care being provided in brick-and-mortar facilities. This predisposition has been a real problem because in-person care is expensive and unwillingness to modernize care delivery can cripple innovation. Telehealth opens the door to many options for improving and extending the provision of services that keep people healthy, help take care of them when they are not and enable clinicians to do more than they might have done otherwise," says Mond Johnson.

(Continued)

In looking ahead, beyond the use of telehealth related to the pandemic, Mond Johnson sees telehealth playing a critical role in addressing other significant challenges the health industry faces.

"Before the pandemic, we faced big problems like the cost of care, access, and a clinical workforce shortage. We have an uneven distribution of quality and evidence-based care. These issues have not gone away. Some are getting worse. When it comes down to it, none of these problems can be solved without telehealth and AI playing vital roles. The key to addressing these issues will be to keep telehealth front and center in the discussions and in its use," says Mond Johnson.

Another important issue is health equity. Telehealth can play a pivotal role in helping create better, more equitable access to health and medical services.

"The ATA is committed to addressing the challenges we face in providing equitable access to services. We have an advisory group focused on how telehealth can help eliminate today's disparities. This starts with addressing technology, such as improving access to smart devices or connectivity, including expanding broadband coverage."

"While such things are important, we must also recognize and address more profound and often unspoken issues for telehealth to be broadly adopted and used to reduce disparities. These include building trust, improving our approaches to inclusiveness, and building up health and digital literacy. This focus on health disparities is critical and long overdue and I am confident we will advance work on eliminating disparities through the use of telehealth," says Mond Johnson.

When it comes to the role of AI in supporting telehealth:

"When I think about AI, I'm reminded of the idea that telehealth helps clinicians practice at 'the top of their license.' You can't

(Continued)

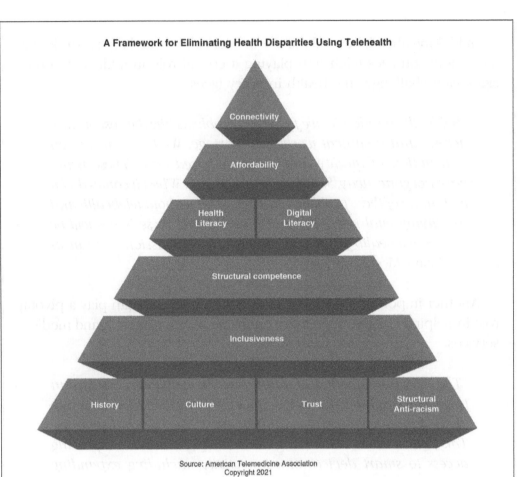

A Framework for Eliminating Health Disparities Using Telehealth

Source: American Telemedicine Association
Copyright 2021

do this without AI. Today, AI-powered telehealth and remote monitoring enables clinicians to more efficiently and effectively monitor more patients, assess their health status and then intervene in time to avoid a serious health event. I liken it to the control tower of an airport."

In looking ahead at the growth of telehealth, the focus should be on what issues or priorities?

"When people talk about telehealth, the discussions often gravitate to technology. When it comes to the work of the ATA and others, it's essential to recognize that we are not talking about delivering

(Continued)

technology. We're talking about delivering better health. It's an important distinction. The technology enables the solution."

"Another topic that often comes up is how payment mechanisms will drive the adoption of telehealth. We agree that fair payment is important. I expect innovative health organizations which operate with a value-based care mindset – even if it doesn't apply to their entire patient population - will be the strongest proponents on the use of telehealth. I also see innovative self-insured employers doing more with telehealth to broaden their offerings to employees," says Mond Johnson.

"In the end, it's important to recognize that telehealth is a modality of care. In this regard, the decision on which modality of care is best should always be made by the clinician and the patient," says Mond Johnson.

For more information on the ATA go to www.americantelemed.org

Notes

1. Medicare Telemedicine Snapshot, Medicare Telemedicine Snapshot (cms.gov)
2. Joann Donnellan, New Survey: Virtual Care Could Keep Low-Acuity Cases Out of Emergency Department, Biprtisan Policy Center, August 4, 2021, https://bipartisanpolicy.org/press-release/telehealth-survey/
3. Oleg Bestsennyy, Greg Gilbert, Alex Harris, and Jennifer Rost, Telehealth: A Quarter-Trillion-Dollar Post-COVID-19 Reality?, McKinsey & Company, July 9, 2021, https://www.mckinsey.com/industries/healthcare-systems-and-services/our-insights/telehealth-a-quarter-trillion-dollar-post-covid-19-reality.
4. Telehealth: Defining 21st Century Care, American Telemedicine Association, https://www.americantelemed.org/resource/why-telemedicine/.
5. Centers for Medicare and Medicaid Services, "Telemedicine and Telehealth." Available online at www.cms.gov/telemedicine.
6. Ibid.
7. Oleg Bestsennyy, Greg Gilbert, Alex Harris, and Jennifer Rost, Telehealth: A Quarter-Trillion-Dollar Post-COVID-19 Reality?, McKinsey & Company, July 9, 2021, https://www.mckinsey.com/industries/healthcare-systems-and-services/our-insights/telehealth-a-quarter-trillion-dollar-post-covid-19-reality.
8. The AI Effect – How Artificial Intelligence is Making Healthcare More Human, MIT Technology Review/GE, https://www.technologyreview.com/hub/ai-effect/.

9. AI-Driven Facial Analysis Equals Better Healthcare for All, FDNA Insights, November 13, 2019, https://www.fdna.com/blog/ai-driven-facial-analysis-equals-better-healthcare-for-all/.

10. Daniel Ackerman, System Detects Errors When Medication Is Self-Administered, MIT Computer Science and Artificial Intelligence Lab, March 23, 2021, https://www.csail.mit.edu/news/system-detects-errors-when-medication-self-administered.

11. Ibid.

12. Henry BW, Block DE, Ciesla JR, McGowan BA, Vozenilek JA. Clinician behaviors in telehealth care delivery. Adv Health Sci Educ Theory Pract. 2017;22(4):869–888. doi:10.1007/s10459-016-9717-2.

13. State Telehealth Laws and Reimbursement Policies Report, Center for Connected Health Policy, Published 2020. https://www.cchpca.org/telehealth-policy/state-telehealth-laws-and-reimbursement-policies-report.

Chapter 11

Care Anywhere

Convenience is the American way.

Cheech Marin

American actor, comedian, and activist

Connected health consumers are the new norm. They increasingly expect personalized, device-enabled services that are smart and convenient. They benchmark their healthcare experiences against their other consumer experiences. In scheduling a virtual or in-person visit, they will compare the ease of doing so with the dinner reservation they just made through apps like OpenTable.

The pandemic accelerated changes in the online habits and expectations of consumers. Forty-one percent now shop daily or weekly using their mobile device or smartphone, compared to 12% five years ago.[1] Another pandemic-driven change is a decline in brand loyalty. Forced to alter shopping behaviors, 73% of consumers who tried a different brand during the pandemic said they would continue seeking out new brands in the future.[2]

Time will tell if such dynamics change consumer behaviors when seeking health services. The trend though is clear: consumer demand and new technology-driven options are rapidly erasing historical industry boundaries. Tech-savvy players are entering the health market with new approaches to giving patients and health consumers what they want.

Most healthcare organizations today have an artificial intelligence (AI) plan or strategy. Not all will be successful. Intelligent Health Systems will successfully differentiate themselves by using AI to innovate services seamlessly *across all touchpoints, experiences, and channels.* They will be

DOI: 10.4324/9781003286103-11

faster and smarter than their competition in using AI-enabling technologies, ubiquitous connectivity, and smart devices. Competitive advantage will be gained by:

■ Blurring or eliminating historical care and service delivery boundaries by utilizing innovative technologies, remote monitoring and wearables, virtual visits, virtual clinical assistants, and a host of other AI-driven solutions.
■ Eliminating the traditional "partitions" between health and wellness services and medical interventions using data and predictive capabilities to dramatically increase the proactive nature of monitoring and managing the health of individuals and populations.
■ Using AI-driven automation to reduce medical bureaucracy and improve experiences for consumers, patients, and staff.

Innovative health leaders are already leveraging their learnings and experience from the pandemic. This is driving changes in business models and service delivery in keeping with the new norms of the market.

An essential part of this is the provision of *care anywhere*.

Driven by the Intelligent Health Revolution, care anywhere means a growing set of choices, including virtual, in-person, at home, or on-the-go. Care anywhere in the future will include fully virtualized experiences for some services delivered through mixed reality, augmented reality, and the metaverse.

Giving Consumers What They Want

Like changes in other industries, healthcare is moving from providing care and services in big institutions to delivering them through a variety of settings and mediums. Health services are already becoming a blend of virtual and physical experiences. As this occurs, health and medical care will become as convenient as banking and shopping.

Such moves will not diminish the importance and value of on-site or face-to-face care *when needed*. Instead, it will shift things that do not require cost-heavy equipment and facilities to options that are more convenient and lower cost.

Today, "digital-first" entrants are pouring into the health marketplace to disrupt traditional health business models. Current higher priced market leaders anchored primarily in a "bricks and mortar" approach will face stiff competition from agile market players focused on gaining market share by demonstrating higher quality, lower costs, and improved convenience.

As this change unfolds, payers and large employers will steer subscribers and employees away from higher cost providers. Consumers will also gain more control over how and when they seek services. As they pay more out-of-pocket costs than ever before, consumers will increasingly choose "*best value*" options. Best value in the eyes of health consumers includes price, perceived quality, and convenience.

AI Is the New UI for Consumers

In the world of software and digital solutions, the term user interface, or UI, describes how a user engages or interacts with a system. Think about apps on your phone or computer that do this well. Now think about apps and websites that increase your blood pressure as you try and to get something done with a UI that is not intuitive, convenient, or personalized. With this concept in mind, consider how easy or difficult your organizational interfaces make it for today's consumers to utilize your services.

It's a useful exercise to apply the UI concept to how patients and consumers interact with your organization today. How might the application of AI plus intelligent processes and systems be used to improve your organization's "UI" for patients, clinicians, and staff?

Today's products, services, and surroundings are increasingly customized with data and AI to cater to the individual. The opportunity in healthcare is to reimagine the processes and touchpoints consumers, clinicians, and staff are run through every day.

Care Anywhere Building Blocks

As noted in the last chapter, telehealth and AI make care more seamless, effective, and personalized. Personalization includes care being provided anywhere. It means that many health services no longer need to be tethered to physical locations or outdated processes.

In the future, health and medical services will seamlessly blend virtual and physical experiences thanks to increasing infrastructure capabilities like 5G and the intelligent cloud. These serve as conduits by which a growing array of intelligent sensors and devices create, gather, and use data from any location to manage health services.

As the market changes, here are some of the ways in which "care anywhere" will play out.

Virtual-First Health Plans

The pandemic brought about a boom in telehealth innovations. In 2020 alone, the Centers for Medicare and Medicaid Services (CMS) approved 80 new types of telehealth solutions.[3] As telehealth and virtual care options improve and consumer demand grows, health payers are capitalizing on these trends by creating virtual-first health plans.

In virtual-first health plans, the first entry point to getting medical care is with a virtual provider. Health maintenance activities and administrative processes are also conducted virtually and streamlined using intelligent technologies.

Major payers are jumping on the virtual-first bandwagon. UnitedHealthcare, for example, has launched a virtual-first health plan that provides members with virtual and in-person primary care and behavioral health visits. It also includes virtual urgent care, chats with providers, online scheduling, and same-day appointments.

The plan is offered with a premium designed to be 15% lower than traditional health plans. Beyond lower premiums, members can join a well-being program, which uses a wearable device to track physical activity and can earn members over $1,000 in annual rewards designed to incentivize good health.[4]

Virtual-First Health Centers

Innovative provider and payer organizations are leveraging intelligent digital technologies to create virtual health centers. Sanford Health is creating a virtual hospital to better serve rural and underserved areas.[5] The initiative is designed to deliver medical services to communities, patients, and long-term care residents around the globe when and where they're most needed.

Anthem Health is leading a collaborative effort to create a nationwide virtual primary care offering. The initiative leverages AI to drive down healthcare costs for consumers and employers. It includes text- and video-based digital primary care and taps into an AI platform to personalize care.[6]

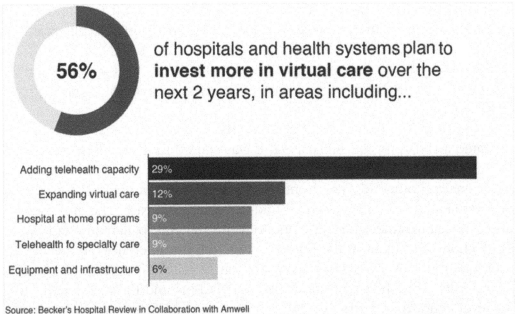

Adding telehealth capacity	29%
Expanding virtual care	12%
Hospital at home programs	9%
Telehealth fo specialty care	9%
Equipment and infrastructure	6%

Source: Becker's Hospital Review in Collaboration with Amwell
https://www.beckershospitalreview.com/hospital-execs-eye-expanded-virtual-care-and-streamlined-platforms-in-years-ahead-2.html

Digital Front Doors

Healthcare has been working to transform the patient experience for years, but the COVID-19 pandemic accelerated the transformation of one key area: the digital front door. "Digital front door" is among the latest buzzwords to be added to the healthcare industry's lexicon. Like other buzzwords, the term lacks a consistent definition.

Generally speaking, a digital front door is not a technology but rather a strategy used by provider and payer organizations to engage patients. It typically consists of a series of intelligent, digital technologies that provide a virtual experience as the first point of contact, streamlining processes for finding and arranging care. Components include symptom checkers, chatbots, provider search tools, scheduling, call centers, and patient check-ins.[7]

Market research company IDC predicts that 65% of patients will have accessed healthcare through a digital front door by 2023.[8]

Hospital at Home (HaH)

Hospital at Home (HaH) programs enables patients to receive hospital-level care in the comfort of their homes. It's an approach that has flourished in countries with single-payer health systems, but its use in the US has been limited until now.

HaH programs are well established in England, Canada, Israel, and other countries where payment policies encourage the provision of healthcare services in less costly venues.

For certain medical conditions, HaH provides well-monitored, at-home treatments that are safer, cheaper, and more effective than traditional hospital care.[9]

Johns Hopkins Medicine (Johns Hopkins), in Baltimore, Maryland, has operated a HaH program since 1994. It was started to treat elderly patients who either refused to go to the hospital or were at risk of hospital-acquired infections and other adverse events. Early results showed that the total cost of at-home care was 32% less than traditional hospital care. The approach also reduced treatment times by one-third. In the end, patient and family satisfaction was higher in the home setting with no differences in the subsequent use of medical services or readmissions.[10]

Innovative health organizations like Mayo Clinic and Kaiser Permanente are leveraging AI and other digital tools to transform healthcare delivery outside hospital settings.[11]

Despite improved outcomes, lower costs, and higher satisfaction, HaH programs face resistance from some providers and payers. Headwinds include

Consumers more willing to receive Virtual Services from traditional providers

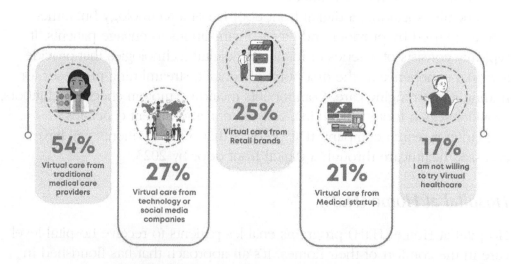

54%
Virtual care from traditional medical care providers

27%
Virtual care from technology or social media companies

25%
Virtual care from Retail brands

21%
Virtual care from Medical startup

17%
I am not willing to try Virtual healthcare

Source : How can leaders make Recent Digital Health Gains Last? Reexamining the Accenture 2020 Digital Health Health Consumer Survey, Accenture

physicians who are reluctant to use the home care model. Chief financial officers worry whether inpatient beds freed by treating patients at home will be filled with patients needing more complex and intensive services.

Medicare and private payers have historically not paid for HaH-type services. With the onset of the pandemic, CMS increased flexibility for hospitals to provide and receive Medicare payments for HaH services.[12] It is unknown whether the temporary flexibility and reimbursement changes will become permanent and adequate in incentivizing widespread HaH use by health providers.

Retail Health

Retail health refers to health and wellness services delivered via a retail store or company. This can include pharmacies, health centers located within a retail site, telehealth services provided via a retail entity, and other health and wellness products available in retail settings or through retail-focused entities.[13]

Within the continuum of the healthcare system, retail health is one of the few points in the system that offers a scalable delivery model of healthcare solutions supporting treatment, prevention, education, maintenance, and general well-being. Retail health centers also provide widespread reach to populations that could not easily access such resources across communities, from urban to rural.[14]

Retail health organizations played a significant role as convenient access points for vaccine distribution and a variety of other services. We'll take a closer look at the future of retail health in the next chapter.

Notes

1. A time for hope: Consumers' outlook brightens despite headwinds, PwC, December 2021, https://www.pwc.com/gx/en/industries/consumer-markets/consumer-insights-survey.html#smartphone-shopping-is-at-an-historic-high.
2. Simon Torkington, The pandemic has changed consumer behavior forever – and online shopping looks set to stay, World Economic Forum, July 7, 2021, https://www.weforum.org/agenda/2021/07/global-consumer-behaviour-trends-online-shopping/.
3. Oleg Bestsennyy, Greg Gilbert, Alex Harris, and Jennifer Rost, Telehealth: A quarter-trillion-dollar post-COVID-19 reality?, McKinsey & Company, July 9, 2021, https://www.mckinsey.com/industries/healthcare-systems-and-services/our-insights/telehealth-a-quarter-trillion-dollar-post-covid-19-reality.

4. Nick Moran, UnitedHealthcare launches virtual-first health plan, Becker's Payers Issues, October 19, 2021, https://www.beckershospitalreview.com/payer-issues/unitedhealthcare-launches-virtual-first-health-plan.html?origin=BHRE&utm_source=BHRE&utm_medium=email&utm_content=newsletter&oly_enc_id=7676G315714512B.

5. Jeremy Fugleberg, T. Denny Sanford gives $350M to Sanford Health for 'virtual care center', The Dickinson Press, September 8, 2021, https://www.thedickinsonpress.com/newsmd/health-news/7186263-T.-Denny-Sanford-gives-350M-to-Sanford-Health-for-virtual-care-center.

6. Nick Moran, Anthem joint venture launches virtual primary care nationwide, Becker's Payer Issues, December 9, 2021, https://www.beckershospitalreview.com/payer-issues/anthem-joint-venture-launches-virtual-primary-care-nationwide.html.

7. Digital Front Door 2021 – A view through the eyes of market leaders, KLAS Research, September 28, 2021, https://klasresearch.com/report/digital-front-door-2021/1830.

8. How to gain a competitive edge through a digital front door strategy: 5 insights, Becker's Health IT, October 18, 2021, https://www.beckershospitalreview.com/digital-transformation/how-to-gain-a-competitive-edge-through-a-digital-front-door-strategy-5-insights.html.

9. B. Leff, L. Burton, S. L. Mader et al., "Hospital at Home: Feasibility and Outcomes of a Program to Provide Hospital-Level Care at Home for Acutely Ill Older Patients," Annals of Internal Medicine, Dec. 2005 143(11):798–808.

10. Ibid.

11. Jacki Drees, Mayo, Kaiser rally 11 systems to launch hospital-at-home coalition, Becker's Health IT, October 14, 2021, https://www.beckershospitalreview.com/digital-transformation/mayo-kaiser-rally-10-systems-to-launch-hospital-at-home-coalition.

12. Hospital at Home – CMS Expands Payments to Hospitals for Care Provided In Patient Homes, McDermot Website, https://www.mwe.com/insights/hospital-at-home-cms-expands-payments-to-hospitals-for-care-provided-in-patient-homes/#:~:text=Under%20the%20hospital-at-home%20model%2C%20hospitals%20can%20receive%20payment,staff%2C%20including%20outpatient%20therapy%2C%20counseling%20and%20educational%20services.

13. Atiya Hasan, Daniel Ruppar, and Greg Caressi, Elevating Retail Health in Healthcare and Well-being via Communication and Collaboration Solutions, Frost & Sullivan White Paper, 2021.

14. Atiya Hasan, Daniel Ruppar, and Greg Caressi, Elevating Retail Health in Healthcare and Well-being via Communication and Collaboration Solutions, Frost and Sullivan, 2020.

Chapter 12

Are Retailers the New Market Makers?

As traditional health systems mobilized to take care of those critically ill from COVID, retail health stepped in to play a vital role in serving the needs of health consumers. They filled an access gap for patients who wanted to avoid high-volume care venues such as emergency rooms or hospitals to lower their risk of exposure to COVID. These retailers provided medications and medical consultations. They became critical access centers for food, healthcare, wellness, hygiene, cleaning products, and other common consumer goods needed by everyone forced to shelter in place. As COVID vaccines became available, retailers were the single most viable option to conveniently vaccinate millions of people.

Within the continuum of healthcare, retail health is one of the few points in the system that offers a scalable delivery model of solutions supporting treatment, prevention, education, maintenance, and general well-being. Retail health centers also provide widespread reach to populations that would not easily access such resources across communities, from urban to rural.[1]

There Are No Swim Lanes in the Blue Ocean

Today retail health organizations are riding the crest of the blue ocean strategy wave.

Blue ocean strategy is an analytical framework used by disruptive, tech-savvy companies to systematically define and capture new market opportunities known as "blue oceans."[2]

The success of Uber, Netflix, and Airbnb are examples of the blue ocean strategy.[3]

It's an approach being used by some health market entrants to focus on creating new solutions that are exponentially more valuable to end users *while also lowering costs*. The end goal for disruptors using a blue ocean strategy is to create new demand and capture uncontested market space in ways that make the historical market players less relevant or less competitive.

For decades, healthcare fit neatly into categories like providers, payers, and retail health. Not today. Changing market demands and economics are driving new and old players in the health space to rethink their offerings. As we are already seeing, the health market will be driven by various old and new players looking to seize opportunities to curate new types of services to serve today's market needs.

Retail health companies are rethinking their strategies to become an integral part of the intelligent health movement. They are investing in artificial intelligence (AI) platforms and digital tools to make deeper consumer connections. When it supports their success, they align with traditional health systems for a more seamless continuum thus gaining even more traction with consumers.

Mobile apps, telehealth platforms, messaging reminders, and even reward programs allow for diverse interactions with consumers as both people and patients. According to the analysts at Frost & Sullivan here are five ways retail health will expand its reach and impact.[4]

The Expanding Role of Retail Health

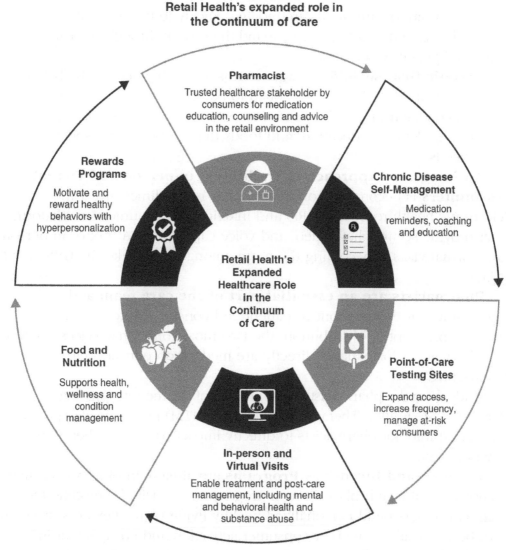

Retail Health's expanded role in the Continuum of Care

Pharmacist
Trusted healthcare stakeholder by consumers for medication education, counseling and advice in the retail environment

Rewards Programs
Motivate and reward healthy behaviors with hyperpersonalization

Chronic Disease Self-Management
Medication reminders, coaching and education

Retail Health's Expanded Healthcare Role in the Continuum of Care

Food and Nutrition
Supports health, wellness and condition management

Point-of-Care Testing Sites
Expand access, increase frequency, manage at-risk consumers

In-person and Virtual Visits
Enable treatment and post-care management, including mental and behavioral health and substance abuse

Source: Elevating Retail Health in Healthcare and Well-being via Communication and Collaboration Solutions, Frost & Sullivan, 2021

Connecting to Patients and Consumers is a key strength of retail health. The pandemic brought to light the need for convenient sites for triage, screening, diagnostics, and community care. Today, there are about 2,000 retail health clinics within the United States.[5] Such clinics are often tied directly to retail outlets and offer value through convenience and improved access. Typical benefits include ease of access due to availability on weekends and longer hours, elimination or better management of wait times for patients, direct access to prescriptions, food, and healthcare goods, all with more locations within communities.

Retail health organizations are moving quickly to use telehealth, telemedicine, and smart apps to expand their reach through pre-care, during care, and post-care services.

Chronic Disease Self-management is a growing need to be better served. Retail health is well-positioned to build loyalty among those with chronic conditions. It provides easy access to medications, medical and monitoring devices, education, and foods that support goals specific to their needs.

An integrated approach to traditional in-person and virtual encounters is becoming more seamless as retail clinics invest in electronic health records (EHRs) and intelligent communication platforms that provide secure chat, video, and voice capabilities. A mix of in-person and virtual visits is becoming the norm among groups like the CVS Minute Clinics.

Pharmacists are an essential part of the care team and are increasingly at the forefront of patient and consumer interactions. Besides prescription distribution, the two most common services offered by pharmacists for patients directly are medication education and counseling.[6]

Aside from the pharmacist role with patients in the retail setting, telehealth Medication Therapy Management (MTM) programs also provide an opportunity for pharmacists to directly impact patients in their home environment.

Rewards and Incentives Programs are already in place within many national retail health players. Such programs can easily be modified to help consumers build personalized healthy living plans. Rewards programs can be a crucial channel for consumer activation and engagement in their health. By crediting rewards points for activities such as filling prescriptions, managing prescriptions online, obtaining vaccines, and retail purchases such as healthy foods, retail health organizations can "nudge" consumers toward healthy behaviors and build loyalty along the way.

> "Within the continuum of the healthcare system, retail health is one of the few points in the system that offers a scalable delivery model of healthcare solutions supporting treatment, prevention, education, maintenance, and general well-being."
>
> **-Frost and Sullivan**

A Sampler of Retail Health

CVS Health and Microsoft have created a strategic alliance to reimagine personalized care and accelerate digital transformation. The plan is to remake CVS into a consumer-centric, integrated health solutions company to better serve more than 100 million people.

Fresh off of delivering 43 million vaccines, CVS will make greater use of data, AI, and the cloud to enhance its omnichannel pharmacy capabilities and provide customized health recommendations when and where consumers need them. CVS is also working to scale up its existing retail loyalty and personalization programs by making deeper use of machine learning.

CVS Health is also improving internal efficiencies by using AI solutions like computer vision and text analytics to automate tasks like filling prescriptions.[7]

Walmart is making several moves to bring its trademark slogan of *"save money, live better"* into the health space. In a short period, Walmart Health has been building and opening brick-and-mortar health clinics and pushing into the health plan space with the launch of a Medicare-focused brokerage plan.[8]

The giant retailer has tapped Epic to use its EHR system to connect records across all healthcare services, including virtual care. Epic's technology will eventually support all of Walmart's health and wellness lines of business.[9] With Epic serving as the top EHR for provider organizations, there may be future opportunities to improve interoperability between retail health and health systems.

In keeping with the needs of many consumers, Walmart also provides a free digital wallet that its customers can use to store and share their health information, starting with their COVID-19 vaccine record. This HIPAA compliant app includes a digital version of vaccine cards issued by the CDC.[10]

With half of all Americans covered by employer-sponsored health plans, Walmart is pushing into this space, making it easier for self-funded employers to access its healthcare services. This includes offering its lowest prices on pharmaceuticals and healthcare services to employers.[11]

A strategic advantage beyond the company's purchasing power and supply chain expertise is its ability to offer convenience. Most Americans live within 10 miles of a Walmart.[12]

Other companies don't fit strictly into the Retail Health definition but are adjacent market plays worth watching. Some of these include:

Best Buy is a company you may associate with purchasing major appliances or electronics, but it's moving quickly to secure a position in serving health consumers and patients. Best Buy Health is a division within the company now focusing on three key areas: consumer health monitoring, active aging, and virtual care.

It recently acquired a remote patient monitoring and telehealth company called Current Health. The company's care platform allows healthcare organizations to monitor patients in their homes. The approach includes combining patient-reported data with data from biosensors to give caregivers real-time insights about a patient's condition and alert them when they need clinical attention.[13]

Beyond remote patient monitoring, Best Buy plans to work with health systems to support "hospital-at-home" (HaH) programs by installing and managing all of the technology associated with HaH. The goal is to be the go-to resource for caregivers and consumers by assembling a team of health IT professionals to form a "health squad" within its existing "Geek Squad" division.[14]

As a digital-first company, Amazon has ambitious plans to expand its virtual care services and in-home care to most major cities in the United States. Based on a pilot launched initially for its employees, the company is going after major employers by offering in-app text chat with clinicians, mobile care visits, prescription delivery from a care courier, and in-person care. When needed, Amazon Care will dispatch medical professionals to a patient's home for services ranging from routine blood draws to listening to a patient's lungs.[15]

Amazon Care's expansion also comes as the tech giant moves into at-home testing. It recently got the green light from the FDA to begin offering its own COVID-19 test directly to consumers. And with the acquisition of the online pharmacy PillPack, the tech giant is launching Amazon Pharmacy, allowing consumers to purchase prescription drugs online and have them shipped to a home or office.[16]

Uber Health is an example of what major companies are doing to adapt their core business models to capture a share of the changing health market. One of the original "shared economy" companies, Uber, is setting its sights on disrupting and streamlining non-emergency medical transportation (NEMT).

Uber Health allows consumers to contact them directly but focuses on working with health organizations to reduce transportation barriers to accessing care. By enabling health organizations to arrange rides on behalf of others, the value proposition is straightforward – fewer no-shows and more on-time appointments.

During the pandemic, the company applied its events and operations expertise to help public health and other health organizations plan designated pickup and drop-off locations at mass vaccination sites.

To automate transportation planning into care coordination, clinicians, case managers, and discharge planners can access Uber Health directly from the Cerner EHR.[17] And just as the company offers food delivery through Uber Eats, Uber Health now gives users the ability to order and have delivered a variety of health and wellness products.[18]

FROST AND SULLIVAN: THE EVOLUTION OF RETAIL HEALTH

Frost and Sullivan is a global market research and advisory firm that focuses on identifying market trends impacting growth opportunities across all business segments, including retail and health and life sciences.

The firm closely follows the retail health sector and recently completed an analysis of this segment's contribution to managing the pandemic. This a brief overview of their findings and views from Greg Caressi, Senior Vice President and Global Leader for Health and Daniel Ruppar, Consulting Director for Health and Life Sciences.

While retail health was already on an upward trajectory, the pandemic came along and put this sector in the spotlight. How has retail health changed as a result of the pandemic?

"We've all seen how the pandemic accelerated trends that were already underway. Retail health is one of the areas where we've seen a significant uptick in consumer awareness and interest. This has been driven by the pandemic giving new experiences to consumers and a better understanding of how health and medical services can be conveniently delivered outside of a hospital, clinic or doctor's office," says Caressi.

"People went to retail health locations to get tested for COVID-19 (COVID) and to get their COVID vaccines and boosters. They made better use of walk-in clinics tied to retail health outlets for a variety of primary care needs. In trying to reduce their exposure risks they did more shopping for food, and other health products at retail health locations. They also got a taste of digital services

---

(Continued)

such as virtual care that are offered by retail health. These are all trends that are going to continue to drive retail health to the forefront of the health market in the future."

How are retail health organizations looking to leverage the new exposure received during the pandemic to expand the base and diversity of what they provide?

"There are a number of moves to be made that are natural extensions of what they do today. A current advantage is having pharmacists who are more available and friendly than a consumer might experience in traditional health settings. If a big part of a retailer's business is selling food and nutritional items, then adding nutritionists to the mix opens the door to nutritional and food counseling to support consumers who are obese, diabetic, prediabetic or just want to have healthier diets. As such services are provided, they can also be tied to existing reward programs that retailers have in place to incent food and nutritional purchases that move people to becoming healthier."

"Going deeper in providing a robust digital experience is also a natural growth area. Most retail health providers already have an app on people's phones for things like pharmacy management. We see the retail health organizations creating a portfolio of other rich digital health apps by building their own apps or creating partnerships with existing popular digital health apps."

"Beyond what is being provided today, retail health has the footprint to deliver more testing and therapeutic services. Their geographic locations and growing digital capabilities mean that they are poised to provide services in the consumer's home and within the communities in which they operate. At some point we may see retail health moving into services previously only within the purview of traditional health providers such as remote monitoring and perhaps even mobile imaging services," says Caressi.

(Continued)

The coverage and reach of many national retail health players also makes them well suited to increasing convenience for everyone, especially populations that are often underserved.

"When you look at the combination of convenient locations combined with the ability to do many things while 'instore' or even online, retail health makes access easy to so many things. This is especially important in serving people in rural locations," says Ruppar.

"Looking ahead, the economics of making small, rural hospitals and clinics work is getting increasingly difficult. I think in the next five years we're going to see the decline of rural hospitals and clinics. As this occurs the gaps in rural health that exist today will widen. This trend creates a market opportunity in those communities for retail health."

"Exposure to retail health channels will become increasingly important for those living in rural areas. Instead of driving longer distances for health services and other activities of daily living, rural consumers will find that the easiest way getting these things done will be one visit to retailers like WalMart who already have a strong bricks-and-mortar presence in smaller communities. Such companies already have the physical locations and infrastructure to capture a larger share of smaller communities. They are also adding digital services like telehealth to their physical infrastructure. In combination, these delivery locations combined with online services make retail health players the easiest place to turn compared to driving longer distances for services," says Ruppar

Going forward, what do you see when it comes to the role of retail health and its relationship with traditional health providers?

"We see the market at three levels. First, there are acute care services to address the needs of those who are sick or injured.

(Continued)

> *These services will stay in the hospital. Then there's general healthcare, which includes parts of sick care that are already getting carved out into retail clinics. Organizations like CVS and others are interested in this space because it supports key parts of their business model such as pharmacy growth. Finally, there's the wellness side of managing health. In looking at these different segments we see retail health being better positioned in the last two segments,"* says Caressi.
>
> *"While there is an element of competition between retail health and traditional health providers, there is also a need for some level of integration between the two. Integration, for example, is needed for many services that are reimbursed by payers.*
>
> *"At the heart of how services are integrated and paid for is the need for data integration. It will be important to create data systems that allow for seamlessly moving data among providers and payers,"* says Caressi.

Notes

1. Atiya Hasan, Daniel Ruppar, and Greg Caressi, Elevating Retail Health in Healthcare and Well-being via Communication and Collaboration Solutions, Frost and Sullivan, 2020.
2. W. Chan Kim, Renée Mauborgne, Blue Ocean Strategy, Harvard Business School Publishing, 2015.
3. W. Chan Kim, Renée Mauborgne, Blue Ocean Strategy, Harvard Business School Publishing, 2015.
4. Atiya Hasan, Daniel Ruppar, and Greg Caressi, Elevating Retail Health in Healthcare and Well-being via Communication and Collaboration Solutions, Frost and Sullivan, 2020.
5. The 2019 Economic Report on U.S. Pharmacies and Pharmacy Benefit Managers, Drug Channels Institute.
6. National Pharmacist Workforce Study 2019, American Association of Colleges of Pharmacy (AACP).
7. CVS Health and Microsoft announce new strategic alliance to reimagine personalized care and accelerate digital transformation, CVS Website, December 2, 2021, https://cvshealth.com/news-and-insights/press-releases/cvs-health-and-microsoft-announce-new-strategic-alliance-to.

8. Tina Reed, Walmart Health announces expansion with new clinics planned in Chicago, Georgia and Florida, Fierce Healthcare, September 17, 2021, https://www.fiercehealthcare.com/practices/walmart-health-announces-expansion-new-clinics-planned-chicago-georgia-and-florida.

9. Heather Landi, Walmart deploys Epic medical records tech across its health centers, virtual care services, Firerce Healthcare, September 27, 2021, https://www.fiercehealthcare.com/tech/walmart-taps-epic-for-medical-records-platform-across-its-health-centers-virtual-care.

10. Jackie Drees, Walmart rolls out digital COVID-19 vaccine record: 4 details, Beckers Health IT, June 16, 2021, https://www.beckershospitalreview.com/digital-transformation/walmart-rolls-out-digital-covid-19-vaccine-record-4-details.html?utm_campaign=bhr&utm_source=website&utm_content=related.

11. Walmart selects transcarent to provide go-to-market solution for self-insured employers, Walmart website, October 15, 2021, https://corporate.walmart.com/newsroom/2021/10/15/walmart-selects-transcarent-to-provide-go-to-market-solution-for-self-insured-employers.

12. Paige Minemyer, Walmart unveils employer market team-up with Transcarent, Fierce Healthcare, October 15, 2021, https://www.fiercehealthcare.com/payer/walmart-unveils-employer-market-team-up-transcarent?utm_source=email&utm_medium=email&utm_campaign=HC-NL-FierceHealthPayer&oly_enc_id=8231D1748001G1C.

13. Katie Adams, Best Buy to acquire remote care monitoring platform: 5 details, Beckers Hospital Review, October 12, 2021, https://www.beckershospitalreview.com/disruptors/best-buy-to-acquire-remote-care-monitoring-platform-5-details.html.

14. Hannah Mitchell, Best Buy unveils its healthcare strategy: 5 insights, Beckers Hospital Review, October 26, 2021, https://www.beckershospitalreview.com/disruptors/best-buy-unveils-its-healthcare-strategy-5-insights.html?utm_campaign=bhr&utm_source=website&utm_content=latestarticles.

15. Heather Landi, Amazon Care may be coming to another 20 U.S. cities: report, Fierce Healthcare, September 8, 2021, https://www.fiercehealthcare.com/tech/amazon-care-may-be-coming-to-another-20-u-s-cities-report.

16. Ibid.

17. Access Uber Health directly from Cerner, Uber Health website, https://www.uberhealth.com/.

18. Hims & Hers Partner with Uber for Largest On-Demand Delivery Partnership of Companies' Health and Wellness Products Across the U.S., BusinessWire, November 29, 2021, https://www.businesswire.com/news/home/20211129005015/en/.

Chapter 13

Health Infonomics: Data Gets Its Due

There were 5 exabytes of information created between the dawn of civilization through 2003, but that much information is now created every two days.

Eric Schmidt
Executive Chairman at Google

It's a catchphrase heard in health circles today: *"Data is healthcare's new currency."* When I hear this, I like to ask, *"If data is healthcare's new currency, are you managing your data the same way you manage your financial assets?"* This usually produces an awkward moment followed by the start of one of the most important conversations health and clinical leaders should be having if they want to leverage artificial intelligence (AI) and the Intelligent Health Revolution to their advantage.

AI needs, feeds, and thrives on data. While most healthcare organizations recognize that the data being collected has value to support things like clinical decisions, value-based care, and personalizing the patient experience, many have not made a commensurate investment in developing a comprehensive data strategy.

In today's world of smart-everything, data is becoming a new form of currency used to redefine business models, fuel process change, and drive market success. Unlocking the power of data is at the heart of today's Intelligent Health Revolution.

Healthcare organizations need to recognize data for what it is: a valuable intangible asset desired by multiple stakeholders that is the key to being competitive in today's market.

DOI: 10.4324/9781003286103-13

The good news is that healthcare produces an enormous amount of data. According to a study by the International Data Corporation (IDC), the volume of data in the healthcare industry will grow faster than in any other industry through 2025. They estimate the volume of health data created annually, which reached over 2,000 exabytes in 2020, will continue to grow year-over-year at a 48% rate.[1]

Healthcare's data explosion is fueling significant advances in AI and machine learning, which rely on large datasets to make predictions ranging from hospital bed capacity to the presence of cancer. Despite torrents of valuable data, many organizations remain behind the curve in harnessing its use. Cross-industry studies show that, on average, less than half of an organization's structured data is actively used in making decisions. Even worse is that less than 1% of its unstructured data is analyzed or used at all.[2]

A contributing factor to these issues is that data in healthcare has traditionally been perceived as merely a byproduct of technology projects or the provision of care rather than being treated as organizational assets. As a result, the belief has been that traditional application and database planning efforts were sufficient to address ongoing data issues. In the world of AI and intelligent health, they are not.

For AI to create the value necessary to move health organizations forward, data must be managed as a strategic asset. Historically, health organizations have used analytics to optimize existing sources of value rather than leveraging data and analytics to innovate and create new value. Creating new value is what AI is all about. This requires treating data as an asset, just like capital and human resources.

As data is recognized as a strategic asset to be leveraged and monetized, we are seeing the early stages of a new discipline known as information economics. This movement is defining frameworks and processes similar to those used in managing financial assets.

Douglas Laney is one of the leaders of this movement. His book, *Infonomics,* provides a framework for treating information as an organization's most valuable asset for creating competitive advantage.[3] It puts forward three management principles:

1. **Measuring Data** is an organization's willingness to invest in and manage data as a valuable asset. From EMRs, imaging, or billing systems, healthcare organizations today generate and store massive amounts of data. Most healthcare systems recognize that much of this data has value, but many fail to treat it as a tangible asset.

2. **Managing Data** is an organization's ability to track and inventory data like a physical asset. What data does the organization have, and how might it be used to improve performance or create strategic advantages? Do you know how many data systems your organization has and relies on to operate? Effective healthcare data management means understanding where the data is and getting the data into some form to be appropriately managed.

3. **Monetizing Data** is an organization's ability to leverage its information assets. How does the organization use data today, and how might it leverage it in new ways to create measurable value in support of its mission, clinical, and business goals?

An example of applying such a framework in service of your goals is Value-Based Healthcare (VBC). This healthcare delivery model is where providers, including hospitals and physicians, are paid based on patient health outcomes. Under value-based care agreements, providers are rewarded for helping patients improve their health, reduce the effects and incidence of chronic disease, and live healthier lives in an evidence-based way.[4]

VBC is a trend gaining momentum in the market. It will continue to change how health organizations approach delivering and evaluating services. This includes incentivizing preventative care services and moving the delivery model to be proactive in managing health status.

Data and AI will play a pivotal role in optimizing VBC by helping organizations better understand the intricacies of their operations, providing more transparency into patient outcomes, and identifying ways to lower costs while still achieving higher levels of quality.

Creating and Managing a Modern Data Estate

Developing an understanding and organizational mindset around "data as a strategic asset" is the starting point for creating value. As you develop a framework for organizing, managing, and measuring the value of data, the single most important factor to get right is creating a modern data estate.

Simply put, a data estate refers to all the data your organization owns, controls, manages, or uses regardless of where it is stored. The goal of migrating this data to the cloud or modernizing your environment on-premises is to make it easier and faster to gain important insights to fuel innovation. A modern data environment allows you to empower employees, engage customers, optimize operations, and transform products repeatedly and at scale. Successful AI programs must have a solid foundation built on a strong organization-wide data estate.

The massive growth in data and the increasing need for everyone to get immediate insights demand fast and highly scalable data platforms. When cloud, data, and AI work together, they offer new opportunities for people and organizations to innovate, grow, and achieve more. The healthcare industry is changing how it interacts with patients through the use of the cloud, data, and AI. This growth of data is driving the need for data modernization.

Data modernization refers to the process of restructuring how data is collected, stored, and managed to take advantage of new technologies. Events such as software end-of-support and datacenter consolidation can be opportunities to modernize an organization's approach to data management.

Anyone who has ever been in the trenches knows that working with real-world data is messy. It often spans various data and media types. It changes constantly and often includes valuable knowledge that is not readily usable.

In most cases, the amount of time and energy spent on data discovery and preparation exceeds the time spent on analytics resulting in actionable insights. As noted below, a study by IDC suggests that 80% of a data specialist's time goes toward getting ready, with only 20% of their time being spent deriving value from the data.[5]

How many hours per week on average do you spend on each of the following data-related activities?

% of Time Spent on Data Activities (Weekly)

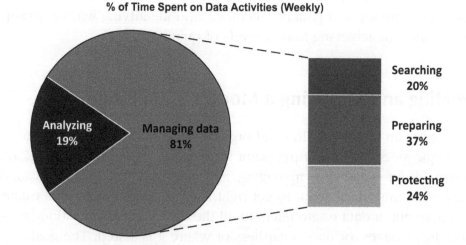

Source: IDC's Data Integration and Integrity End-User Survey, November 2017

While the "plumbing" aspects of data management are not as sexy as creating predictive models, getting your data estate in order is foundational to the success of any enterprise-wide AI strategy. Here are several areas to consider in your move to becoming a data-enabled organization.

Data Unification: One of the most valuable benefits of unifying data is to create a single holistic view of a patient or consumer for care planning. Such efforts lay the foundation to perform many types of behavioral analytics. This includes creating an aggregated view to assess a population of patients within a service area.

Interoperability: Data unification is highly dependent on data interoperability. This relates to creating a standard health information technology infrastructure that allows seamless electronic access, exchange, and use of health information.

For example, data on social determinants of health (SDOH) is increasingly incorporated into AI health initiatives. SDOH are the conditions in which people are born, grow, work, live, and age, and the broader set of forces and systems shaping the conditions of daily life.[6] These forces and systems include economic policies and procedures, development agendas, social norms that may be causal factors in current health status and health inequities that should be factored into AI programs to better manage the health of individuals and populations. More information on this is available in the next chapter.

Real-time Insights Delivery: Most traditional analytical initiatives in health organizations have been focused on old data and processes that summarize what happened in the past. This is akin to looking in the rear-view mirror. The process tells you where you've been but doesn't necessarily help you understand how to get to your destination. There is an increasing ability, especially with cloud-based solutions, to aggregate and present data and information in near real-time, thus allowing greater opportunity for rapid understanding and response. And with the help of machine learning, we can extend the intelligence process from looking at what just happened to predicting what will occur in the future.

Knowledge Mining: An organized data estate provides the opportunity to retrieve information and extract insights within a vast amount of data. A variety of powerful, intelligent tools enable knowledge mining by using built-in AI capabilities to uncover latent insights from documents, images, and media, including the ability to discover patterns and relationships in content, as well as understand sentiment, extract key phrases, and more.

Data Governance

Data governance is a set of processes that ensures that data assets are formally managed throughout the enterprise so that data can be trusted and that people can be made accountable for adverse events caused by low data quality. It's the management of your organization's data asset availability, usability, integrity, and security.[7]

While all health organizations have data staffing expertise as well as policies and monitoring activities for privacy and security, many do not have an organizational-wide data governance program managed in a way to maximize its value against clinical and operational goals.

One study focusing on the role and importance of data governance notes that the single greatest challenge to the success of data governance programs is the difficulty of identifying its costs and benefits.[8]

Today, best practice data governance programs include a governing body that works to set standards, refine procedures, and creates accountability for all data assets.

A Data Governance Committee should practice a cultural philosophy that believes in governing data to the least extent necessary to achieve the greatest common good. Often, organizations will either over-apply data governance in their enthusiasm for the new function; or under-apply data governance due to their lack of experience. The best approach is to start with a broad vision and framework but limit application initially and expand the governance function incrementally, only as needed.

Like a finance committee, a data governance committee should be a subcommittee of an existing governance structure, with the oversight responsibility to influence and make changes to workflows, resolve data quality conflicts, and develop complex data acquisition strategies to support the strategic clinical and financial optimization of the organization.

Increasingly, health organizations are enlisting the expertise of Data Stewards who are knowledgeable about collecting data in source transaction systems such as EHRs, cost accounting, scheduling, registration, and materials management systems. Data stewards are integral to the mission of a data governance committee as their role is to ensure that data governance processes are followed, guidelines enforced, and that recommendations for improvements to data governance processes are brought forward for action.

Creating a Data Culture

A well-curated data estate will only create value if it's used by those responsible for the ongoing activities of the enterprise.

As data volumes increase, the importance of an enterprise data culture grows. To promote an enterprise "value of data" culture, organizations often need to make behavioral, cultural, and operational improvements.

A data-driven culture within an organization is created by leaders who recognize and promote data as a critical business asset to empower clinicians and staff by providing them with knowledge and tools to access and turn data into actionable insights and impactful intelligence.

In creating and executing an AI strategy, some organizations build a team of data scientists and top data talent to advance their goals. On their own, such groups can develop and deploy AI capabilities within the organization. Still, such efforts will have higher failure rates if the organization has not created an enterprise-wide culture that embraces and uses data.

Creating a data-driven culture is a balancing act that requires both the approval and advocacy of top leaders and the acceptance and adoption by front-line staff. This requires ongoing communications and engagement with stakeholders to help them understand and believe that the culture you're trying to foster will further empower them in their work.

A data-driven culture begins by putting those business users in the driver's seat and furnishing them with the tools to quickly and easily extract meaningful insights from data.

Good Governance, Good Data, Great Results

AI initiatives often start with great optimism but end with less-than-satisfactory results. A key predictor of success almost always is the condition of the data estate on which any projects are built.

Health organizations that are serious about AI can no longer afford to treat data management as anything less than what it is – the linchpin for making intelligent health real and practical. Organizations seeking to thrive in the intelligent health world will connect the "data dots" through investments in staffing, expertise, and systems so that their data is accurate, complete, and consistent to empower people and processes in doing more.

Notes

1. Top 3 Data-Growth Challenges in the Healthcare Industry, TechTalkTuesday, First Light, https://www.firstlight.net/top-3-data-growth-challenges-in-the-healthcare-industry/#:~:text=According%20to%20a%202018%20report%20 published%20by%20IDC%2C,the%20challenge%20of%20managing%20 extremely%20large%20data%20sets.
2. Leandro DalleMule, Thomas H. Davenport, What's Your Data Strategy?, Harvard Business Review, 2017, https://hbr.org/2017/05/whats-your-data-strategy
3. Douglas Laney, Infonomics: How to Monetize, Manage, and Measure Information as an Asset for Competitive Advantage, 2018, Taylor and Francis Publishing
4. What Is Value-Based Healthcare?, NEJM, January 1, 2017, https://catalyst.nejm. org/doi/full/10.1056/CAT.17.0558
5. Stewart Bond, Data Intelligence in Context: Enabling Data Governance for Digital Transformation, IDC TECHNOLOGY SPOTLIGHT, 2018, http://idcdocserv.com/ us44514218
6. About social determinants of health, World Health Organization, 2017, https:// www.who.int/social_determinants/sdh_definition/en/
7. James Gaston, A Recipe for Analytics, Key Ingredient #3-Data Governance, HIMSS Analytics, 2018, https://www.himssanalytics.org/news/analytics-key-ingredient-data-governance
8. The Future of Enterprise Information Governance, The Economist Intelligent Unit, 2008, http://graphics.eiu.com/files/ad_pdfs/EMC_InfoGovernence.pdf

Chapter 14

Genetic Code vs. Zip Code: The Social Determinants of Health

The future is already here. It's just not evenly distributed.

William Gibson
Futurist

As we learned in the last chapter, health, medical, and other data are growing exponentially. This is fueling artificial intelligence (AI)'s ability to do good.

With so many types of data available today to help monitor and manage health, here's a question: Which is a better predictor of health status – your genetic code or your zip code?

Where you live affects how you live. It impacts whether you have access to healthy food, places to exercise, or health services when needed. Your "living location" also affects your personal and family's economic prosperity based on the availability of jobs, unemployment rates, educational, and training opportunities. These "social" factors shape and determine health and longevity across your lifespan.

Social determinants of health (SDOH) matter when it comes to understanding and addressing how we improve the health status of individuals, communities, and nations. SDOH are conditions where people live, learn, work, and play that affect a wide range of health and quality-of-life-risks and outcomes.[1]

DOI: 10.4324/9781003286103-14

Here's an example: Two 60-year-old women live 10 miles apart in the Washington, DC area. They've both been prescribed beta-blockers for high blood pressure, both have family histories of Type 2 diabetes, and both have missed their last few annual check-ups. Shouldn't their care plans be the same?

Clinically, they're identical images of each other. However, one piece of data can dramatically tilt the equation. It's their zip code. One will likely live 33 years longer (63 years versus 96 years) based on their location. This dramatic life expectancy gap can be chalked up to differences in income, education, and access to grocery stores with fresh food.[2]

SDOH have a significant impact on people's health, well-being, and quality of life. Examples include access to health services, economic stability, education, social and community context, and environmental factors.

Social Determinants of Health (SDOH)

CATEGORY	SUBCATEGORIES
Economic Stability	Economic stability Poverty Food security Housing stability
Education	High school graduation Enrollment in higher education Language and literacy Early childhood education and development
Social & Community Context	Social cohesion Civic participation Discrimination Incarceration
Health & Healthcare	Access to health care Access to primary care Health literacy
Neighborhood & Built Environment	Access to healthy food Quality of housing Crime and violence Environmental conditions

Source: The Social Determinants of Health: Applying AI & Machine Learning to Achieve Whole Person Care, Cognizant

Data Provides the Full Picture

Traditional Health Systems have historically gathered and used data to understand the physiologic aspects of a health or medical condition. This includes capturing and using data going in an electronic health record (EHR), diagnostic images, and lab results.

This data is vitally important in making diagnoses and managing health. But, on its own, the data only shows part of the picture. Social and environmental factors are much more indicative of a patient's health outcome than once thought. One study suggests that 60% of a patient's health-care outcome is driven by their behavior and social and economic factors, 10% by their clinical care, and 30% by their genetics.[3]

Negative SDOH contribute to wide health disparities and inequities. Without access to grocery stores with healthy foods, nutrition suffers, raising the risk of health conditions like heart disease, diabetes, and obesity. It lowers life expectancy relative to people who have access to healthy foods.

The Color of Coronavirus

Neighborhoods with large populations of African Americans tend to have lower life expectancies than majority white, Hispanic, or Asian communities. Such racial differences reflect the places where different races live, not the individual characteristics of people themselves.[4]

COVID helped give voice to these issues. For example, at the beginning of the pandemic, we began seeing that Black Americans were twice as likely to die from COVID even though they were a smaller percentage of the overall population. In taking a closer look at the situation, two things became self-evident – first, higher death rates related to where people lived. Second, the *"twice as likely to die"* was a statistical average. Underneath this average was the true story. In reality, if you were Black and living in Washington, DC, you were six times more likely to die of COVID at that time. Living in Michigan meant that you were four times more likely to die of COVID.[5]

Research shows that Black communities are less likely to have access to resources that promote health, like grocery stores with fresh foods, places to exercise, and quality health care facilities. This is true even in middle-class neighborhoods.[6,7,8]

These communities also have fewer opportunities for economic prosperity, with higher unemployment rates and fewer opportunities to work and lower quality education, all of which shape health outcomes across a lifespan. Working two jobs means there is less time to exercise and shop for groceries.

How well a place is doing economically affects how long people can expect to live. Economically distressed areas tend to have the lowest life expectancies.[9] As new research from the Census Bureau and researchers at Harvard and Brown universities shows, children from economically disadvantaged neighborhoods tend to have worse outcomes as adults.[10]

These data demonstrate the importance of understanding and factoring SDOH into planning and delivering health services.

AI as a Turning Point

The Intelligent Health Revolution gives us the ability to better understand and proactively address social determinants impacting health. Understanding and incorporating SDOH in health planning is at the heart of moving us toward healthier citizens and communities.

To factor SDOH into health planning, health organizations must first be able to identify consumers facing adverse SDOH. Once identified by data, such factors can be incorporated into personal health management and population health strategies. Until now, such identification at scale has proven difficult and although the Center for Medicare and Medicaid Services (CMS) has introduced standardized medical codes for capturing SDOH as part of the ICD-10 code set, they are not being widely used.

AI and machine learning (ML) help automate the identification of people whose health is likely impacted by their living situation. Opportunities include adding intelligent features to EMRs and proactive assessments of populations of people. Such activities identify and triage target populations and enable organizations to build intelligent workflows for referrals and follow-up.

Data that is readily available can serve as "clues" to which consumers or patients are affected by SDOH. While readily available, such information is often not included in health data systems or is hidden in unstructured data like clinical notes or discharge plans.

Forward-thinking health systems are changing this. To better understand and leverage SDOH, leaders at Mount Sinai Medical Center in New York City utilized Natural Language Processing (NLP) to detect patients' special social needs from unstructured data found in its EMR. They specifically targeted identification in four categories: economic stability, education, physical environment, and healthcare. In doing this, they found that one-third of patients analyzed had at least one social factor with the potential to negatively affect their health that had not been uncovered by other means.[11]

At Providence St. Joseph, health analytics are used to identify social conditions that impact patients' care, access to care, and overall health status. Their work found four social factors most likely to correlate to a future medical event: homelessness, mental illness, substance abuse, and domestic violence. Their work also incorporates "hot spot" analysis to identify specific ZIP codes where factors like employment rates, education levels, income, and access to food and mental health centers can contribute to poor health outcomes.[12]

A study published in the *American Journal of Managed Care* found that AI accurately predicted inpatient and emergency department utilization using only publicly available SDOH data such as gender, age, race, and address. In this study, researchers also found that local air quality and income were more important health predictors than age, gender, or ethnicity.[13]

AI promises to make it more practical to incorporate SDOH into individual care management and population health strategies. AI and ML can use existing data sets to identify patients with adverse SDOH. It can identify consumers whose health issues are related to SDOH. It can also customize targeted interventions to help them better manage their health while maximizing the use of resources.

In the future, the use of AI will improve the ability to identify and help individuals and populations whose health may otherwise be adversely affected by SDOH.

Notes

1. Centers for Disease Control (CDC). https://www.cdc.gov/socialdeterminants/index.htm.
2. Greg Kefer. Zip Codes Have Become a Better Predictor of Health Outcomes than Genetic Codes. Technology May be Ready to Fix That. Medcity News, August 24, 2021. https://medcitynews.com/2021/08/zip-codes-have-become-a-better-predictor-of-health-outcomes-than-genetic-codes-technology-may-be-ready-to-fix-that.

3. Shroeder, SA. We Can Do Better – Improving the Health of the American People. New England Journal of Medicine, 2007, 357:1221–8.
4. U.S. Small-Area Life Expectancy Estimates Project: Methodology and Results Summary, National Center for Health Statistics, September 2018. https://www.cdc.gov/nchs/data/series/sr_02/sr02_181.pdf.
5. APM Research Lab. The Color of Coronavirus: COVID-19 Deaths by Race and Ethnicity in the U.S. Data Updated as of June 10, 2020. Accessible via: https://www.apmresearchlab.org/covid/deaths-by-race.
6. Ibid.
7. Nicole I. Larson, Mary T. Story, Melissa C. Nelson. Neighborhood Environments Disparities in Access to Healthy Foods in the U.S.. American Journal of Preventive Medicine. November 03, 2008. https://doi.org/10.1016/j.amepre.2008.09.025.
8. Rayshawn, Ray. An Intersectional Analysis to Explaining a Lack of Physical Activity among Middle Class Black Women, Wiley Online Library, September 2014. https://doi.org/10.1111/soc4.12172.
9. When It Comes to Your Health, Where You Live Matters, The Conversation, January 2018. https://theconversation.com/when-it-comes-to-your-health-where-you-live-matters-89352.
10. Detailed Maps Show How Neighborhoods Shape Children for Life, The New York Times, October 1, 2018 https://www.nytimes.com/2018/10/01/upshot/maps-neighborhoods-shape-child-poverty.html.
11. Laura Ramos Hegwer. Using Artificial Intelligence to Uncover Social Determinants of Health, HFMA, April 24, 2019. https://www.hfma.org/topics/technology/article/using-artificial-intelligence-to-uncover-social-determinants-of-.html.
12. Laura Ramos Hegwer. How Data Provides Vital Insight into the Social Determinants of Health. HFMA, April 24, 2019. https://www.hfma.org/topics/technology/article/how-data-provides-vital-insight-into-the-social-determinants-of-.html.
13. Soy Chen, Danielle Bergman, Kelly Miller, Allison Kavanagh, John Frownfelter, John Showalter. Using Applied Machine Learning to Predict Healthcare Utilization Based on Socioeconomic Determinants of Care. The American Journal of Managed Care, January 2020, 26, 01. https://www.ajmc.com/view/using-applied-machine-learning-to-predict-healthcare-utilization-based-on-socioeconomic-determinants-of-care.

Chapter 15

Achieving Health Tequity

We can do a lot of measurement, but eventually you have to do something about it, right?

Aswita Tan-McGrory
Director of the Disparities Solution Center
at Massachusetts General Hospital

It was 1961, and America was a nation divided by racial strife. Segregation had just been deemed unconstitutional. Despite this ruling by the highest court in the land, little notice or action was taken. This was especially true in the Deep South, where separate bus seats, lunch counters, and restrooms were deeply entrenched as the historical and cultural norm.

To call attention to the injustices and inaction, people of all colors and ages banded together to participate in Freedom Rides. They put themselves at risk by taking bus trips through the south to protest segregated bus terminals. They foisted themselves into "white-only" restrooms and lunch counters along the way. These Freedom Riders were confronted by arresting police officers and violence. In the end, their efforts drew international attention and gave a greater voice to the civil rights movement.

Present Day

While great strides have been made since the 1960s, we remain engaged in an important societal debate about entrenched inequalities and the impact such disparities have on Black Americans and others. Nowhere is this more evident than in our approach to health.

DOI: 10.4324/9781003286103-15

The impact of these disparities on African Americans is well documented:

■ Compared to their white counterparts, African Americans are generally at higher risk for heart diseases, stroke, cancer, asthma, influenza and pneumonia, diabetes, and HIV/AIDS.[1]
■ Infants are three times more likely to die of accidental death and four times more likely to develop SIDS.[2]
■ Mothers are three times more likely to die during pregnancy.[3]

On the matter of health, this is not a political issue but rather an important humanitarian issue. As we grapple with systemic health inequities, there are three things anyone interested in mitigating or resolving these issues should consider:

First, racial disparities in healthcare exist. This is the conclusion of the Institute of Medicine's (IOM) study, *Unequal Treatment: Confronting Racial and Ethnic Disparities in Health Care.* The study found measurable differences in the quality of healthcare received by racial and ethnic minorities and nonminorities.[4]

Second, extensive, peer-reviewed studies of population health show that social determinants of health profoundly impact a wide range of healthcare outcomes.[5,6] As discussed in the previous chapter, economic and social conditions affect healthcare status. When financial stability, healthy food access, safe and stable neighborhood and work environments, health literacy, and quality education are lacking, health inequalities are created even within commercially insured populations.[7]

Third, the use of AI to support health services holds the promise of reducing or mitigating many of these issues. It can be used to level the playing field and improve the health status of people of all colors and socioeconomic groups. Accomplishing this goal requires that we develop and deploy intelligent health solutions that are inclusive and free of bias.

Correctly planned and applied, AI can reduce existing inequities and improve health for all. Failure to understand and act on this opportunity poses a risk of perpetuating the existing biases of the system.

As we look at how the Intelligence Revolution will unfold in health, a fundamental question is: Will AI in health be a force for good for some citizens or all citizens?

Whether a clinician or consumer, the answer to this question rests with each of us.

It Starts with Awareness

The COVID pandemic was the tipping point for a dramatic uptick in the planning and use of digital health services. Many of these were AI-powered solutions that automated or augmented the delivery of health services while improving convenience and effectiveness for consumers and clinicians.

As AI and digital services become more pervasive, we must take steps to recognize and address the fact that the biases and inequities of the physical world are crossing over to the digital world. If we are not mindful, AI will be the carrier.

In the digital world, bias is most often introduced through algorithms. Algorithmic bias is the application of an algorithm that compounds existing inequities in socioeconomic status, race, ethnic background, religion, gender, disability, or sexual orientation. Such bias can also amplify inequities in the current health system.[8]

We are already seeing and documenting how bias creeps into algorithms used to make predictions that guide diagnostic and treatment decisions in healthcare.

In one situation, a commercially available algorithm was being used to assess which patients already undergoing treatments would graduate to receive additional specialized care.

This widely used algorithm was four times more likely to recommend that white patients receive additional specialty care than Black patients, even though Black patients were often sicker.

This occurred because developers of the algorithm had correlated *health spending with health status.* This meant that a patient's past health expenditures became pivotal in predicting the risk of worsening health and the need for additional services. This was flawed logic as white Americans have had historically higher health expenditures than Black Americans *even when their health situations were identical.*

This algorithm was used over a million times to determine whether patients had access to additional care. Had it reflected accurate proportions of the sickest Black and white patients, 46% of Black patients would have been referred to more specialized care.[9]

Note: While this algorithm has been corrected, it is a real-world example of the *"correlation vs. causation"* issue noted in Chapter 6.

In the groundbreaking article, *Hidden in Plain Sight – Reconsidering the Use of Race Correction in Clinical Algorithms,* the New England Journal of Medicine outlines and documents bias found in other algorithms used to guide the treatment of obstetrics, cardiology, oncology, and other specialties.[10]

Finding and Fixing Bias

An algorithm is nothing more than a mathematical technique rooted in logic that is assigned or programmed by humans. In understanding this, the question becomes, what causes algorithms to have a bias that can lead to discrimination?

Most often, bias creeps into algorithms and AI in general in one of three ways:

First, we naturally have biases developed through our own history and experiences as humans. The conscious and unconscious biases of those developing an algorithm can be reflected in what they create.

The second way bias is introduced comes from the data used to develop and train predictive capabilities. For example, regardless of one's beliefs as to whether healthcare should be a right, it is not a legal right in the United States, though in places like the United Kingdom healthcare is constitutionally guaranteed to all citizens. With this in mind, many of the datasets used for developing algorithms to predict healthcare events under-represent those who are uninsured or underinsured.

The third way bias is introduced in how an algorithm is used in practice. This includes whether access and use of AI is selectively applied to populations based on where they live or whether a public entity can access and use AI solutions compared to private healthcare organizations.

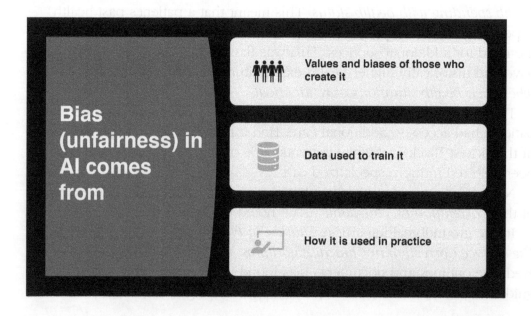

Creating a universal understanding of bias in AI is an important starting point. With understanding comes the ability to be more purposeful in developing and deploying intelligent solutions to reduce inequities.

Beyond understanding is the need for tools and approaches to AI development that lower the risks of bias and other factors in developing, deploying, and managing AI solutions.

Tools

There are several assessment tools in the market that allow teams to assess the predictive algorithms they are creating. One example is an open-source toolkit called Fairlearn.[11] Data scientists and developers use this free resource from Microsoft to assess and improve the fairness of their AI systems. It includes unfairness mitigation algorithms designed to help navigate trade-offs between fairness and model performance. A process has been created to have the capabilities of this approach shaped by a diverse community of stakeholders, ranging from data scientists, developers, and business decision-makers to the people whose lives may be affected by the predictions of AI systems.

Team Composition

The composition of teams developing and deploying AI is another crucial factor impacting outcomes. Ideally, such teams should include a diversity of backgrounds and perspectives. In the field of intelligent health, this includes having clinicians and representative end users as part of the team. This helps to ensure an understanding of the clinical context of the problem to be solved and the people who will be served by it.

A Responsible AI Framework

Not too long ago health systems operated in a pre-algorithm world where humans and organizations made decisions about who could access care and the services they received. In the future, algorithms will increasingly harness the power of macro- and micro-data sources to influence the decisions of the people both giving and receiving health services.

It is imperative to recognize the overall good this change could produce. At the same time, we must be mindful of how this change can replicate and even amplify human biases that work against the goal of using the intelligence revolution to improve the health and well-being of all citizens.

Prioritizing fairness and inclusion in AI systems is a socio-technical challenge. From a historical perspective, technology capabilities often get ahead of lawmakers and regulators tasked with standards by which society can best benefit from such breakthroughs.

Today, artificial intelligence is spawning a new set of issues for governments and regulators and to a new set of ethical considerations in the field of computer science. Ultimately the question is not only what AI can do, but rather, what AI *should* do. The real question is not whether AI law will emerge but how it can best come together – and over what time frame.

AI technology will continue to develop and mature as rules are crafted to govern its use.

Inevitably, this creates a gray zone for innovators who are harnessing the power of new technology to do good.

As regulators and legislators work to catch up, it's essential to recognize that it is possible for AI solutions in health and medicine to be legal and compliant with all regulations yet still be applied unethically.

While this is an area that will be sorted out, it is incumbent upon those developing or deploying AI in health settings to ensure that data is being used in keeping with principles for Responsible AI.

Health organizations using AI today should have a defined set of Responsible AI principles in place to guide the development and use of intelligent solutions. Most often, these principles or guidelines are incorporated into an organization's overall approach to Data Governance.

Today, organizations ranging from the American Medical Association to the Organization for Economic Cooperation and Development (OECD) are putting forward guidelines by which AI should be governed and managed.

With many organizations putting forward Responsible AI guidelines, there is currently no universal standard for what is covered. Until a set of universal guidelines are developed and approved, it is best to review various versions and then select or develop a set of policies in keeping with your organization's mission, goals, and ethics.

The remainder of this chapter outlines five principles for responsible AI that are adapted from Responsible AI principles developed and used by Microsoft's Office of Responsible AI.[12]

Responsible AI Principles

Fairness – AI Systems Should Treat All People Fairly

AI systems should treat everyone in a fair and balanced manner and not affect similarly situated groups of people differently. For example, when AI systems guide medical treatments, they should make accurate recommendations for everyone with similar symptoms. If appropriately designed, AI can help make fairer decisions because computers are purely logical and, in theory, are not subject to the conscious and unconscious biases that inevitably influence human decision-making.

And yet, AI systems are designed by human beings, and the systems are trained using data that reflects the imperfect world in which we live. Without careful attention, AI systems can wind up operating unfairly without careful planning due to bias that enters the system. To ensure that fairness is the foundation for solutions using this new technology, it's imperative to understand how bias can be introduced into AI systems and how it can affect AI-based decisions and guidance.

Because AI-driven systems are trained using data that reflect our imperfect world, those systems can actually amplify biases and unfairness within datasets without proper awareness and control. They also can "learn" biases through their processing. "Under-representation" in datasets may also hide population differences in disease risk or treatment efficacy.

For example, researchers recently found that cardiomyopathy genetic tests were better able to identify pathogenic variants in white patients than patients of other ethnicities, the latter of which had higher rates of inconclusive results or variants of uncertain significance.

Even data that are representative can still include bias because they reflect the discrepancies and biases of our society. This includes racial, geographic, or economic disparities in access to healthcare.

Nonrepresentative collection of data also can produce bias. For example, reliance on data collected through user-facing apps and wearables may skew toward socioeconomically advantaged populations. Those who use such devices may have greater access to connected devices and cloud services.

Similarly, genetic testing remains cost-prohibitive for many consumers. As such, AI systems that leverage such genetic datasets may be skewed toward more economically advantaged consumers. And data obtained from electronic health records (EHRs) will reflect disparities in the patient populations treated by health systems implementing EHR systems;

the uninsured or underinsured and those without consistent access to quality healthcare (such as some patients in rural areas) often will be underrepresented in EHR datasets. EHR data themselves may introduce bias because they were collected for clinical, administrative, and financial purposes (patient care and billing) rather than for research. Therefore, they may be missing critical clinical contextual information.

How can we ensure that AI systems treat everyone fairly? There's almost certainly a lot of learning ahead for all of us in this area, and it will be vital to sustain research and foster robust discussions to share new best practices that emerge.

Reliability – AI Systems Should Perform Reliably and Safely

AI-enabled systems deployed in the healthcare sector not only offer great promise but also the potential for injury or even death if they do not operate reliably and safely. In some senses, the healthcare sector has a head start here, in that many of the systems we envision will be considered medical devices and subject to existing and new regulations.

The complexity of AI technologies has fueled fears that AI systems may cause harm in the face of unforeseen circumstances or that they can be manipulated to act in harmful ways.

As is true for any technology, trust will ultimately depend on whether AI-based systems can be operated reliably, safely, and consistently – not only under normal circumstances but also in unexpected conditions or when they are under attack.

This begins by demonstrating that systems are designed to operate within a clear set of parameters under expected performance conditions. In all cases, there should be a way to verify that they are behaving as intended under actual operating conditions. This means consistently producing the correct or intended results.

Because AI systems are data-driven, how they behave and the variety of conditions they can handle reliably and safely largely reflects the range of situations and circumstances that developers anticipate during design and testing.

For example, an AI system with a vision component designed to assess skin lesions for cancer may have difficulty consistently spotting patterns of concern based on race or skin coloration. This means designers should conduct tests across all skin types. Rigorous testing is essential during system development and deployment to ensure that systems can respond safely to unanticipated situations, do not have unexpected performance failures, and do not evolve in ways that are inconsistent with original expectations.

Equally important, because AI should augment and amplify human capabilities, people should play a critical role in deciding how and when an AI system is deployed and whether it's appropriate to continue using it over time. As noted throughout this book, since AI systems often do not see or understand the bigger societal picture, human judgment is key to identifying potential blind spots and biases in AI systems.

In one example, a system designed to help decide whether to hospitalize patients with pneumonia "learned" that people with asthma have a lower rate of mortality from pneumonia than the general population. This was a surprising result because people with asthma are generally considered at greater risk of dying from pneumonia than others.

While the correlation was accurate, the system failed to detect that the primary reason for this lower mortality rate was that asthma patients receive faster and more comprehensive care than other patients because they are at greater risk. Suppose researchers hadn't noticed that the AI system had drawn a misleading inference. In that case, the system might have recommended against hospitalizing people with asthma, an outcome that would have run counter to what the data revealed.[13]

Such examples highlight the critical role that people, particularly clinicians and those with subject matter expertise, must play in observing and evaluating AI systems as they are developed and deployed.

The dynamic nature of continuous learning AI means we will need to develop new ways to ensure the safety and reliability of such systems. We will need to establish a regulatory regime that ensures that changes the continuous learning system makes to itself, ostensibly improvements, do not instead introduce errors into the model that could injure subsequent patients. But at the same time, that new regime must be more agile to not require nearly constant revalidation of a medical device using AI.

Privacy and Security – AI Systems Should Be Secure and Respect Our Privacy

As more of our lives are captured in digital form, the question of how to preserve our privacy and secure our personal data is becoming more important and more complicated. While protecting privacy and security is important to all technology development, recent advances require that we pay even closer attention to these issues to create the levels of trust needed to realize the full benefits of AI.

As we collect an increasing volume of sensitive data about people through an expanding array of devices, we will have to do more to ensure that this data is stored in secure systems. Such systems will be managed by stewards guided by clear rules that protect this sensitive data from improper uses. At the same time, such systems will need to be managed to enable new AI-powered innovations that benefit individual patients and society as a whole.

Simply put, people will not share data about themselves – data essential for AI to drive value in healthcare decisions – unless they are confident that their privacy is protected and their data is secured. The advances and benefits that AI-enabled technologies will drive in the healthcare sector will not be possible without data governance. So we must ensure that we proceed in ways that build and reinforce patient trust.

These dual objectives of security (ensuring that unauthorized parties cannot access the data) and privacy (ensuring that neither authorized nor unauthorized parties access and use the data for a nonpermitted purpose) are increasingly intertwined with the technology platforms on which the data is captured, stored, processed, and retrieved. The same technology platforms that have resulted in tremendous strides in AI capabilities are also proving to be the foundation for advances in properly managing patient privacy and security expectations.

From a security standpoint, modern cloud platforms enable sensitive datasets to benefit from massive security investments by the companies that build and operate these systems. From a privacy standpoint, these modern cloud systems provide a deep and nuanced set of technical controls that allow data stewards to control access at a granular level and create robust access logs that enable audits to ensure data has not been improperly accessed or used.

Such platforms can replace past practices of shipping large health datasets on portable media. It can potentially be downloaded by many different parties and onto multiple local servers, with little ability to log or audit access and use. Techniques such as differential privacy and homomorphic encryption provide additional protections, ensuring that sensitive data is less visible and accessible to prying human eyes. Moreover, the machine-based access that these systems enable greatly diminishes the need and opportunity for humans to have "eyes on" reviews of sensitive data.

Such techniques will reduce the risk of privacy intrusions by AI systems to use personal data without accessing or knowing the identities of individuals. It will be critical for AI researchers, policymakers, and even patients to understand the privacy and security promoting advances in technology platforms and how those can be overlaid on law and regulation to result in more robust security and privacy protections for patient data.

Privacy issues associated with patient health information have proven to be some of the most challenging problems. At root, we know that the information contained in a patient's health records can be some of the most sensitive information about a person, and all of us have a strong interest in keeping that information private. But as we move into more complex areas of healthcare research, we also see the emergence of new and more challenging privacy issues.

Research using genetic information can unleash ever deeper layers of information not just about a patient but also about the patient's distant relatives. Some research projects may also represent a dilemma to a particular patient, raising ethical issues that are in tension with an otherwise altruistic sense of sharing personal health data for research purposes that could benefit society.

These nuanced privacy issues will require policymakers and data stewards responsible for maintaining and managing patient health information to have a deeper understanding of technology and its interplay with data privacy requirements for patient health data.

Inclusiveness – AI Systems Should Empower Everyone and Engage People

If we are to ensure that AI technologies benefit and empower everyone, they must incorporate and address a broad range of human needs and experiences. Inclusive design practices will help system developers understand and address potential barriers in a product or environment that could unintentionally exclude people. This means that AI systems should be designed to understand the context, needs, and expectations of those who use them.

AI experiences can have the greatest positive impact when they offer both emotional intelligence and cognitive intelligence, a balance that can improve predictability and comprehension. AI-based personal agents, for example, can exhibit user awareness by confirming and, as necessary, correcting understanding of the user's intent. Personal agents should provide information and make recommendations in ways that are contextual and expected. They should provide information that helps people understand what inferences the system makes about them. Over time, such successful interactions will increase usage of AI systems and trust in their performance.

Transparency and Accountability

Underlying the principles of reliability, fairness, and security are two fundamental principles: transparency and accountability. Because decisions made by AI health systems will impact patients' health and care, everyone relying on these systems (healthcare professionals, patients, managed care organizations, regulators) must understand how the systems make decisions.

Equally important, as AI health systems play a greater role in diagnosing and selecting treatment options by healthcare professionals, we will need to work through existing rules around accountability, including liability. As a threshold matter, these systems should provide "holistic" explanations that include contextual information about how the system works and interacts with data. This enables the medical community to identify and raise awareness of potential bias, errors, and other unintended outcomes.

AI health systems may create unfairness if healthcare professionals do not understand the limitations (including accuracy) of a system or misunderstand the role of the system's output. Even if it is difficult for users to understand all the nuances of how a particular algorithm functions, healthcare professionals must understand the clinical basis for recommendations generated by AI systems. As discussed above, even where the results of AI systems may be technically reliable, they may not always be clinically relevant to a particular patient. This is why healthcare professionals will need to continue to exercise their judgment between the two.

Transparency is not just how the AI system explains its results. It's also about teaching healthcare providers and users how to interrogate the results. The goal is to ensure that doctors and others relying on these systems understand the limitations of the systems and do not put undue reliance on them.

Recent court cases involving the use of algorithms by state officials to assess and revise benefits for citizens with developmental and intellectual disabilities under a state Medicaid program provide a glimpse of how accountability issues will arise and be adjudicated. In these cases, courts required the states to provide patients with information about how the algorithms were created to challenge their individual benefit allocations.

Beyond transparency, developers of AI-driven health systems should have some degree of accountability for how the systems operate. At the same time, there is also accountability among those that deploy these systems in medical practice to exercise appropriate judgment when integrating them into medical decision-making. At this point, there remain more questions than answers about how accountability should be addressed.

For example, how should the balance of responsibility for using suggestions provided by AI-driven precision health systems fall between system developers, healthcare institutions implementing the systems, and healthcare professionals utilizing the systems in clinical decision-making? Are healthcare institutions required to evaluate each system independently, and if so, how?

The introduction and use of AI in healthcare continues to evolve. We must maintain an open and questioning mind on emerging policy and ethical issues as we look to the future. At the same time, we seek to take advantage of the opportunities and address the challenges that this new technology creates.

Health leaders, policymakers, researchers, academics, and representatives of nongovernmental groups must work together to ensure that AI-based technologies are designed and deployed in a manner that will earn the trust of the people who use them and the individuals whose data is being collected.

Notes

1. Office of Minority Health Resource Center. "Profile: Black/African Americans." Black/African American – The Office of Minority Health, 22 Aug. 2019, www.minorityhealth.hhs.gov/omh/browse.aspx?lvl=3&lvlid=61.
2. CDC: Infant mortality rates https://www.cdc.gov/reproductivehealth/maternalinfanthealth/infantmortality.htm.
3. NIH-funded study highlights stark racial disparities in maternal deaths, National Institute of Health, August 12, 2021, https://www.nih.gov/news-events/news-releases/nih-funded-study-highlights-stark-racial-disparities-maternal-deaths.
4. Institute of Medicine (US) Committee on Understanding and Eliminating Racial and Ethnic Disparities in Health Care; Smedley BD, Stith AY, Nelson AR, editors. Unequal Treatment: Confronting Racial and Ethnic Disparities in Health Care. Washington, DC: National Academies Press (US); 2003. EXECUTIVE SUMMARY. Available from: https://www.ncbi.nlm.nih.gov/books/NBK220355/.

5. Graham, H., & White, P. C. L. (2016). Social determinants and lifestyles: integrating environmental and public health perspectives. Public Health, 141, 270–278.
6. Sederer, L. I. (2016). The social determinants of mental health. Psychiatric Services, 67(2), 234–235.
7. Pera, M. F., Cain, M. M., Emerick, A., Katz, S., Hirsch, N. A., Sherman, B. W., & Bravata, D. M. (2021). Social determinants of health challenges are prevalent among commercially insured populations. Journal of Primary Care & Community Health, 12, 1–10.
8. Panch, T., Mattie, H., & Atun, R. (2019). Artificial intelligence and algorithmic bias: implications for health systems. Journal of Global Health, 9(2), 010318. doi:10.7189/jogh.09.020318 https://www.ncbi.nlm.nih.gov/pmc/articles/PMC6875681/#:~:text=Trishan%20Panch%2C1%2C2%20Heather%20Mattie%2C3%20and%20Rifat%20Atun4.
9. Obermeyer, Z., Powers, B., Vogeli, C., & Mullainathan, S. (2019). Dissecting racial bias in an algorithm used to manage the health of populations. Science, 366(6464), 447–453.
10. Vyas, D. A., Eisenstein, L. G., & Jones, D. S. (July 2020) Hidden in plain sight — reconsidering the use of race correction in clinical algorithms. New England Journal of Medicine, https://www.nejm.org/doi/full/10.1056/NEJMms2004740.
11. Sarah Bird Miro Dudík Richard Edgar Brandon Horn Roman Lutz Vanessa Milan Mehrnoosh Sameki Hanna Wallach Kathleen Walker, Fairlearn: A toolkit for assessing and improving fairness in AI, Microsoft, May, 2020, https://www.microsoft.com/en-us/research/publication/fairlearn-a-toolkit-for-assessing-and-improving-fairness-in-ai/.
12. Microsoft AI principles, Microsoft, https://www.microsoft.com/en-us/ai/responsible-ai?activetab=pivot1:primaryr6.
13. Can A.I. Be Taught to Explain Itself?, Cliff Kuang, The New York Times Magazine, 2017, https://www.nytimes.com/2017/11/21/magazine/can-ai-be-taught-to-explain-itself.html.

Chapter 16

AI-Driven Leadership

Change will not come if we wait for some other person or some other time. We are the ones we've been waiting for. We are the change that we seek.

Barack Obama

With all the hype about artificial intelligence (AI) changing every aspect of living and working, you would think that everyone investing in AI is riding a wave of success.

Think again.

Strip away the gushy superlatives used to describe what's happening, and you see that success, especially at scale, can elude even those making sizable investments in AI.

A recent report from Boston Consulting Group and MIT Sloan Management Review offers a sobering dose of realism. It also provides a glimpse at why some organizations are reaping significant returns on their AI investments while others are pouring money down the drain.

According to this report, only a small minority of organizations from all business sectors – Just 11% – are reaping *significant* returns.[1]

Successful organizations see AI as more than a path to automation. Instead, it's an integral strategic component of their business models. Organizations implementing AI as part of a bigger rethink in what they do and how they operate are seeing greater returns. These organizations build teams and curate learning cultures that focus on AI-driven innovation. They continue experimenting even when initial projects don't yield a big payoff.

DOI: 10.4324/9781003286103-16

They learn and adjust as they go. Seventy-three percent of organizations that get this right go on to see significant returns on their investments.[2]

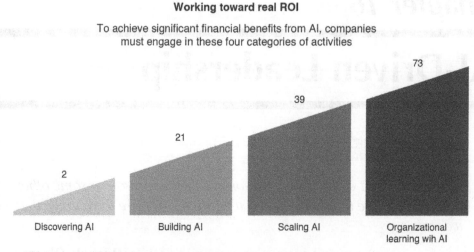

Working toward real ROI

To achieve significant financial benefits from AI, companies must engage in these four categories of activities

73

39

21

2

Discovering AI   Building AI   Scaling AI   Organizational learning wih AI

Chance of achieving significant financial benefits with each activity (%)

When you net out the specific findings of this and other studies, the most critical factor separating AI winners from losers is leadership.

Those who are successful are leveraging AI to create new approaches in which the activities, people, culture, and structure of the organization are better aligned with new market expectations. Just as AI-supported agile transformation in our response to the pandemic, it will serve as the backbone for innovating how we address the challenges of a rapidly changing market.

Many health leaders are excited about the opportunities to use AI and intelligent systems to drive systemic change in keeping with their mission and goals. At the same time, there is a growing recognition that their organizations are not adequately prepared for the industry disruptions that are ahead.

Preparing for and navigating through such change is not for the faint of heart. While some health leaders take a narrow view of AI by relegating it to being another technical improvement to be managed by capable IT leaders, the move toward becoming an Intelligent Health System requires leaders to think and act differently.

Q: Which of the following are top challenges for your organization's AI initiatives?

Integrating AI into the organization

30%

Managing AI-related risks

28%

The high cost of AI technologies/solutions

36%

Data challenges

28%

Challenges implementing AI technologies

28%

Choosing the right AI technologies

27%

Lack of executive commitment

21%

Challenges proving business value

19%

Difficulty identifying the use cases with the greatest business value

19%

Lack of skills

17%

☐ Operational ■ Technology
■ Organizational

Note: Total number of respondents, N = 120

Source: Deloitte's State of AI survey.
www2.deloitte.com/content/dam/insights/us/articles/6872_AI-in-healthcare/6872_AI-in-healthcare.pdf

Characteristics of AI Leaders

In the ever-increasing world of intelligent health, AI-driven leadership will require the following skills and characteristics.

Planning Visionary

Effectively managing the introduction and pursuit of AI-driven transformation starts with defining a vision and then backing it up with razor-sharp clarity about the new market demands, future operating models, the rationale for why change is needed, and how success will be defined and measured.

Strategically Ambidextrous

Large-scale change and disruption are on the horizon as people and organizations move into the next phase of the Intelligent Health Revolution. Successful leaders understand that and are leading organizations to pursue a dual strategy. This includes protecting and repositioning current core service lines while actively investing in transformation activities that seed the new growth opportunities in keeping with the market and consumer demands. This pursuit of "two journeys" sets an organization in a new direction while recognizing that a transition period is needed to accommodate the move to new processes and ways of doing business.

Customer Obsessed

As noted in Chapter 8, shifting expectations are pushing health organizations to improve the consumer experience across all touchpoints, channels, and experiences. Excellence in one area is insufficient as consumers expect the same frictionless experience across all interactions and touchpoints.

An obsession with improving the consumer experience is foundational to creating an Intelligent Health System. Leadership should aspire to evaluate and fix every error or bad experience. This includes the experiences of existing patients, consumers in the markets you serve, medical staff, employees, and referral sources.

Internal Evangelist

The single most important determinant in early success for enterprise-wide AI and intelligent heath is how effectively you bring everyone along in the move to reinvent the organization.

Transformational AI leaders understand that success depends on the entire team's effort. This starts with the total commitment of clinical and business leadership. Leaders must understand and commit to a strategy and actively communicate that strategy to all employees and constituents. To drive cultural change and stimulate new growth, it is essential for everyone to understand not only what is happening but also why it is in everyone's best interest to embrace the change that is occurring and the benefits it will bring.

Agile Adaptor

AI-driven leaders must be prepared to think differently about how AI and the Intelligent Health Revolution will change clinical and operational processes. Setting aspirations that on the surface may at times seem unreasonable can be a means of jarring an organization into viewing AI as a way to create value in a changing marketplace.

A Framework for AI-Driven Leadership

In adopting these leadership characteristics and putting them into practice, here is a leadership framework to consider[3]:

Lead rather than delegate: The key to the success of any AI initiative is for leaders to actually lead. This is a statement of the obvious, but time and time again, clinical and business leaders often "delegate" technology matters to IT. And while IT and data professionals are critical to success, leaders must be prepared to define a vision for change and create an environment in which the work of the technical and data specialists will be successful.

Learn the technologies: When leading with AI, it helps to know what AI is and does (which may be why you are reading this book). Recognize that AI is different from other technologies used in the past. It is not just one technology, but many – each with its own application types, stage of development, strengths, and limitations. Leaders don't have to become IT experts or data scientists. They should, however, know enough about the technologies to weigh in on which ones will be most critical to their organization's success.

Establish clear objectives for what will be achieved and how it will be measured: As with any other technology, it's important to have clear objectives for using AI. Applications for AI in health and medicine are almost unlimited. The time and resources available to you are not. As a leader, it's important to create a clear set of objectives and a process by which ideas for the use of AI can be evaluated. When embarking on an enterprise-wide approach to AI, it is critical to select initial use cases where AI will be used to drive change and value.

Look beyond pilots and proofs of concept: AI projects in health and medicine have been heavily weighted toward pilots. Driving AI value at scale requires that such projects move into full production status. Doing so requires careful evaluation of process improvements to be gained. It also requires figuring out how to integrate AI technologies into existing applications, IT architectures, and human-driven workflows.

Prepare people for the journey: In healthcare, most AI projects will involve "augmentation." This means looking at how people will collaborate with smart machines, a process that is different from full-on automation. This means that employees will have to learn new skills and adopt new roles. Such change doesn't happen overnight. Good leaders are already preparing their people for AI by developing training programs, recruiting for new skills when necessary, and integrating continuous learning into their models.

Get the necessary data: AI-driven leaders know that data is their most important asset if they want to do substantial work in AI. Many organizations will need to turn to external data to augment their internal sources, while others will need to improve data quality and integration before using it with their AI projects. In other words, AI-driven leaders need to start now, to improve their data by creating and managing modern data estates (Chapter 13).

Orchestrate collaborative organizations: C-level executives aren't always at the head of the pack when it comes to technology initiatives. But roles like CEO, HR, and other operational leaders must create a close collaboration to establish priorities, determine the implications for technology architectures and human skills, and assess the implications for critical functions such as marketing and supply chain.

AI should be viewed and treated as an essential catalytic technology. As such, senior executives should form strategic and operational collaborations that involve key stakeholders who can best provide input on goals, deliverables, and the impact that change will have on the organization.

Creating such internal collaborations facilitates progress in AI and communicates to the organization that a new way of working and managing is being adopted.

Managing Decisions About Decisions

As AI becomes pervasive in clinical and organizational work processes, leaders must recognize how this will impact decision-making at all levels of the organization.

Eventually, AI will make, aid, or impact thousands of granular decisions made each day. The value of AI comes in automating or augmenting certain decision types. This includes improving the accuracy or outcome of decisions. Examples range from complex decisions about a single patient or a population of patients to decisions that impact supply chain, throughput, and financial performance.

AI-powered decisions made at the atomic level are known as "micro-decisions."[4] Realizing value from AI requires leaders to make a paradigm shift *from "making decisions"* to creating processes to guide making *"decisions about decisions."*[5]

This shift is happening across every industry and all kinds of decision-making.

Over time AI-driven leaders will create frameworks and new management models that optimize the use of AI in making decisions.

One model gaining traction today is that put forward by Michael Ross, an executive fellow at London Business School, and James Taylor, author of *Digital Decisioning: Using Decision Management to Deliver Business Impact from AI*. The model creates a taxonomy well suited to the types of decisions made in providing health and medical services. It proposes four decision types to be managed[6]:

Human in the loop (HITL): A human is assisted by a machine. In this model, the human is making the decision, and the machine provides only decision support or partial automation of some decisions or parts of decisions. This is often referred to as intelligence amplification (IA).

Human in the loop for exceptions (HITLFE): Most decisions are automated in this model, and humans only handle exceptions. For the exceptions, the system requires some judgment or input from the human before it can make the decision, though it is unlikely to ask the human to make the whole decision. Humans also control the logic to determine which exceptions are flagged for review.

Human on the loop (HOTL): Here, the machine is assisted by a human. The machine makes the micro-decisions, but the human reviews the decision outcomes and can adjust rules and parameters for future decisions. In a more advanced setup, the machine also recommends parameters or rule changes approved by a human.

Human out of the loop (HOOTL): The machine is monitored by the human in this model. The machine makes every decision, and the human intervenes only by setting new constraints and objectives. Improvement is also an automated closed loop. Adjustments, based on feedback from humans, are automated.

Defining and Demonstrating Value

The creation and execution of an AI strategy is a multi-year event and, in some ways, a continuous process that never ends. Whether at the launch of your strategy or a review several years down the road, it's important to develop and measure success against specific goals. There are three areas around which specific key performance indicators should be developed in broad terms.

New growth: How successful is your organization in creating new services, solutions, and business models? This can be gauged by assessing the percent of revenue outside historical core services attributed to new growth.

Core repositioning: How effectively is your organization adapting its legacy business to change and disruption? Internally this can be gauged by evaluating volume and key performance indicators (KPI's) pre- and post-change. Externally this can be measured by assessing the retention and growth of specific patient populations (using AI to better manage populations covered under Value-Based Care), increases in market penetration both geographically (increasing volumes from core service area or generating increased volumes in new geographies), and demographically (e.g., attracting a higher volume of millennials).

Financial performance: How are the organization's growth, operating expenses, and gross and net revenue changing compared to previous operating periods or relevant industry benchmarks during a transformation period?

While measuring and quantifying the impact of AI investments is important, recognize that the value of AI shouldn't be limited to quantitative metrics. Additional qualitative measures to be considered addressing when determining the value of AI include:[7]

- Improved quality and safety
- Improved customer experience
- Skills and employee retention
- Increased competitive advantage
- Increased agility and operational resilience
- Enhanced brand reputation
- Improved accuracy and effectiveness

There should be little doubt that companies aspiring to be AI-driven need themselves to be led by AI-driven leaders – meaning motivated, knowledgeable, and engaged in the intelligent health movement.

For most organizations today, AI is a source of evolutionary benefits. Over the long run, it will be a revolutionary force. AI will change how work is done, how decisions are made, and how organizations harness knowledge and information to achieve their goals.

With AI and the digitization of data, the nature of jobs and work is changing again. In their book *"No Ordinary Disruption,"* authors Richard Dobbs, James Manyika, and Jonathan Woetzel estimate that change today is happening 10 times faster and at 300 times the scale of the First Industrial Revolution, which works out to about 3,000 times the impact.

Accenture has created a "disruptability index," which analyzes the disruption of smart technologies across 20 industries. Healthcare is among the top sectors that AI will significantly disrupt.[8]

Health leaders are always on the front lines of understanding and managing change. If there is one factor to consider when it comes to managing change coming about by AI, it's this: Throughout time, no matter what technology was driving change, decision-making authority has always remained with humans. AI has the potential to change this age-old management paradigm. It will move us toward how we use and relate to our new intelligent tools.

Notes

1. Will Knight, Companies Are Rushing to Use AI—but Few See a Payoff, Wired, October 10, 2020, https://www.wired.com/story/companies-rushing-use-ai-few-see-payoff/?utm_source=onsite-share&utm_medium=email&utm_campaign=onsite-share&utm_brand=wired.
2. Are You Making the Most of Your Relationship with AI?, BCG, October 20, 2020, https://www.bcg.com/publications/2020/is-your-company-embracing-full-potential-of-artificial-intelligence.
3. Adapted from AI-Driven Leadership, Thomas H. Davenport, Janet Foutty, MIT Sloand Management Review, August 10, 2018, https://sloanreview.mit.edu/article/ai-driven-leadership/.
4. James Taylor, Neil Raden, Smart Enough Systems: How to Deliver Competitive Advantage by Automating Hidden Decisions, 2019, Pearson Education.
5. Michael Ross and James Taylor, Managing AI Decision-Making Tools, Harvard Business Review, November 10, 2021, https://hbr.org/2021/11/managing-ai-decision-making-tools.
6. Ibid.
7. Elizabeth Mixson, AI ROI: Calculating the Value of Machine Intelligence, AI Data and Anaytics Network, August 11, 2021, https://www.aidataanalytics.network/data-monetization/articles/ai-roi-calculating-the-value-of-machine-intelligence.
8. Digital Health Tech Vision, Kaveh Safavi, Accenture Consulting, 2019, https://www.accenture.com/_acnmedia/PDF-102/Accenture-Digital-Health-Tech-Vision-2019.pdf#zoom=50.

Chapter 17

Adopting AI Requires Adapting

Without deviation from the norm, progress is not possible.

Frank Zappa

American musician, singer, composer

If history is to be our teacher, a lesson to be learned is this: Don't be the next Kodak.

Founded in 1888, Kodak dominated the photographic film market for more than a century. Then, in 1975, one of its engineers named Steve Sasson developed the world's first digital camera. When presented to Kodak's leadership team as a game-changing technology that would allow them to lead the industry for the next 100 years, the reaction, according to Sasson, was, *"that's cute—but don't tell anyone about it."*[1]

Kodak blew its chance to lead the digital photography revolution. Its demise was summarized by a former (unemployed) vice president: *"We developed the world's first consumer digital camera, but we could not get approval to launch or sell it because of our fear of the effects on the film market."* Kodak filed for bankruptcy in 2012.

Nokia is another cautionary tale. In 2007, a close-up of CEO Olli Pekka Kallasvuo was splashed across the cover of Forbes with a headline proclaiming *"Nokia – One Billion Customers – Can Anyone Catch the Cell Phone King?"* Meanwhile, Apple had just become an upstart in the phone business. Its newly released iPhone featured a novel touchscreen instead of a keyboard and focused on how data, not voice, was the future of communication. Nokia executives balked at such ideas. The iPhone was brushed off as a novelty item. Nokia never recovered.

DOI: 10.4324/9781003286103-17

As the Intelligent Health Revolution takes hold, it will produce winners and losers. Emerging as a winner will not happen by accident. The secret to winning will not be about adopting artificial intelligence (AI). Instead, success will come by first recognizing that change is imminent and then adapting to what is coming.

Navigating the change already happening starts with understanding how the Intelligence Revolution is different from other technological breakthroughs.

As represented in the chart below, broad tech trends typically produce change over time. Progress or growth is linear, which means changes occur at a constant rate. As linear growth occurs, small gaps are created between technology, individuals, businesses, governments, and society. Over time these gaps are closed through normal processes like creating public policies to provide safeguards as businesses incorporate new technologies into existing workflows.

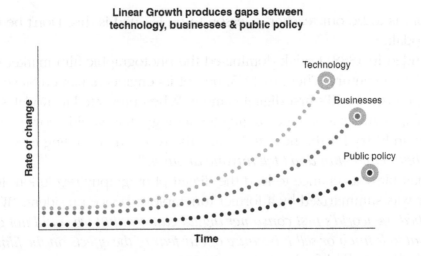

The Intelligence Revolution is different. As noted in Chapter 2, AI is a *general-purpose technology*. This means that it has the power to continually transform itself. As this happens, it will progressively branch out and drive rapid, systemic change across all sectors. As this occurs, it will unleash a wave of change that produces *exponential growth*.

In math circles, there is something known as the Exponential Curve. This is a visualization of what happens when rapid growth is plotted on a chart. Typically, something being measured starts out appearing to follow a linear growth pattern then the rate of change becomes exponential. It starts increasing so fast that the plotline becomes vertical.

One only needs to look at any graph plotting the rise of COVID cases in the initial phase of the pandemic to understand exponential growth.

How the world operates is geared mostly toward managing linear change. This includes the training, systems, and processes we use to manage our work and personal lives.

Exponential growth puts everyone in new territory when it comes to understanding and managing change. It's a rapid paradigm shift that often catches people and organizations off guard.

An important tenet of exponential growth is that it is not sustainable. Eventually, things settle down but what is left in place is a new normal brought about by exponential change.

Exponential growth matters because it's easy to underestimate. As noted in the chart below, it starts out following an expected linear growth pattern. Then it shifts.

When exponential growth happens, how you or your organization adapt to the space underneath the growth curve is where winners and losers are made.

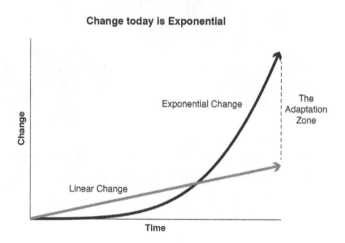

When it comes to the disruptive nature of AI and the transition to intelligent health systems, there's a lesson to be learned in a pair of photographs taken in New York City in the early part of the last century. The images are of the Flatiron Building, and they are strikingly similar except for one crucial feature.

In the first image, taken in 1905, the primary mode of transportation is equine – horses haul carts laden with freight, horse-drawn carriages convey people, and horse-drawn cabs sit curbside waiting for fares.

In the second image, taken 20 years later, not a single horse can be seen. Instead, a long line of automobiles snakes down Broadway, parked cars jam the curbs, and a stretch of pavement in front of the Flatiron Building has been converted to a parking lot.

What happened in between was a period of profound transformation and disruption. In 1905, it took more than 100,000 horses to move goods and people through New York City. Tens of thousands of people were employed feeding and cleaning up after them. Thousands more worked as blacksmiths, wheelwrights, saddlemakers, and carriage builders. Nationwide, one-quarter of the country's agricultural output was dedicated to growing crops to feed horses.

Two decades later, a new form of horsepower predominated fueling innovation that gave rise to new industries, generated vast numbers of new jobs, and transformed the economy. It also ended a long-standing way of life and created a new kind of society – not just in New York but in cities around the world. During that time, entire categories of work that had previously provided a good living for people for centuries all but disappeared. Entirely new ways of working and living emerged that carried us forward for decades. The realities of a society that suddenly moved at the speed of cars rather than the trot of horses meant that new laws had to be enacted, new infrastructures built, and new social norms developed.[2]

These two images are a good reason to pause and consider the sweeping implications of the Intelligent Health Revolution. It will challenge old ways and be the catalyst for change.

The Benefits of Adopting and Adapting

Done right, the benefits of adopting and adapting to AI go beyond improving efficiencies and decision-making. Such change also produces cultural as well as financial benefits. In a groundbreaking study by MIT and BCG, researchers identified a wide range of AI-related cultural benefits at the team and organizational levels. Study results included:

■ Seventy-five percent of teams with AI implementations that improved efficiency and decision-making also saw improvements in team morale, collaboration, and collective learning.
■ Teams that saw financial benefits from their AI initiatives were ten times more likely to change how they measure success than those who saw no such benefits. In some cases, AI helped leaders identify new performance drivers. AI also helped these organizations realign behaviors and become more competitive.
■ Organizations that use AI primarily to explore new ways of creating value are far more likely to improve their ability to compete with AI than those that use AI primarily to improve existing processes.[3]

Utilizing AI strategically creates the opportunity to reexamine fundamental assumptions about business operations and organizational effectiveness. Revising performance measures is also typical of organizations that adopt AI. Sixty-four percent of organizations integrating AI into work processes say it led to changes in the organization's Key Performance Indicators (KPIs). In some cases, it enables stronger performance and makes legacy measures or KPIs that no longer reflect an organization's desired goals obsolete.[4]

The Cultural-Use-Effectiveness Dynamic

Improving each component of the C-U-E dynamic
can lead to a virtuous cycle of cultural improvement

Source: The Cultural Benefits of Artificial Intelligence in the Enterprise, MIT Sloan, BCG

Reaping measurable benefits from AI depends on employees working with and trusting AI. AI-based solutions that generate new ways of working often face resistance from teams entrenched in existing cultures. The MIT study notes that the top reasons for resistance come from a lack of understanding of AI (49%) or training (46%). Effective leaders lower resistance by including end users in the development process, building trust in AI system performance, and encouraging teams to change their work processes.

Beyond helping teams become more efficient and make better decisions, AI can have a positive effect on the "soft measures" of a company's culture, including:

Collective Learning: Culture reflects the accumulated learning that a given group acquires and passes on to newcomers. Eighty-seven percent of teams that improved their efficiency and decision quality with AI also improved their collective learning. AI implementations influence both what teams learn and how learning occurs.

Collaboration: The increased efficiency from AI implementations frequently leads to improved collaboration. Among those who saw an increase in efficiency and decision quality from AI, 78% reported enhanced collaboration.

Morale: Among teams that improved their efficiency and decision quality with AI implementations, 79% reported an increase in morale.

In the end, innovating new processes with AI increases the effectiveness of teams and can improve an organization's competitiveness with both existing and new rivals.

Moderna is a great example of adopting and adapting to AI. Before the pandemic, they began using AI to automate work previously done by humans. This included testing the design sequence of messenger RNA (mRNA) used in the COVID-19 vaccine. One of the significant bottlenecks was having mRNA for the scientist to run testing. Through an investment in AI, robotic automation, and digital systems, Moderna went from manually producing about 30 mRNA a month to producing a thousand in the same period. It was this capability that helped the company to develop the COVID-19 vaccine rapidly.[5]

Notes

1. 50 Examples of Corporations That Failed to Innovate, Valuer, July 2, 2019, https://www.valuer.ai/blog/50-examples-of-corporations-that-failed-to-innovate-and-missed-their-chance.
2. Modified and used with permission from A Cloud for Global Good, Microsoft, 2017.
3. Sam Ransbotham, François Candelon, David Kiron, Burt LaFountain, and Shervin Khodabandeh, The Cultural Benefits of Artificial Intelligence in the Enterprise, MIT Sloan Management Review – Big Ideas Research Report, November 2021, https://sloanreview.mit.edu/projects/the-cultural-benefits-of-artificial-intelligence-in-the-enterprise/#:~:text=The%20benefits%20of%20artificial%20intelligence%20go%20well%20beyond,cultural%20as%20well%20as%20financial%20benefits%20for%20organizations.
4. Ibid.
5. Ibid.

Chapter 18

From Aspiration to Execution

There is no instant pudding.

Dr. W. Edwards Deming
on the matter of transformation

Most health leaders understand that artificial intelligence (AI) has the power to change how health services are provided. Many don't know how to transition from deploying a few AI pilots to delivering transformational AI at scale. Moving from aspiration to execution is where many organizations flounder in having their investment of time and money produce the payoffs that are promised with AI.

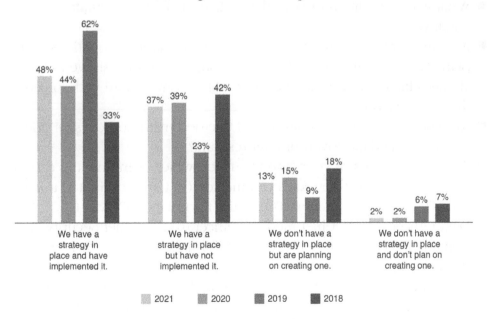

Health organizations' AI strategies

Source: Still on the Rise: How AI in health care continues to grow, 4th Annual Optum Survey on AI in Health Care, Optum.

DOI: 10.4324/9781003286103-18

The difference between AI leaders and laggards often comes down to the strength of an organization's AI strategy. That strategy must define the goals and expected deliverables and provide an operational road map to achieve these goals. In developing an enterprise-wide AI plan, here are things to consider:

Complete an AI Reality Check

No matter how far along you believe your organization to be in its AI journey, it's essential to have a clear and realistic view of your starting position with AI. Completing an assessment should go beyond an inventory of AI pilots and projects underway. Instead, you should evaluate critical aspects of your readiness to execute by addressing the following questions:

■ What interactions with consumers, patients, and staff provide the best opportunities to use AI to improve consumer satisfaction and quality?

■ Is it clear how existing and new AI projects will measurably support your mission and goals? What are the metrics you will use to measure value and success?

■ How will AI be used to differentiate your organization in the market and reduce the risk of losing out to a competitor?

■ What is the condition of your data estate to efficiently curate new initiatives?

■ Are clinicians and staff aware of your organization's aspirations and planning efforts in using AI? Are they supportive or resistive to the changes likely to occur as the use of AI becomes more widespread in the organization?

■ Are your organization's culture and decision-making processes oriented toward being data-driven or data resistant?

■ What is the status of your "top talent" on which planning and execution will be dependent? Key roles can include (but are not limited to) your Chief Technology Officer (CTO), Chief Information Officer (CIO), Chief Data Officer (CDO), Chief Medical Officer (CMO), Chief Security and Compliance Officer (CISO), Clinical Informaticists, and Chief Human Resource Officer. Important: Executing an enterprise-wide AI initiative does not require all of the positions noted above (especially in smaller organizations). Instead, it's important to have staff capable of managing the various components of an initiative.

- Beyond compliance with privacy and security standards, is your organization's use of AI being evaluated to ensure it is in keeping with the ethical standards and values of the organization?
- Strategic direction – Are you focused on using AI to get better at what you do (remain traditional health system) or forging ahead with a new model assuming exponential growth and change described in this book?

Creating a snapshot of what is occurring in your organization today provides a starting view of organizational attitude and skills, technology infrastructure, process improvement opportunities, and general level of readiness on which to build.

Lay a Solid AI Foundation: This Means People + Data

Your organization's ability to successfully plan and launch an enterprise-wide AI program will be built on a foundation that includes the following cornerstones:

Enterprise AI is a team sport: Early AI initiatives in health organizations often begin with AI specialists and IT leaders who are early adopters. Such efforts are important but often struggle to gain broad traction. At the same time, AI initiatives bubbling up from the clinical or business side of the organization often fail because they have limited focus and don't take full advantage of the data and IT talent required to successfully drive and sustain such projects. Simply put, the success of AI pilots can be done with a small group of motivated, like-minded team members, but the success of a sustainable, enterprise-wide AI program cannot.

The success of AI across your organization is highly dependent on empowering a team of diverse stakeholders to plan and execute your AI strategy. This requires including people representing clinicians, IT, AI and data specialists, business process owners, HR, security and compliance, marketing, and consumer experience.

Once you define a team to drive the planning and implementation of your AI strategy, it's important to define and communicate an organizational operating structure that enables this group to lead efforts within the organization. Some organizations create a planning and operational steering committee. Others may add AI responsibilities to existing departments or divisions (e.g., Office of Chief Digital Officer or automation group).

Increasingly, health organizations are establishing AI Centers of Excellence (CoE) to build a foundation and give added visibility to AI efforts. Some organizations are also establishing stronger lines of accountability for AI initiatives by creating board committees related explicitly to AI.

Whatever form is given to the team chosen, a clear charter should be established that defines its role and responsibilities. Typical responsibilities for this group include education and advocacy within and outside the organization, identification, and prioritization of use cases, and development of policies for governance and accountability.

Finally, the AI team should create and manage a digital platform for collaboration, support, and resource management. Think of it as the one-stop-shop for AI efforts: a virtual environment where business and tech professionals share resources (data sets, methodologies, and reusable components) and collaborate on initiatives.

Data is the currency for AI – Be ready to spend it: All AI initiatives start with great optimism, but many end with less-than-satisfactory results. A key predictor of success is the condition of the data estate on which projects are built and maintained. As noted in Chapter 13, AI runs on data and has an almost endless appetite. This includes having data available in the right formats at the right time.

Equally important is recognizing that AI must be integrated into technologies and workflows that operate around the clock. Algorithms and AI applications usually require a continuous flow of new data to learn and perform.

You can increase both the success and time to value of initial AI projects by engaging early with your data and IT leaders to understand and invest in connecting the "data dots" that AI requires. This includes an evaluation of your staffing, in-house expertise, and systems. The goal is to have AI projects supported by data that is current, accurate, complete, and free of biases.

Nix Moonshots in Favor of Well-Curated Use Cases That Drive Value

Imagine being a Saturday morning jogger and, in a moment of excitement, deciding to sign up to run a full marathon the following weekend. Such is the case with some health leaders who are so excited about the possibilities with AI that they commit to projects that are unrealistic in scope or complexity.

The late Mark Hurd was an early tech leader who helped grow big companies like Oracle and Hewlett Packard. While somewhat harsh, he summarized the danger of moonshots: *"Without execution, 'vision' is just another word for hallucination."*[1]

Recognize and champion that the Intelligent Health Revolution will transform how people work and services are provided. In doing this, think big but start with well-defined opportunities to use AI in ways that have a high probability of early success in keeping with your clinical, operational, and customer goals.

Initial AI projects should be selected based on each opportunity's potential value, cost, and speed of delivery. Once you've locked in on which projects to pursue, treat them as "test and learn" opportunities. Each project undertaken helps create an operational framework that can then be used as the launchpad for future projects and use cases. Done right, pursuing an AI use case for one specific task can solve a well-defined business problem while simultaneously creating the potential to scale what you learn to other use cases.

Recognize that every new initiative creates risk. AI projects are no different. When selecting initial AI projects, a variable that determines risk is the complexity of the scenario or use case. One way of "de-risking" early projects is to evaluate the complexity of the use case. There are several components of project complexity to be considered, including:

Technical: What level of technical complexity exists for a given project? In addition to traditional hardware/software considerations, this includes determination of computing model (cloud, on-prem, hybrid, or edge) as well as which approach to be used for developing and managing the "intelligent" component of the project (type of algorithm or AI component plus method for developing/delivering/maintaining).

Data: Data complexity includes the type of data (structured/unstructured), availability (does it exist?), location, integration, and interoperability, security and compliance considerations (data required to predict and reduce claims denials may have compliance requirements different from other data needed to predict clinical outcomes).

People and processes: How many people are involved in a process that will be changed due to an AI initiative? What level of effort will be required to revamp the set of activities, interactions, and handoffs within the old or existing process to be improved by introducing AI? Breaking down processes into six-sigma-like elements uncovers ways in which AI can add value while also identifying just how much change will be required to realize its value.

Different use cases have different levels of complexity. A high-value project may be low in data and technical complexity but high in complexity based on the number of people whose work will have to change to realize value. Use these criteria to select projects that match an organization's initial readiness and then increase the complexity of projects undertaken over time.

Expect imperfection in your initial efforts and use early projects to identify areas for improvement. The dual benefit of initial projects should be to deliver measurable value against your goals while defining what the organization needs to do to replicate the process for future projects.

Understand and Manage Workforce Impact

The very nature by which AI creates value (automation and augmentation) will, at some level, impact every clinician and employee. Many will have concerns about how AI will affect their work, practice, and career. AI often creates stress for staff and, over time, requires the organization to plan for large-scale retraining.

Engage early in exploring AI and its impact on the future of work. It's an opportunity to evaluate what changes you should be prepared to make. It also helps to bring your people along in supporting change. While some jobs may eventually be eliminated through AI automation, other jobs will be created, and most jobs will be improved or enhanced as AI will take over many repetitive and time-consuming tasks.

AI will influence the structure of how work is done. Invest early in planning and education activities to increase the capacity of your people to adapt and change with the times.

Focus on Delivering Secure and Responsible AI

The AI legal and policy landscape is in its infancy worldwide. Health leaders, policymakers, and legislators are working to ensure that AI-based technologies are designed and deployed to be safe and earn the trust of the people who use them. As this occurs, recognize that laws and regulations governing AI in health will continue to evolve.

Most countries are revising existing laws and regulations that govern general protections for security and data privacy in the healthcare world.

New initiatives are also popping up in various countries to address privacy, data sovereignty, and ethical issues specific to AI algorithms.

Beyond complying with the laws and regulations specific to your geography, there are situations when AI can be used in keeping with existing laws and regulations but miss the mark in addressing critical ethical principles such as fairness and transparency.

Your AI strategy should consider the current and evolving laws, regulations, and ethical standards that will govern your actions and ensure that your efforts are safe and trustworthy.

The top resources for managing this part of a plan include the Chief Security and Compliance Officer, the Chief Data and Information Officer, Chief Medical Informatics Officer, and the Chief Diversity, Equity and Inclusion Officer.

Become Your Organization's AI CEO (Chief Evangelist Officer)

An important factor in driving a cultural change in support of your AI strategy is having employees and other key constituents understand what is happening and why it is in their interest. Leaders committed to successfully developing and deploying the organization's AI strategy are the most persuasive evangelists in educating and influencing key people to embrace the changes necessary for the strategy to succeed.

Ideally, every team member appointed to plan and execute your organization's AI strategy will become a Chief Evangelist Officer. The role includes articulating the vision outlined in the plan, soliciting input and involvement, countering misperceptions, and changing the mindset of employees to lower the fear factor and increase the excitement factor for what is ahead.

In this regard, an essential role of leaders is to be compelling storytellers. While professional communications staff (HR, PR, marketing) can support the packaging and positioning of change, organizational leaders must be on the frontlines to effectively communicate the "what and why" messages surrounding transformation. Telling that kind of story about the future is not a one-time event. Leaders should be consistent and persistent in bringing the core message home to all. Additionally, the message being delivered should be tailored to fit with the many internal constituents found within the organization.

AI Leaders and Laggards

Most health leaders recognize the potential of AI. The question is not whether AI is used but how well and widespread is its use in a given organization? As time moves on, there will be AI leaders and laggards.

AI leaders will be characterized as those who mobilize to embrace the changes AI brings even in the uncertainties of the currently emerging market.

AI leaders will enlist a select group of clinicians and staff to lead an organizational transformation effort that benefits and empowers all staff to better leverage their expertise and capabilities. It will include using the power of AI to reimagine and redevelop the patient and consumer journey to provide more personal experiences.

AI leaders will set clear goals for AI and use early projects to support these goals. They will create a continuous learning cycle that benefits future projects and builds momentum internally that becomes a competitive advantage externally. They will leverage the value of their data as a true asset that can be monetized in service of the organization's mission and goals.

AI laggards will likely adopt a "wait and see" attitude while moving at traditional industry speed. They will spend too much time within the safety of their "pilot period" while figuring out which way the market is moving. AI will mainly be treated as another technology initiative with that is tied to making existing processes incrementally more efficient rather than reimagining and reinventing how work will be done differently.

AI laggards will treat data mainly as a byproduct of existing activities primarily used to look at what happened rather than what is to come. Clinicians and staff will be left wondering about their future in light of what they see and hear about the impact of AI in other organizations and how it will affect their work or whether they will even have a job.

The Choice Is Yours

What role will AI ultimately play in the future of health and medicine? No one really knows the exact form it will take, but it will be both disruptive and transformational.

In the end, AI is a tool. Whether it's a hammer or a heuristic analytics engine, the value of any tool comes from the skills and intended purpose of the user whose hands it's in. For those who choose to use its power wisely, AI will make health organizations and practitioners smarter, processes more efficient, experiences more personalized, and consumers more satisfied.

We are witnessing a new shift in computing. It's moving away from static systems and toward a mobile-first and AI-first world. It is forcing us to imagine a new order in the health world that allows us to create a more natural, seamless way of interacting and caring for those served by healthcare.

AI in health is a new journey for all of us. And like any new journey, the initial steps you take will be some of the most important when it comes to where this journey will take us.

Note

1. Mark Hurd, Wikipedia, https://en.wikipedia.org/wiki/Mark_Hurd.

Chapter 19

The Role of the Intelligent Cloud

Cloud is about how you do computing, not where you do computing.

Paul Maritz
Computer Scientist, and Software Executive

Prior to the COVID-19 pandemic, Moderna decided to build the company's mRNA research and development platform in the cloud to create what CEO Stéphane Bancel calls *"software for life."*[1] Moderna's leadership team saw the cloud as a means to accelerate therapeutic discovery and development. When the pandemic hit, this strategy proved prescient. Thanks mainly to the cloud and AI, Moderna delivered the first clinical batch of its vaccine candidate to the US National Institutes of Health for phase one trials in just 42 days. According to Bancel, this was made possible by the cloud *"because you don't have to reinvent everything, you just fly."*[2]

The cloud is at the heart of AI's growing capabilities to fuel the Intelligent Health Revolution. And while everyone talks about the cloud these days, much of what it is and how it drives value is not well understood outside of IT.

Essentially, cloud computing and artificial intelligence are partners. One enables the other. Without cloud computing, current AI capabilities would be limited.

The pandemic produced many success stories like Moderna's that illustrate the transformational opportunities made possible by the cloud and AI. Done right, cloud-delivered intelligence enables agile innovation at a near-limitless scale.

DOI: 10.4324/9781003286103-19

The value proposition of cloud-based AI comes at a time of increasing competitive pressures on health and medical organizations. Stimulated by the pandemic, fast-moving digital strategies are changing the health services landscape.

Creating and implementing a strategic cloud strategy is more than an efficiency play for IT. It's the engine that will drive the speed, scale, productivity, and level of innovation that an organization achieves now and in the future.

The success of any organization in achieving its desired AI-driven outcomes is impacted by leadership's understanding of what the cloud is and its role in agile innovation.

Research by McKinsey and Company identifies three "pools of value" for cloud adoption that fit well with healthcare.[3] These include:

Rejuvenate: In this category, organizations break from traditional legacy approaches by using the cloud to lower costs and risks across IT and core operations. Older on-premises models are inherently inefficient for managing data, applications, and infrastructure. They are highly manual and typically use expensive technology that often runs at less than full capacity. Organizations building new cloud-based systems are seeing dramatic efficiency improvements.

Benefits include cost optimization of application development and maintenance, improved business resilience, and faster "time to value" when investing in the latest technologies.

Innovate: This involves using the cloud to accelerate innovation using technologies such as advanced analytics, IoT, and automation at scale. These provide organizations with ways to pursue innovation-driven growth and optimize business operations costs. The cloud enables organizations to experiment with applications and new business models at lower costs and greater speed.

Leaders who embrace cloud avoid sizeable up-front capital outlays when launching or expanding clinical and business services. To support this shift, organizations need new operating models that are focused on managing consumption, gaining visibility into future demands, and forming integrated financial operations teams to maintain fiscal control, among other things. New cloud apps draw on ever-evolving data sets at a lower cost and greater speed.

Pioneer: As its name suggests, the third dimension of cloud adoption is where an enterprise can extend the cloud's value once it has reached a certain level of cloud maturity. Companies can harness the cloud to experiment with new technologies, such as AI, blockchain, quantum computing, augmented and virtual reality, and 3-D printing.

With agile operating models, organizations in the pioneer mode can set up nimble "SWAT teams" to develop proofs of concept. This advanced level of cloud maturity has the additional benefit of attracting and retaining top talent to work on emerging technologies. While the impact of nascent technologies is difficult to calculate, leaders need to account for potential applications and commit to understanding their potential value.

What Mature Cloud Adopters Get Right

The cloud offers tremendous value, but the benefits don't appear magically. Fully realizing its value requires a well-defined, value-oriented strategy and coordinated execution by IT, clinical, and business leaders.

Organizations with high cloud maturity exhibit different adoption mindsets than their peers. One study of organizations with higher cloud maturity shows that they share several traits: They were early adopters of cutting-edge technology (71%), they aggressively innovate (72%), and view technology as a competitive differentiator and critical enabler for launching and building new services and solutions (79%). By being the first to move, these organizations gain considerable experience, outstripping their peers in cloud outcomes.[4,5]

Impact of cloud use cases and improvements
Estimated 2030 EBITDA[1] run-rate impact

■ 1. Rejuvenate ■ 2. Innovate

	#of companies	EBITDA impact, $ billion
High tech	30	110–160
Oil & gas	45	80–160
Retail	64	90–140
Healthcare systems & services	30	70–140
Insurance	45	70–110
Banking	36	60–80
Automative & assembly	23	40–60
Telecom	12	40–60
Advanced electronics & semiconductors	25	30–50

[1]Earnings before interest, taxes, depreciation, and amortization.
Source: Independent third-party research data (Omnicom Group and Known), industry and McKinsey expert interviews, McKinsey D2020 IT cost benchmarking, McKinsey Global Institure research

Today, it is estimated that about half of all health information technology workloads are deployed in the cloud. Eight out of 10 healthcare stakeholders now consider cloud a strategic priority. For those organizations choosing to leverage the power of the cloud to gain strategic advantage, McKinsey and Company suggests following three best practices[6]:

■ Executing a well-defined, value-oriented strategy across IT and businesses and installing a cloud-ready operating model.
■ Developing firsthand experience with the cloud and adopting a more technology-forward mindset than their peers.
■ Excelling at developing a cloud-literate workforce.

The remainder of this chapter is designed to serve as an at-a-glance review of fundamental cloud concepts.

A Bright Cloudy Future

Cloud computing – also known simply as "the cloud" – is a model for enabling ubiquitous, convenient, on-demand network access to a shared pool of configurable computing resources. This includes networks, servers, storage, applications, and services. All of the resources needed or required can be rapidly provisioned and flexibly scaled to meet the changing needs of an organization.[7]

The cloud has many distinguishing features compared to conventional "on-premises" systems that people traditionally use to do computing.[8]

The cloud's system of networked datacenters offers users access to immense computing storage capacity. Users can access this storage in a scalable fashion, paying for more capacity when they require more storage. Think, for example, of a rapidly growing organization that can smoothly scale the amount of computer storage and computing power it needs without having to upgrade its infrastructure as it grows.

In addition to storage capacity, a cloud provider's network of datacenters offers users the ability to draw on large amounts of computing capacity, again in a scalable fashion. This is very convenient for organizations that experience fluctuations in their computing needs. For example, consider clinical research projects involving genomic data that have to scale up capacity during the research rapidly but then return to a lower capacity once the study is completed.

It is the cloud's ability to store and process immense amounts of data with vast amounts of computing power that is at the core of data-driven technologies like AI and data analytics.

Due to the distributed and networked nature of the cloud, users can access it anywhere, allowing them to work, record, and access data wherever they happen to be. This is especially valuable in allowing for the global reach of any cloud-based services and work that enables establishing global working research communities.

Benefits of AI in the Cloud

Artificial intelligence was once the stuff of science fiction. However, it is no longer simply a promise; it is happening now, enriching our personal lives through intelligent assistants such as Cortana, Siri, and Alexa. It is helping hospitals more easily detect errors by recognizing anomalies in best clinical practices, improving throughput efficiencies in hospitals, and a variety of other value-driven use cases.

Such things are possible today because of the cloud's computing power and storage.

To give a sense of the speed at which cloud-based AI can complete tasks, a system from Microsoft can now translate the entire English-language version of Wikipedia into another primary language in less than one-tenth of a second, or the time it takes to blink an eye. It has also learned the ability to process human speech at the same level as a human and provide for real-time translation of conversations.[9]

AI's ability to learn and process huge amounts of data because of the cloud offers immense potential to develop systems that allow us to improve the quality and efficiencies in providing health and medical services in a personalized manner.

Simply put, AI is computational intelligence. As we learned in Chapter 5, artificial intelligence gives machines the ability to depict or mimic human brain functions, including learning, speech, problem-solving, vision, and knowledge generation. The value of this comes when it helps humans complete tasks and make decisions more quickly and effectively. All of this is driven by the advances made in the cloud. Beyond speed and power, here are other benefits:

Availability of advanced AI capabilities: Many AI applications generally depend on high performance environments, including servers with multiple and high-speed Graphics Processing Units (GPUs). Such systems are expensive to purchase and unaffordable for many organizations. AI as a service in the cloud becomes accessible to most organizations at a more affordable price.

Cost-effectiveness: With computational capabilities and storage always available online, the cloud eliminates expenses for on-site hardware, software licenses, and set up for AI and advanced analytic solutions. It also eliminates the need for on-site data centers and the costs that come with them. An additional benefit is the shift of expenditures from a capital expense model to an operating expense model from a budgeting perspective.

Increased productivity: Unlike an on-site server, hard drive, or local storage devices, which require IT management, cloud computing is internet-based and reduces or eliminates the need for managing activities like hardware setup, software patching, racking, and stacking. The key to productivity gains is how the cloud frees up valuable IT staff to focus on higher-value activities and allows data scientists and informaticists to be more agile in developing and managing AI solutions.

Reliability: Cloud computing solutions typically ensure a higher degree of business continuity. When managing hardware, software, and connectivity in a physically accessible infrastructure, the risk of crashes, lost files, and other risks are higher than cloud computing. Cloud computing makes data backup, disaster recovery, and business continuity easier and less expensive because data can be mirrored at multiple redundant sites on a cloud provider's network.

Rapid elasticity: This cloud feature is especially important for situations where the volume or computing load varies. This means that when demand for computational or transactional services increases, you can automatically scale by adding more resources. When demand wanes, you can shrink or decrease the resources and costs to fit, thereby not ending up with unneeded resources.

Performance: The large, global cloud computing service providers run on a worldwide network of secure data centers, regularly upgraded to the latest generation of fast and efficient computing hardware. This offers several benefits over maintaining a single corporate data center, including reduced application latency and greater economies of scale.

On demand self-service: Most cloud computing services are provided as self-service and on demand, so that even vast amounts of computing resources can be provisioned on a "just-in-time" basis, typically with just a few mouse clicks, providing health organizations with a lot of flexibility and taking pressure off of capacity planning.

Security: Many cloud providers offer a broad set of policies, technologies, and controls that strengthen your security posture overall, helping to protect your data, apps, and infrastructure from potential threats. This includes specific policies, protocols, and activities to manage data according to security and privacy standards such as HIPAA (United States) and GDPR (Europe).

Cloud Computing Delivery Models

There are three core types of cloud service models in use today:

Infrastructure as a service (IaaS): Processing, storage, networks, and other fundamental computing resources. The customer does not manage or control the underlying cloud infrastructure but controls the operating systems, storage, and deployed applications. This allows customers to outsource their core computing functions, utilizing the reliability, scalability, and cost-effectiveness of the cloud.

Platform as a service (PaaS): This allows the customer to create and deploy custom applications that run in the cloud using programing languages and tools supported by the provider. The customer does not manage or control the underlying cloud infrastructure but controls the deployed applications.

Software as a service (SaaS): The provision of "off-the-shelf" applications running on cloud infrastructure. The applications are accessible from any device with an internet connection via a web browser.[10]

Lastly, public cloud providers typically offer different cloud service models or "service types." It is important to understand these, as they play a crucial role when selecting a cloud deployment model. Here are the three most common cloud service models:

Software as a service (SaaS): Software hosted in the cloud by a 3rd party or cloud provider that users can access over a web browser via the internet. "SaaS" eliminates the need for individual users to install software on their personal computers. Examples include Google Apps and Microsoft O365.

Platform as a service (PaaS): A common/core platform hosted and maintained by the cloud provider. "PaaS" allows users to develop software without maintaining the underlying infrastructure. It often includes version control and compile services and computing and storage resources.

Infrastructure as a service (IaaS): Referred to as the aggregate of services (network, compute, storage) hosted and maintained by the cloud provider. "IaaS" makes it simpler for companies to onboard to the cloud and is often more cost-efficient than purchasing and maintaining hardware on-site. An example would be Amazon's AWS EC2 or Google's Compute Engine.

Cloud Deployment Types

The models described above can be deployed in several ways depending on the type of service and data used and the level of security required. These include:

Public cloud: As the title suggests, this model is openly available to the general public, creating and storing data on third-party servers. Public cloud services providers typically offer resources for a low fee or pay-per-use basis and allow users to scale them when required.

Private cloud: A private cloud refers to cloud computing resources used exclusively by a single business or organization. A private cloud can physically be located in a company's on-site data center. Some companies also pay third-party service providers to host a private cloud. There is little to no difference between public and private clouds from a technical perspective. The main difference is that a private cloud is one in which the services and infrastructure are maintained on a private network. As such, the advantages of a private cloud include greater control over system performance and scalability.

This one is often referred to as "internal" or "corporate cloud." Unlike the public cloud, it provides a dedicated environment and services to a single company. A private cloud can either be hosted on premises (meaning on hardware running in a data center owned by that company) or at a data center owned and managed by a third party on behalf of the customer. As you might imagine, on-premise vs. third-party data centers have very different operational costs and responsibility models. The focus is typically on how services are made available to a single company, thus allowing logical and physical access to authorized users.

Hybrid cloud: The hybrid deployment model uses a mix of on-premise, private and third-party public cloud services. This creates a setup where one or many touchpoints exist between the environments and gives providers the freedom to choose which apps and resources to keep exclusively in their data center and which to place in the cloud. By allowing data and applications to move between private and public clouds, a hybrid cloud provides organizations with greater flexibility, more deployment options. It helps optimize existing infrastructure, security, and compliance protocols.

Multi-cloud: A multi-cloud deployment model refers to one that leverages cloud computing services (storage, computing, applications, etc.) from more than a single cloud provider.

A common question is: "What is the difference between hybrid and multi-cloud?" A hybrid cloud refers to the pairing of both private and public clouds. As previously mentioned, it relies on a private data center (third-party hosted or on premises), typically used to host sensitive data, while also leveraging the computing power/resources of a public cloud. A multi-cloud model can include using a hybrid cloud, but it relies on more than a single cloud. For example, a company may choose to store sensitive data in their on-premise data center, leverage one cloud provider for the "IaaS" services and a second public cloud provider for their "SaaS" services.

While the benefits of data and AI in the cloud are clear, it's essential to recognize that there will continue to be dependencies with on-premises data and solutions in real-world health settings. Knowing how and when to tie together your cloud and on-premise strategy is key to driving sustainable value.

IT leaders are in the best position to plan and map data to the optimal configuration for performance and security. Today's environment typically makes this discussion a moving target influenced by factors such as security standards, migration plans for moving applications and workloads to the cloud, and other scenarios managed by IT leadership.

The Opportunities and Challenges of Cloud and AI

If the cloud is the engine that underpins the growth of intelligent health systems, data is the fuel that will power it. The analytic tools that will generate insights on how we can build healthier populations are data-driven and data-hungry. The more data these systems can process, the more valuable their outputs are, allowing health organizations to improve health and medical services at scale.

Cloud computing represents a seismic shift from traditional computing – not just in what it enables but in how it is built, managed, and used. To address the risks and threats of the cloud computing era, health organizations will need to adapt existing security programs and policies and enhance current approaches to ensuring the security and resilience of their systems in keeping with existing laws and regulations such as HIPAA and GDPR, but also to new policies and laws being created to address new issues emerging from the use of AI (Chapter 20).

The shift will require closer cooperation with cloud vendors to ensure the security and compliance outcomes required in health and a change in how the regulatory landscape is managed.

Cloud computing and artificial intelligence are partners in the move toward Intelligent Health Systems. The benefits of melding these two technologies should be evident to any health organization that wishes to harness their combined power. Cloud computing is the engine that drives the value and power of AI. With this pair of technologies constantly reinforcing each other, the power and clarity of cloud and AI strategies will become exponentially more important in the coming years.

EDGE COMPUTING AND THE CLOUD

Edge computing is fueling the growth of intelligent health solutions. It's an important building block to making "care anywhere" real. So, what exactly is edge computing?

Gartner, a global research and advisory firm, defines edge computing as solutions that facilitate data processing at or near the source of data generation.[11] Think about remote monitoring. An Internet of Things (IoT) example is data is generated via sensors or embedded devices. Edge computing moves computing to the edge of the network, where it's closest to users and devices. Most important it allows computation to be done as close as possible to data sources.

In cloud computing, data is generated or collected from many locations and then moved to the cloud, where computing is centralized. Centralized cloud computing makes it easier and cheaper to process data together and at scale. But there are situations when sending data to the

---

(Continued)

cloud for processing doesn't make sense or is not possible. This includes situations where a device needs to analyze data quickly to make split second decisions or when data can't be transferred offsite due to security or privacy regulations.

Edge computing acts on data at the source. Think of it as a distributed computing framework that brings enterprise applications closer to data sources such as Internet of Things (IoT) devices or local edge servers. This proximity to data at its source enables AI applications by providing the following benefits[12]:

Better data control: There is greater control in preserving data fidelity tapping directly into the source. It also the point where controls to address data privacy can be added.

Speed: Edge computing is always on and has low latency thanks to reduced network uptime, round-trip times, and bandwidth constraints.

Lower costs: Processing at the edge makes cloud uploads and storage cheaper.

A question that often arises is whether edge computing will replace cloud computing?

The simple answer is that the cloud and edge computing are distinct but complementary. The cloud centralizes data to create new analytics and applications. These can be distributed on the edge. By residing on-site or with the consumer, it generates more data that is fed back into the cloud to optimize the experience.

Instead of seeing cloud and edge computing as rivals they should be viewed as part of an intelligent cloud continuum.

A BRIEF HISTORY OF THE CLOUD – AKA THE INTERGALACTIC COMPUTER NETWORK

When it comes to the evolution of the cloud, much of what we know and use today has its **roots going back to the 1950s.** It started with the emergence of mainframe computing that allowed multiple users to access a centralized computer through "dumb terminals." Providing shared access to a single computer resource was pretty revolutionary at the time.

(Continued)

With the arrival of the 1960s, and in keeping with the times, came some "totally-far-out-ideas" on where shared computing might go. Four years before the TV Series Star Trek debuted and first popularized the concept of Intergalactic Travel, Dr. Joseph Carl Robnett Licklider (to his friends simply known as "Lick"), was imagining and postulating ideas around the creation of what he called an "Intergalactic Computer Network."

Lick was a psychologist and an early computer scientist who put out a series of memos in 1962 outlining what then was considered science fiction-grade material. At a time when computers were only thought of as mathematical devices for speeding up computations, he wrote about the concept of a global network of time-sharing computers that would include graphical computing and user-friendly interfaces to drive everything from digital libraries to e-commerce.

While serving as director at the US Department of Defense Advanced Research Projects Agency (ARPA), it was Dr. Licklider's persuasive and detailed description of the challenges to establishing a time-sharing network of computers that ultimately led to the creation of the ARPAnet, considered by tech historians as the precursor to the internet as it was the first network to implement TCP/IP protocols, the rules that govern how computer systems communicate in a network and how data is transferred from one system to another.

With the 1970s came the concept of virtual machines (VMs). Essentially VMs took the 1950s concept of shared access to a new level by permitting multiple distinct computing capabilities and environments to reside in one physical environment. Virtualization was an important catalyst for the communication and information revolution that was to come in the 1990s.

The 1980s brought about the personal computer revolution upon which cloud computing and shared access would be dependent. This meant there would eventually be devices to connect together. In the late eighties something known as the "internet" began to come into the public consciousness as a new type of space whereby personal computers could be connected together to communicate and share information. Companies like AOL, CompuServe and Prodigy began springing up to provide connections and prepackaged services like email. As we rolled into the nineties these top service providers were now offering modem connections that promised an anemic top speed of 9,600 bits per second.

(Continued)

With the 1990s came telecommunication companies that began leveraging virtualization to offer virtual private networks (VPNs). Up until that point, telecommunications companies only offered single dedicated point-to-point data connections. The newly offered virtualized private network connections had the same service quality as dedicated services at a reduced cost. A VPN extended a private network across a public network, enabling users to send and receive data across shared or public networks as if their computing devices were directly connected to the private network. The use of virtual computers became the starting point for the creation of the cloud's computing infrastructure.

As the story goes, it was 1997 when Professor Ramnath Chellapa gave an identity to this set of things happening between computers operating on public and private networks by defining cloud computing as a new computing paradigm, where the "boundaries of computing would be determined by economic rationale, rather than technical limits alone."[13] In this early stage, this definition of the cloud was used to express the empty space that existed between the end user and the provider.

As we came into the 2000s the rest is history. Salesforce was an early example of using the cloud to deliver software to end users. Amazon introduced and first popularized the use of online retail services and later altered their business model by introducing Amazon Web Services to offer its online services infrastructure to other clients. Microsoft began moving delivery and maintenance of its core software from shrink-wrapped discs to the cloud while curating a host of other cloud-native services that are now the company's core solutions and offerings.

Today, most global providers of cloud services are releasing and managing cloud services specific to health and medicine. This includes Microsoft, Google, and AWS. The goal of these health-centric cloud platforms is to facilitate rapid deployment of AI and other solutions through the provision of health-specific configurations, connectors, and applications. They are also deployed and managed in compliance with health specific privacy and security standards. Additionally, they are configured in ways that better accommodate health-specific data interoperability standards such as Fast Healthcare Interoperability Resources (FHIR). FHIR is a standard describing data formats and elements and an application programming interface for exchanging electronic health records.

Notes

1. Tyler Clifford, "How Moderna is using Amazon cloud to produce personalized cancer vaccines," CNBC, January 15, 2020, cnbc.com
2. Clifford, "How Moderna is using Amazon cloud," 2020.
3. What matters most? Five priorities for CEOs in the next normal, McKinsey & Company, September 2021, https://www.mckinsey.com/business-functions/strategy-and-corporate-finance/our-insights/what-matters-most-five-priorities-for-ceos-in-the-next-normal.
4. Source: Data from cloud-migration experience of AWS and independent third-party research data (OmnicomGroup and Known).
5. What matters most? Five priorities for CEOs in the next normal, McKinsey & Company, September 2021, https://www.mckinsey.com/business-functions/strategy-and-corporate-finance/our-insights/what-matters-most-five-priorities-for-ceos-in-the-next-normal.
6. Ibid.
7. A Cloud for Social Good, Microsoft, https://news.microsoft.com/cloudforgood/spotlight/what-is-cloud.html.
8. A Cloud for Social Good, Microsoft, https://news.microsoft.com/cloudforgood/spotlight/what-is-cloud.html.
9. Ibid.
10. Ibid.
11. Rob van der Meulen, What Edge Computing Means for Infrastructure and Operations Leaders, Gartner, October 3, 2018, https://www.gartner.com/smarterwithgartner/what-edge-computing-means-for-infrastructure-and-operations-leaders.
12. Teresa Tung, What is edge computing? Accenture, February 15, 2021, https://www.accenture.com/us-en/blogs/cloud-computing/what-you-need-to-know-about-edge-computing.
13. Keith Foote, A Brief History of Cloud Computing, Dataversity, 2017, https://www.dataversity.net/brief-history-cloud-computing/.

Chapter 20

Intelligent Health Needs Gas and Guardrails

Give me a place to stand, a lever long enough and I can move the Earth.

Archimedes

While we are early in the journey to apply artificial intelligence (AI), there is no turning back. Instead, it's about moving forward with plans to harness its power. It's about having a societal discussion that creates pathways for AI to do good while building appropriate guardrails to keep it from running amok.

Doing so allows us to embrace healthcare's future with imagination and a sense of hope for genuine change and reform.

To track the societal change coming about from AI, Stanford University launched the One Hundred Year Study of Artificial Intelligence (AI100). It's a longitudinal study to anticipate and report on how artificial intelligence will ripple through every aspect of how people work, play, and live.[1,2]

One focus area is the cause of delays in translating AI advances into real-world value.

Healthcare is called out in the framing of this initiative:

Numerous advances in AI can reduce costs, introduce new efficiencies, and raise the quality of life. For example, machine learning and inference can play a significant role with reducing costs and enhancing the quality of healthcare. However, the methods have not come into wide use. The sluggish translation of these technologies into the world translates into unnecessary deaths and costs. There is an urgent need to better understand how we can more quickly translate valuable existing AI competencies and advances into real-world practice.[3]

Getting AI up and running to its fullest potential in healthcare could fuel some of the greatest achievements in health and medicine in our lifetime.

Here are some of the things that can be done to accomplish that while smoothing out the speed bumps and creating guardrails to ensure it produces positive results while minimizing the potential for harm.

Actions That Support AI as a Positive Force for Change

Reimagining healthcare through applied design thinking: In the rapidly changing health and medicine markets, innovation gives organizations the upper hand. It's the ability to conceive actionable and effective ideas to make an organization more competitive and better at achieving its goals.

And while many of us consider ourselves innovators, true innovation doesn't always come easily. That's where reimagining through applied design thinking comes in.

Design thinking began as a way of teaching engineers how to approach problems creatively as designers do. Today it is a discipline and process used to drive change in products, organizations, and social innovation.

Design thinking is both an ideology and a process that seeks to solve complex problems in a user-centric way. It focuses on achieving practical results and solutions that are as follows:

- ■ Technically feasible: They can be developed into functional products or processes;
- ■ Economically viable: The business can afford to implement them;
- ■ Desirable for the user: They meet a real human need.

Design thinking adopts a designer's mindset and approaches the problem from the user's perspective. At the same time, design thinking is all about getting hands-on; the aim is to turn ideas into tangible, testable products or processes as quickly as possible.[4]

Many health organizations use design thinking to reimagine and redevelop services and workflow processes to support their missions, clinical and business goals.

The value of AI comes from innovating the way we work; design thinking is an approach that supports the process of change to help organizations realize greater value from their AI investments. There are many resources available today to assist organizations in using design thinking to innovate.

Financial incentives that drive new health models: In the time it takes to read this sentence, $7 million will be spent on healthcare in America. On average, this is the amount of money that trades hands as you read each sentence in this book.

America spends an average of $12,530 yearly on healthcare for every citizen.[5] It's a big number that might be considered a worthy expense *if* the health status of individuals and the nation reflected that investment. But as we learned in Chapter 3, the United States ranks last in every key health measure compared to other countries.

Fifty percent of all health expenditures in the United States are spent on just 5% of the population.[6] What this means is that healthcare spending is highly concentrated among a very small number of high-cost users.[7] At the other end of the spending spectrum, half of the population accounts for just 3% of healthcare spending.[8]

Follow the trail of how healthcare dollars are spent today, and you see that most dollars are spent reactively, paying to treat people after they become ill or injured.

To be clear, physicians and medical professionals are the best trained and dedicated to keeping people healthy and meeting their needs when they are not. Unfortunately, they too are caught in a system designed decades ago that still incentivizes the number of procedures performed once there is an illness or injury to manage.

Consumers want a system that is more proactive than reactive and focuses more on keeping people healthy, not just fixing them when they are sick. Making this happen will require financial incentives and reimbursement policy changes to create economic parity for intelligent health services that proactively support new ways of managing health in addition to managing care when people are injured or ill.

Value-based care is a promising delivery model where providers are rewarded for helping patients improve their health, reduce the effects and incidence of chronic disease, and live healthier lives in an evidence-based way.

Today, we're used to a health system that takes care of people after they are already sick. Traditional fee-for-service models today pay providers based on the number of healthcare services they deliver. The "value" in value-based healthcare is derived from measuring health outcomes against the cost of delivering the outcomes.[9]

Value-based health care benefits

PATIENTS	PROVIDERS	PAYERS	SUPPLIERS	SOCIETY
Lower costs & better outcomes	Higher patient satisfaction rates & better care efficiencies	Stronger cost controls & reduced risks	Alignment of prices with patient outcomes	Reduced healthcare spending & better overall health

NEJM Catalyst (catalyst.nejm.org) © Massachusetts Medical Society
https://catalyst.nejm.org/doi/full/10.1056/CAT.17.0558

In a value-based care model, providers are rewarded for things like successful surgical procedures, reduced side effects, symptoms, and incidences of chronic disease, and measurably healthier lives. In value-based care models, it's all about the quality of care rather than the number of services provided. It's a patient-centered approach that focuses on prevention, wellness, and improved coordination of services provided throughout the care continuum.

We learned from the pandemic that telehealth works and effectively provides high-quality services that are convenient and cost-effective. According to a study by McKinsey & Company, 58% of physicians continue to view telehealth more favorably now than they did before COVID. As of the spring of 2021, 84% of physicians were offering virtual visits, and 57% would prefer to continue offering virtual care. However, 54% would not offer virtual care if they have to provide it at a 15% discount to in-person care.[10]

Hospital-at-Home (HaH) is another model that leverages AI and digital solutions to effectively provide care and services that keep people out of high-cost hospitals. A growing body of evidence shows that for some medical conditions; HaH is more effective in producing good outcomes while also being more cost-effective and convenient.

With the pandemic came a temporary loosening of federal regulations and reimbursement policies to expand telehealth and Hospital-at-Home programs. Looking ahead, service and payment parity must be established across all payers to increase access to such services for patients and incentivize providers to provide and expand such services.

Ensuring equitable access: As healthcare organizations embrace telehealth, several fixable issues will ensure that the benefits of digital and other services benefit all populations rather than certain groups. Here are three areas to be addressed:

- **Connectivity:** The lack of broadband access still exists, including rural communities that stand to benefit the most from telehealth and other intelligent health solutions. A study by the Harvard School of Public Health showed that 21% of rural Americans reported access to high-speed internet is a problem for them or their family.[11]
- **Digital literacy:** Health consumers who lack digital literacy skills may soon find themselves at just as much of a disadvantage as those who cannot read or write. This term encompasses a wide range of skills necessary to succeed in a digital world. It's the ability to find, evaluate, utilize, share, and create content using information technologies and the internet.[12] Many younger people grew up learning these skills. Some older people or those with limited access to technology may lack the necessary skills to benefit from telehealth and virtual care services. For example, Pew Research notes that 27% of US adults reported not using the internet.[13]
- **Access to technology:** Access to telehealth via smartphones or computers is particularly challenging for older and low-income people. A study by the Kaiser Family Foundation notes that only 68% of adults age 65 and older say they have a computer, smartphone, or tablet with internet access at home, compared to virtually 100% of adults age 30–49 and 85% of adults age 50–64.[14]

Interoperability of data and systems: The lack of interoperability is a critical barrier to adopting intelligent and widescale digital transformation of healthcare. Liberating data from silos and generally making it easier to use produce significant returns, including:

- Ready-to-use patient-centric information enables advanced clinical decision support in diagnostics and treatment.
- Better care coordination can greatly benefit from sharing data in uniform formats that all players can interpret.
- Patients' access to their health data can empower them to pursue a healthy life and actively manage their condition.
- Operational data can help smoothen workflow and enable outcomes-driven improvement cycles.

Better interoperability will help deliver better care at lower cost. Interoperability issues to be solved come in two forms:

■ **Data interoperability:** Unifying data to improve health decisions and processes is highly dependent on data interoperability. This means creating a standard health information technology infrastructure that allows seamless electronic access, exchange, and use of information from multiple sources.

■ **System and device interoperability:** As noted in Chapter 11, there is a need to join together those information systems and devices used by traditional health systems with the growing array of digital devices and solutions that reside outside the walls of healthcare organizations used by consumers to monitor and manage health.

Much of this chasm has been created by default. Medical practitioners did not see the value of outside data or did not have the means or expertise to bring them together.

As the market moves toward new models, the challenge is that there is no single digital health interoperability standard. Instead, there is a diversity of standards, specifications, and profiles coming from various organizations and initiatives. Many of these have organically emerged to meet interoperability needs around specific uses. This has resulted in a fragmented environment that holds back the adoption of information and communication technologies (ICT) in healthcare. Other industries, including mobile communications, consumer electronics, banking, and commerce, have delivered interoperable data flows and standards while preserving competition. The health and medical industry must do the same.

Decision Makers: Importance of moving to a single telehealth platform integrated into other systems such as EHRs

Extremely important — 20%
Very important — 57%
Somewhat important — 20%
Not very important — 3%
Not at all important — 0%

Source: Amwell and HIMSS Analytics survey, October 2021
www.beckershospitalreview.com/hospital-execs-eye-expanded-virtual-care-and-streamlined-platforms-in-years-ahead-2.html

Education, training, and career planning: Today, many traditional organizational training programs are limited in scope and focused on maintaining or improving existing competencies. While some innovative training and development programs are emerging, new training solutions that match the scale of change produced by AI will be needed.

The move toward an AI-enabled work environment puts new pressures on existing workforce skill challenges. These challenges include:

- Increasing demand for advanced technology and cognitive skills such as critical thinking and complex information processing.
- As intelligent machines are integrated more deeply into the workplace, workflows will change and require skill sets that allow employees to effectively interact and collaborate with intelligent systems.
- Automation of human-driven processes means some workers will likely need to change occupations.

Scaling and reimagining job retraining and workforce skill development is a crucial area for investment for those organizations that successfully transition to become intelligent work environments. This includes the need for learning and development programs to be integrated into the technology strategies.

A successful AI plan must include how to best match people and machines as the decisions being made today will have a long-tail effect on workforce composition, productivity, and operating margins for years to come.

Guardrails to Put in Place to Prevent Harmful or Unintended Consequences

Privacy, security, and compliance: As previously noted, AI solutions are developing faster than regulatory agencies can keep up. The result is that AI-related issues are emerging beyond the security and compliance regulations that health organizations manage today. In the United States, this includes HIPAA. In Europe, this includes GDPR.

AI is governed by the same laws and regulations as any system involving Personal Health Information (PHI). The massive quantity of data used by AI and how the use of the data can change over time is one of the new challenges.

For example, HIPAA provides parameters for the de-identification of data. The problem is that intelligent technologies can now re-identify such data. Current guidance provided by HIPAA and other policies and regulations doesn't consider these new developments.[15]

Various privacy issues are coming forward that are not addressed by current policies. For example, AI can predict private health information about a consumer even though the algorithm never received that information. An AI system might accurately infer that a person has Parkinson's disease based on the trembling of a computer mouse or movement pattern measured from a mobile app or device, even if the person had never revealed that information to anyone or sought treatment for the condition.

Despite AI's potential benefits, policy-making bodies, including the Food and Drug Administration (FDA), the Federal Trade Commission (FTC), and other agencies, must work to provide guidance and regulations that create appropriate safeguards for AI without significantly stifling its use.

Mobile app governance (privacy, security, and classification): Thanks to a cornucopia of health and medically themed apps, personal health is becoming increasingly mobile. From lifestyle planning to managing chronic conditions, there are thousands of apps from sites like Apple App Store or Google Play.

But here is the question: Can you trust these apps the same way you would trust a prescribed drug or a medical device regulated by the FDA? Perhaps scrutiny of a step counter or something simple like a diet planner doesn't concern you, but do you know what is being done with the data being collected by the app?

Health and medical apps hold the promise of improving health, reducing medical errors, and avoiding costly interventions. They also have the potential to broaden access to care. But to reach their potential, these products must be safe, effective, and hold up to the same rules and regulations used to validate product claims.

Today the jurisdiction of the FDA is limited. The line is blurry between what constitutes a medical app and a health and fitness app. The situation frustrates legitimate developers while opening the door for unscrupulous opportunists to cash in on the digital health space.

Beyond the annoyance of downloading and using an app that doesn't work as claimed or the dangers of using a product that makes potentially harmful mistakes are other issues relating to the collected data. Many developers of mobile apps are less than transparent about how collected data is managed and used.

A study of 21,000 health apps published in the British Medical Journal (BMJ) found that[16]:

- 28.1% of the apps provided no privacy policies;
- 23.0% of the apps transmitted user data insecurely;
- 1.3% of user reviews raised concerns about privacy.

As the health and medical app explosion continues, the federal government is taking a deeper look at how to respond. The Federal Trade Commission (FTC) recently resurrected a decade-old transparency rule requiring health apps to tell users about data breaches. Many health apps often have poor data protection systems or violate their own privacy policies by sharing data with outside groups without informing users. New guidance from the FTC clarifies that the Health Breach Notification Rule applies to these platforms as well and failure to comply will result in hefty fines.[17]

Universal standards for Responsible AI: From a historical perspective, technology capabilities often get ahead of the lawmakers and regulators in creating standards by which society can best benefit from such breakthroughs. One only needs to look at the advent of the internet to understand the likely trajectory of legal and ethical issues arising from AI.

As the internet began to be widely used by consumers and businesses in the late 1990s, it generated a plethora of issues on privacy and other matters not covered by existing laws and regulations. At that time, one would have been hard-pressed to find a full-time "privacy lawyer."

This legal specialty emerged as governments began assessing and creating privacy laws and regulations to guide and govern the appropriate use of consumer and patient data.[18]

Today, the International Association of Privacy Professionals, or IAPP (founded in 1997), has over 20,000 members in 83 countries.[19]

Just as in the early days of the internet, there are areas where better definition is needed. While the system works to catch up, it is essential to define a set of standards and principles that guide the use of AI. And while the capabilities and use of AI will continue to evolve, the creation and use of principles for responsible AI should remain fixed and used to guide its use going forward.

There are many legal and ethical issues arising from AI in health and medicine. At this time, legislators and regulators are working to identify and address issues that balance the opportunities to use AI to improve health and medicine with safeguards to protect the rights of citizens and ensure that other standards like fairness are defined and codified.

While an important topic, AI ethics lacks benchmarks and consensus. Many public and private groups are producing a range of qualitative or normative outputs in the AI ethics domain. A challenge with this is that the field generally lacks agreed-upon benchmarks that can be used to measure or assess the relationship between broader societal discussions about AI development and how it is applied responsibly.[20]

There are new and emerging issues regarding the legal and ethical considerations of deploying AI. Such issues go beyond the security and compliance rules and regulations that health organizations must manage today. And while AI is governed by the same laws and regulations as any systems involving PHI, new issues are arising from AI, which are currently not addressed by existing laws and regulations.

AI is enabling humans to harness vast amounts of data and make breakthrough advances in medicine and the delivery of health services. This is happening across the continuum of needs, service offerings, and care settings. But as we already see in other industries, advances in the use of AI that bring us daily benefits are also raising a host of questions and concerns. These issues will affect how all goods and services, including healthcare, are provided.

Keeping in mind that there currently is not a universally agreed set of standards, the following are a shortened version of Microsoft's Principles for Responsible AI worth considering:

> *Fairness – AI systems should treat all people fairly;*
> *Reliability – AI systems should perform reliably and safely;*
> *Privacy and Security – AI systems should be secure and respect privacy;*
> *Inclusiveness – AI systems should empower everyone and engage people;*
> *Transparency and accountability – AI systems should be transparent in how systems make decisions.*

Notes

1. Artificial Intelligence and Life in 2030, Stanford University, 2016, https://ai100. stanford.edu/sites/g/files/sbiybj9861/f/ai100report10032016fnl_singles.pdf.
2. Artificial Intelligence and Life in 2030, Stanford University, 2016, https://ai100. stanford.edu/sites/g/files/sbiybj9861/f/ai100report10032016fnl_singles.pdfOne-Hundred Year Study on Artificial Intelligence: Reflections and Framing.
3. Ibid.
4. Emily Stevens, What is design thinking, and how do we apply it?, Invision, January 30, 2020, https://www.invisionapp.com/inside-design/what-is-design-thinking/.

5. National Health Expenditure Data, CMS, https://www.cms.gov/Research-Statistics-Data-and-Systems/Statistics-Trends-and-Reports/NationalHealthExpendData/NationalHealthAccountsHistorical#:~:text=U.S.%20health%20care%20spending%20grew%204.6%20percent%20in,for%2017.7%20percent.%20For%20additional%20information%2C%20see%20below.

6. "UNDERSTANDING U.S. HEALTH CARE SPENDING". National Institute of Healthcare Management, July, 2011. http://www.bcnys.org/inside/health/2011/HealthCarePremiumsNIHCM0711.pdf.

7. "The High Concentration of U.S. Health Care Expenditures". Agency for Healthcare Research and Quality. https://archive.ahrq.gov/research/findings/factsheets/costs/expriach/.

8. ibid.

9. What Is Value-Based Healthcare? NEJM Catalyst, January 1, 2017.

10. McKinsey Physician Insights Survey, April 2021.

11. Life in Rural America, Harvard TH Chan School of Public Health, 2019, https://catalyst.nejm.org/doi/full/10.1056/CAT.17.0558https://media.npr.org/documents/2019/may/NPR-RWJF-HARVARD_Rural_Poll_Part_2.pdf.

12. WHAT IS DIGITAL LITERACY?, The Tech Advocate, https://www.thetechedvocate.org/what-is-digital-literacy/

13. ANDREW PERRIN AND SARA ATSKE, 7% of Americans don't use the internet. Who are they?, Pew Research Center, April 2, 2021, https://www.pewresearch.org/fact-tank/2021/04/02/7-of-americans-dont-use-the-internet-who-are-they/.

14. Juliette Cubanski, Possibilities and Limits of Telehealth for Older Adults During the COVID-19 Emergency. Kaiser Family Foundation, April 13, 2020, https://www.kff.org/policy-watch/possibilities-and-limits-of-telehealth-for-older-adults-during-the-covid-19-emergency/.

15. Jill McKeon, Security, Privacy Risks of Artificial Intelligence in Healthcare, Health IT Security, December 1, 2021, https://healthitsecurity.com/features/security-privacy-risks-of-artificial-intelligence-in-healthcare.

16. Tangari G, Ikram M, Ijaz K, Kaafar MA, Berkovsky S. Mobile health and privacy: cross sectional study BMJ 2021; 373:n1248 doi:10.1136/bmj.n1248, https://www.bmj.com/content/373/bmj.n1248.

17. Nicole Wetsman, FTC resurrects a decade-old rule as a guardrail on the health app explosion, The Verge, September 22, 2021, https://www.msn.com/en-us/news/technology/ftc-resurrects-a-decade-old-rule-as-a-guardrail-on-the-health-app-explosion/ar-AAOIlsk.

18. The Future Computed: Artificial Intelligence and its Role in Society, Brad Smith & Harry Shum, Microsoft, 2018, https://news.microsoft.com/futurecomputed/.

19. Ibid.

20. Artificial Intelligence Index Report, Stanford University Human Centered Artificial Intelligence, 2021.

Chapter 21

The Future Is Not What It Used to Be

Any sufficiently advanced technology is indistinguishable from magic.

Arthur C. Clarke
Co-author, 2001: A Space Odyssey

If we perfected time travel, I would add Pasadena, California, on April 10, 1953, to my list of desired destinations. Mark Sullivan, President of Pacific Telephone and Telegraph, was giving a talk on the future of the telephone. Here is his prophecy from 60 years ago: *"In its final development, the telephone will be carried about by the individual, perhaps as we carry a watch today. It probably will require no dial or equivalent and I think users will be able see each other if they want as they talk. Who knows but it may actually translate from one language to another."*[1]

Fast forward to 1985. A young and relatively unknown Bill Gates predicted that someday there would be a personal computer in every home. This pronouncement was met with quite a few snickers from the tech titans of the day.

And so it goes. Predicting where the Intelligent Health Revolution will take us in the future is like predicting where a tornado will land. We may know it's coming but can't know where it will land until it happens. And so, with the evolution and use of artificial intelligence (AI), what is hard to imagine today will likely become commonplace in the next decade.

Just as the early stages of other major tech trends eventually impacted the world in profound ways, there will be many experiments and discoveries in using AI. Some will fail, while others will make initial headway only to become

DOI: 10.4324/9781003286103-21

niche solutions. A few will positively change the world of health at scale. The trick is to know which ideas will be transformational in the years ahead.

The "Nexus of Forces"

Looking ahead, it's essential to understand not only what will change because of AI but also the "how and why" of such change. There will be no singular technology or application that will drive the transformation of health systems. Instead, it will be the convergence of many factors. Understanding this is key to seeing and managing the changes ahead.

The *Nexus of Forces* is a term that describes the convergence and mutual reinforcement of AI, social media, mobile computing, cloud computing, and information (Big Data).

As the concept goes, social media and mobile apps provide a platform for effective social and business interactions. At the same time, the cloud offers a convenient and cost-effective computational and delivery infrastructure. The integration of these forces rapidly decreases the gap between ideation of a concept and actions to make new concepts real. This happens through near-global connectivity, pervasive mobility, industrial-strength computing services, and instant access to vast amounts of information.[2]

We caught a glimpse of the Nexus of Forces using AI and other technologies to respond and adapt to the pandemic quickly. This level of adaptation will continue taking hold in health and medicine. It's already driving us toward more agile change and brings us closer to the realization of Intelligent Health Systems.

Intelligent Trends to Watch

Chapter 7 provided examples of AI adding value today and over the short term. Here's a look at some of the things that will likely drive substantial change in the next decade.

Precision Medicine

While we are already in the early stages of precision medicine, the intelligence and tech forces at work will move us deeper into the realm of precision medicine and health.

As the National Institutes of Health (NIH) puts it, Precision Medicine is *"an emerging approach for disease treatment and prevention that takes into account individual variability in genes, environment, and lifestyle for each person.'*[3] This approach will allow doctors and researchers to predict more accurately which treatment and prevention strategies for a particular disease will work in which individuals or groups of people. This is in contrast to a historical one-size-fits-all approach, in which disease treatment and prevention strategies are developed for the average person, with less consideration for the differences between individuals.

Based on this definition, artificial intelligence will be at the center of any health and medical solutions that personalize health and medical services down to each patient and consumer. AI will drive precision medicine to identify the right treatment for a particular patient and individualize all aspects of healthcare for that patient, including disease risk and prognosis prediction.

What if, at some point in the future, every baby received a DNA report card at birth that would rate risks and offer predictions about their chances of developing diabetes or cancer or their risk of developing addictions to things like tobacco, alcohol, or opioids? Having such a "life map" would allow us to personalize health and medical services down to the individual level. It would also open the door to a host of ethical and legal issues.

In the foreseeable future, AI will support the actual practice of precision medicine in intelligent health organizations by being deployed to analyze big medical data sets, draw conclusions, find new correlations based on patterns found in the data that are specific to an individual patient, and support the doctor's ability to develop and decide on care pathways that are specific to each patient.

For maximum impact, clinicians will also use AI algorithms to consider the latest academic research evidence and regulatory guidelines before recommending personalized treatment pathways to high-risk, high-cost patient populations. AI will also be used to expedite the process of clinical trial eligibility assessment and generate a plan that suggests evidence-based drugs.

Additionally, AI will also factor in nonmedical variables, including Social Determinants of Health. This will ensure that these factors are part of an individual's personalized plan for achieving health and well-being.

A Quantum Leap for Health

While quantum computing is heavily hyped, it should not be ignored as it holds great promise in a technology paradigm shift that most people can't imagine.

Quantum computing is a type of nonclassical computing based on the quantum state of subatomic particles. Quantum computing is fundamentally different from classic computers, which operate using binary bits. The bits are either 0 or 1, true or false, positive or negative. However, the bit is called a quantum bit or qubit in quantum computing. Unlike the strictly binary bits of classic computing, qubits can represent a range of values in one qubit. This representation is called "superpositioning."[4]

In case that definition lost you, imagine your laptop having the combined powers of every superhero in the Justice League. Quantum Computing would open the door to increased computing powers that would move us from taking years to solve complex data problems to hours. Its application to everything from cancer research to drug development would be immense.

Three Dimensional (3D) Bioprinting

Bioprinting (also known as 3D bioprinting) combines 3D printing with biomaterials to replicate parts that imitate natural tissues, bones, and blood vessels in the body. It is mainly used today in connection with drug research. It also has been used recently to create "cell scaffolds" to help repair damaged ligaments and joints.

Bioprinting has been used in medicine since 2007 to study or recreate almost every tissue, cartilage, and organ in the body.

At the Wyss Institute at Harvard, researchers have developed a 3D bioprinter that can produce vascularized tissues of living human cells printed on a chip. They use this tissue on a chip to connect to a vascular channel, which lets researchers give the tissue nutrients to monitor growth and development. The ability to grow tissue on a chip helps researchers examine new regenerative medicine and drug testing techniques.[5]

Researchers at Swansea University in Wales use bioprinting to create artificial bone materials in specific shapes using regenerative and durable materials.[6]

Steady advancements are being made in 3D bioprinting. This includes progress in the ability to bioprint bones, skin, blood vessels, cartilage, and even organs. While there is still much progress to be made before most of these practices are adapted into human medicine, this trend holds the promise of collecting data as well as noninvasive ways to see how the human body interacts with certain substances, which could lead to more personalized medicine for patients and fewer side effects.

Smartdust

Speaking of 3D printing, imagine a complete sensing and computing platform smaller than a grain of sand. Welcome to the world of "smartdust." The *"dust"* itself is a set of microelectromechanical systems (MEMS), more commonly known as motes, which pack an incredible punch considering their limited size. They can detect light, vibrations, and temperature, magnetism, or chemicals; they combine sensing, autonomous power supplies, computing, and wireless communication.

Smart dust components can be 3D printed and collect data on acceleration, stress, pressure, humidity, sound, and more with their sensors. This data can then be processed with what amounts to an onboard computer system, as well as stored and communicated to the cloud or other MEMS. Smart dust can collect information in incredible detail. Think of it as the pinnacle of the Internet of Things.

With its ability to measure anything nearly anywhere, smart dust can aid with diagnostic procedures and make the entire care process less invasive for the patient and provide new and intuitive interfaces for the disabled.

Researchers at UC Berkeley recently built what is thought to be the smallest volume, most efficient wireless server simulator. Known as StimDust (short for *simulation neural dust*), it is intended to one day be implanted in the body through minimally invasive procedures to monitor and treat disease in a real time, patient-specific approach. StimDust is just 6.5 cubic millimeters in volume and powered wirelessly by ultrasound, which the device then uses to power nerve stimulation at an efficiency of 82%.[7]

The vision is to enlist such tiny devices to monitor or diagnose medical conditions and modulate or stimulate the peripheral nervous system, which is efficacious in treating several diseases.

Emotional AI

Imagine a time in the not-too-distant future when your personal device will know more about your emotional state than your friends or family. The ever-improving components of AI that allow machines to identify or predict what humans are feeling are giving rise to what is now being called artificial emotional intelligence or Emotion AI. This is where devices can detect emotions from multiple channels like voice, facial recognition, email, and texts just the way humans do…maybe even better.

Today, innovative retailers are already putting AI-enabled technology in their stores to evaluate shoppers' sentiment and emotional state. In the future, this information will likely be used to have in-store displays change to match the state of mind of shoppers.

When it comes to consumer and patient feedback, emotional signals can provide valuable insights based on changes in facial expressions, tone and pitch of voice, body language, and even neurophysiological activity conveyed through biometric markers that could automatically be built into the care process.

In the world of health, there are many potential applications for emotion AI including the ability to help clinicians diagnose and treat diseases such as depression and dementia. It also provides an opportunity for consumers to self-monitor and manage their own physical health emotional and wellbeing.

Biohacking

Biohacking often conjures up images of a rogue, amateur scientist in their dark basement attempting to create something nefarious or unsafe. What is happening in the medical biohacking community is quite different.

Biohacking refers to applying IT hacks to biological systems – most prominently, the human body. These opportunities range from simple diagnostics to deep neural implants. For example, biochips hold the possibility of detecting or predicting diseases from cancer to smallpox before the patient even develops symptoms. Such chips would be made from an array of intelligent molecular sensors that can analyze biological elements and chemicals.

In the United Kingdom, a woman recently was the recipient of what may be the world's first in-heart microcomputer that is designed to improve the care of those with heart failure. The wireless device allows clinicians to track patients in real time and predict when a patient is approaching a situation that requires medical attention or intervention. Heart failure is the number one reason for hospital admissions in the United Kingdom. Researchers believe that such technology can improve the health of patients in the future while reducing hospital admissions by 40% and saving the National Health Service (NHS) 75 million pounds annually.[8]

There are many legal, ethical, and societal questions that arise from biohacking. Still, AI capabilities will increasingly bring this to the forefront of medicine in the not-to-distant future.

The Advent of Data Whisperers

Among the data science and informaticist communities are those who believe that large data sets are constantly "whispering" valuable things to us that we either aren't paying attention to or do not currently have the tools to hear.

In keeping with this concept, the World Economic Forum recently defined predictive AI for population health as one of the top three ways AI will have the most significant long-term impact on global health.

One company, Cuezen, is already leveraging large data sets from governments to identify citizens at risk of chronic conditions such as diabetes and then using AI and applied "nudge theory" to create individualized plans for each citizen identified as at risk. Based on the work of Nobel Prize winner Richard Thaler, digital therapy plans are created that consumers can opt into that include a series of intelligent "microsteps" that guide citizens to actions that prevent, manage or slow the progression of a health issue.

Augmented Reality/Mixed Reality

Simply put, augmented reality (AR) or mixed reality (MR) is the process of putting digital images on top of a user's natural surroundings. In doing this, AR technology enhances the surrounding environment by overlaying digitally generated images on various surfaces around a user, which can bridge the gap between reality and imagination. And while it's often related to its own category in the tech world, it is fully dependent and driven by many components of AI.

AR is in use today to assist surgeons in providing simulations and ancillary information on demand and enhancing training by providing highly interactive experiences. It is also used to train physicians by providing a 360° view of ailments or replicating real-world procedures.

Mount Sinai Health System serves the greater New York metropolitan area. It's known for providing world-class care to those who live in the area. But there are many places on the planet where people don't have access to simple, sometimes lifesaving surgical operations.

One of these places is Uganda. To solve for this, physicians at Mount Sinai are now extending their expertise through AR tools to help surgeons perform operations 7,000 miles away. Through AR, surgeons share real-time views from the operating room and collaborate hands-free in real time with MR annotations as if they were in the same room.[9]

The Health Metaverse

Fantastic Voyage is a 1966 sci-fi movie where a submarine and a group of scientists are shrunk to a microbial size and injected inside a humans' body. Take away the sci-fi and maybe the sub, and you have a conceptual example of the metaverse.

Facebook CEO Mark Zuckerberg recently decided that the company would transition from a social media company to a metaverse company in the coming years. They even changed the name of the parent company to Meta. Microsoft is also rolling out its approach to create the metaverse.

So, what exactly is the metaverse? Today it's a fairly broad term used to describe a shared virtual world environment that people can access via the internet (and eventually other mediums) including Electronic Health Records.[10]

The term can also refer to digital spaces that are made more lifelike by using virtual reality (VR) or AR.

Some people also use the word metaverse to describe gaming worlds, in which users have a character that can walk around and interact with other players. Many science fiction books and films are set in fully-fledged metaverses – alternative digital worlds indistinguishable from the real physical world. While this is the stuff of science fiction today, it may be more real and closer in the future than you think.

People interact with each other online by going to websites such as social media platforms or using messaging applications. The idea of the metaverse is that it will create new online spaces in which people's interactions can be more multidimensional, where users can immerse themselves in digital content rather than simply viewing it.

Back to the Fantastic Voyage example. Imagine a time when, before a complicated cardiovascular surgical procedure takes place, the team performing it could simulate by being shrunk down and together walk through the problem and procedure from inside the heart. Or, through the use of a digital twin, perform the procedure virtually before operating on the patient.

The metaverse race has begun. CVS Health for example is looking to be the first pharmacy in the metaverse. The company has filed for a trademark to sell virtual goods and bring the health services it provides in its in-store clinics and its telehealth platform to this emerging virtual setting.[11]

Expect a lot of hype about it in the near term. And while it holds great long-term promise, today's current capabilities and experiences are akin to where the gaming world was 20 years ago.

Unifying Mind and Machine with Brain-Computer Interfaces

Using computers to communicate is not a new idea by any means but creating direct interfaces between technology and the human mind is a cutting-edge area of research that has significant applications in health and medicine.

Brain-computer interfaces (BCIs), backed by AI, acquire brain signals, analyze them, and translate them into commands relayed to output devices that carry out desired actions.[12] The main goal of BCI is to replace or restore useful function to people disabled by neuromuscular disorders such as cerebral palsy, stroke, or spinal cord injury.

Until recently, the dream of controlling one's environment through thoughts had been in the realm of science fiction. However, the advance of technology has brought a new reality. Today, humans can use electrical signals from brain activity to interact with, influence, or change their environments. The emerging field of BCI technology may allow individuals unable to speak or use their limbs to once again communicate and operate assistive devices for walking or manipulating objects.

Researchers from the Weill Institute for Neuroscience at the University of California, San Francisco, recently developed an implant that allowed a man with severe paralysis due to a stroke to "speak" again by translating his brain signals into text.[13]

BCI also holds promise for people with disabilities to mentally control robotic limbs or move computer cursors to "type" text on a screen. This is done by implanting electrodes in specific areas of the brain. When a person imagines executing a movement, the relevant brain cells start firing. Wires then transmit those signals to a computer, where they are "decoded" by sophisticated algorithms and translated into action.

New technologies are being developed that blur the lines between computers and biology. The emerging field of neurotechnology involves brain-machine interfaces, neuroprosthetics, neurostimulation, and implantable devices that not only augment nervous system activity but expand its capabilities.

Conversational AI

As noted in Chapter 4, intelligent voice capabilities have reached parity with the skill levels of humans in the ability to speak, listen, and comprehend conversations. Add a dose of medical intelligence with natural language capabilities with a healthy dose of compliance constructs, and you enable an AI-powered, personalized conversational healthcare experience that can scale across all experiences between consumers, providers, and payers.

Today, many organizations are moving toward using conversational AI to leverage and extend information and services currently provided by humans.

In the future conversational AI will be increasingly enhanced with the addition and integration of knowledge management capabilities. Combining this with deep learning to help bots improve responses for every interaction will allow for context-based replies through Natural Language Generation, making it increasingly hard to differentiate between the intelligent machines and intelligent clinicians.

As this occurs, the application of conversational AI will become more pervasive in its uses, including automation through clinical assistance, companions for seniors living alone, new parents in need of "just-in-time" guidance, and a variety of on-demand services by clinicians in operating theaters and procedure rooms.

AI and the Intelligent Health Revolution allow us to create a healthier world. To be a place where human abilities are amplified. It's not that this change will happen overnight or necessarily be linear in its progress. But it is happening as you read the words on this page.

AI's march toward changing the world reminds me of a sign that hangs outside the Netflix Headquarters. It reads: *"Don't give up on your dreams. We started with DVDs."*

**A CENTURY-LONG LOOK AT HOW AI
WILL CHANGE OUR WORLD**

Throughout this book, I've made references to and predictions on how AI and the Intelligence Revolution will change health and medicine. It is already changing the way we as individuals live and work. Along the

---

(Continued)

way AI will impact societal norms and give rise to new opportunities and issues.

While the media is chronicling the changes being driven by AI, Stanford University has launched a longitudinal study to anticipate and report on how AI will ripple through every aspect of how people work, play, and live.

Launched in 2014, the One Hundred Year Study of Artificial Intelligence (AI100) is a long-term investigation of the field of AI and its influences on people, their communities, and society. It considers the science, engineering, and deployment of AI-enabled computing systems.[14,15]

The initiative is managed by a standing committee of AI experts from institutions worldwide. The 2021 AI100 Report was written by a panel of 17 study authors, each of whom is deeply rooted in AI research.

Over the next century, AI 100 will monitor, assess and report on all aspects of AI and its impact on our world. A sampling of interrelated topics of interest includes the following:

Technical trends and surprises: What can we expect in terms of the advancing competencies of technology in the near term and at more distant points in time?

Key opportunities for AI: How can AI advances and implementations help transform the quality of such critical areas as education, healthcare, science, government, and the overall vitality of society? Where might AI be most useful?

Delays with translating AI advances into real-world value: Numerous advances in AI can reduce costs, introduce new efficiencies, and raise the quality of life. For example, machine learning and inference can play a significant role in reducing costs and enhancing healthcare quality. However, the methods have not come into wide use. The sluggish translation of these technologies into the world translates into unnecessary deaths and costs. There is an urgent need to better understand how we can more quickly translate valuable existing AI competencies and advances into real-world practice.

Privacy and machine intelligence: What potential challenges to privacy might come to the fore with advances in AI research and development, including efforts in machine learning, pattern recognition, inference, and prediction?

(Continued)

Law: Advances in AI methods may have numerous implications for laws and regulations. What aspects of common, statutory, and regulatory law may need to be revised in light of advances in the power and applications of AI systems?

Ethics: What ethical challenges and questions might come to the fore with advances in the competencies and uses of AI systems for inferences and robotic actions in the world?

Economics: What are the economic and societal implications more broadly of automated reasoning and robotic systems that take on increasingly sophisticated jobs, replacing or shifting the distributions and nature of human work?

Collaborations with machines: What challenges may arise as collaborations between people and intelligent machines on tasks become more commonplace?

Safety and autonomy: What are key technical opportunities with the specification and verification of ranges of desired or safe behaviors of autonomous systems?

Psychology of people and smart machines: We don't have a good understanding of how people will feel about and respond to intelligent applications, services, and robots in their environments and lives. What are the psychological implications of implementations of intelligence in our various environments?

Communication, understanding, and outreach: What do computer-science nonexperts, including experts in other fields and people in different spheres of life (e.g., political leaders), understand about key issues and developments with AI?

Neuroscience and AI: We have little genuine knowledge about how the human brain performs its computational magic despite many decades of research. While people have been using phrases like "brain-inspired" (e.g., with regard to neural network models, including network models referred to as "deep learning"), we have a surprisingly poor understanding of the operation of the nervous system and the computational methods that it may employ.

The excellent work of Stanford and the global team of AI experts may be found at https://ai100.stanford.edu/.

Notes

1. "There will be no Escape from the Telephone in the Future. Tacoma News Tribune new report, April 11, 1953.
2. Irena Bojanova, The Digital Revolution: What's on the Horizon?, Researchgate, January, 2014, https://www.researchgate.net/publication/260604267_The_Digital_Revolution_What%27s_on_the_Horizon#:~:text=The%20Digital%20Revolution%3A%20What%27s%20on%20the%20Horizon%3F.
3. What is Precision Medicine? National Institute of Health, 2018, https://ghr.nlm.nih.gov/primer/precisionmedicine/definition.
4. Kasey Panetta, The CIO's Guide to Quantum Computing, Gartner, 2019, https://www.gartner.com/smarterwithgartner/the-cios-guide-to-quantum-computing/.
5. 3D Bioprinting of Living Tissues, Wyss Institute Website, Accessed November 10, 2021, https://wyss.harvard.edu/technology/3d-bioprinting/.
6. University-Developed 3D Tissue Bioprinting Technology Now Commercially Available, Swansea University Website, Accessed November 10, 2021, https://www-2018.swansea.ac.uk/press-office/news-archive/2014/university-developed 3dtissuebioprintingtechnologynowcommerciallyavailable.php#accept.
7. Brett Israel, Berkeley Engineers Build Smallest Volume, Most Efficient Wireless Nerve Stimulator, Berkely News, April 10, 2018, https://news.berkeley.edu/2018/04/10/berkeley-engineers-build-smallest-volume-most-efficient-wireless-nerve-stimulator/.
8. Laura Donnelly, British Woman Given World's First In-Heart 'microcomputer', The Telegraph, 2019, https://www.telegraph.co.uk/news/2019/08/31/british-woman-given-worlds-first-in-heart-microcomputer/amp/.
9. Microsoft Customer Stories, arch 2, 2021, https://customers.microsoft.com/en-us/story/858292-mount-sinai-health-system-health-provider-teams-hololens-remote-assist-dynamics-365.
10. Matt O'Brien and Kelvin Chan, What Is the Metaverse and How Will It Work?, AP News, October 28, 2021, https://apnews.com/article/meta-facebook-explaining-the-metaverse-f57e01cd5739840945e89fd668b0fa27.
11. Bertha Coombs, CVS files to trademark its pharmacy and health clinics in the metaverse, CNBC, March 4, 2022, https://www.cnbc.com/2022/03/04/cvs-files-to-trademark-its-pharmacy-and-health-clinics-in-the-metaverse-.html
12. Jerry J. Shih, Dean J. Krusienski, and Jonathan R. Wolpaw, Brain-Computer Interfaces in Medicine, Mayo Clinic Proceedings, 2012, https://www.ncbi.nlm.nih.gov/pmc/articles/PMC3497935/.
13. David A. Moses, Sean L. Metzger, Jessie R. Liu, Gopala K. Anumanchipalli, Joseph G. Makin, Pengfei F. Sun, Josh Chartier, Maximilian E. Dougherty, Patricia M. Liu, Gary M. Abrams, Adelyn Tu-Chan, Karunesh Ganguly, et al., Neuroprosthesis for Decoding Speech in a Paralyzed Person with Anarthria, NEJM, July 15, 2021, https://www.nejm.org/doi/full/10.1056/NEJMoa2027540.

14. ARTIFICIAL INTELLIGENCE AND LIFE IN 2030, Stanford University, 2016, https://ai100.stanford.edu/sites/g/files/sbiybj9861/f/ai100report10032016fnl_singles.pdf.

15. ARTIFICIAL INTELLIGENCE AND LIFE IN 2030, Stanford University, 2016, https://ai100.stanford.edu/sites/g/files/sbiybj9861/f/ai100report10032016fnl_singles.pdf

Index